POP-ROCK MUS

To Nusi

POP-ROCK MUSIC

Aesthetic Cosmopolitanism in Late Modernity

MOTTI REGEV

polity

First published in 2013 by Polity Press

Polity Press
65 Bridge Street
Cambridge CB2 1UR, UK

Polity Press
350 Main Street
Malden, MA 02148, USA

ISBN-13: 978-0-7456-6172-8
ISBN-13: 978-0-7456-6173-5(pb)

A catalogue record for this book is available from the British Library.

Typeset in 10.5 on 12 pt Sabon
by Servis Filmsetting Ltd, Stockport, Cheshire
Printed and bound in Great Britain by the MPG Printgroup

The publisher has used its best endeavors to ensure that the URLs for external websites referred to in this book are correct and active at the time of going to press. However, the publisher has no responsibility for the websites and can make no guarantee that a site will remain live or that the content is or will remain appropriate.

Every effort has been made to trace all copyright holders, but if any have been inadvertently overlooked the publisher will be pleased to include any necessary credits in any subsequent reprint or edition.

For further information on Polity, visit our website: www.politybooks.com

CONTENTS

v

PREFACE

This book grew out of my long time involvement with the International Association for the Study of Popular Music (IASPM), a unique academic organization, where I have encountered generations of researchers, listened to and read numerous papers that introduced me to the wealth of national styles and genres of pop-rock music, beyond the Anglo-American axis. Therefore, my thanks go, in the first place, to the individuals – too many to list here by name – who founded IASPM and who kept it going for three decades (as these lines are being written), as well as to all the researchers whose presentations in IASPM conferences ignited my interest and curiosity, and provided the initial knowledge that allowed me to engage in this work.

Numerous individuals have contributed – either in passing or upon my request – tips, ideas, insightful comments and advice, pieces of knowledge and bits of data, as well as hints and inspiration that in intricate and nuanced ways had an effect on the final text. Amongst them, Pertti Alasuutari, Julio Arce, Sarah Baker, Jeroen de Kloet, Fernán del Val, Tia DeNora, Paul DiMaggio, Christine Feldman, Hector Fouce, Dafna Hirsch, Franco Minganti, Richard Peterson, Rosa Reitsamer, Zeev Rosenhek, Roger Martinez Sanmarti, Hyunjoon Shin, Marco Solaroli, Pinhas Stern and Ian Woodward deserve special mention. My thanks to each of the above and to many others to whom I apologize for not mentioning them here.

Many thanks also to my home institution, The Open University of Israel, for being a great academic habitat.

I am greatly indebted to the Institute of Advanced Studies at the University of Bologna and to the Griffith Centre for Cultural Research at Griffith University (Queensland), whose hospitality and facilities provided the perfect setting for writing substantial parts of this book. Thanks so much to my respective hosts there, Marco Santoro and Andy Bennett, for extending the invitations, keeping great personal and professional company, and providing valuable feedback. Thanks also to Tim Dowd, John Street, and other reviewers, for their comments and endorsement, as well as to Jennifer Jahn, John Thompson, India Darsley, Ian Tuttle and others at Polity for trusting this book and handling it so efficiently.

Work on this book has benefited enormously from conversations and discussion with Natan Sznaider, who embarked me on the cosmopolitan wagon and whose invaluable friendship and collegiality I highly cherish. Similar gratitude goes to Ronen Shamir, for his support and inspiring sociological insights. A special personal gratitude is due to Vered Silber-Varod, for her close friendship and companionship. Finally and primarily, I am deeply grateful to my partner-in-life Irit, and to our daughters Ronny and Noa, for being a never-ending source of vitality and warmth.

Parts of this book have been adapted and reworked from the following previously published articles, for which kind permission has been granted by the publishers:

- "Cultural Uniqueness and Aesthetic Cosmopolitanism," *European Journal of Social Theory* 10(1): 123–38, Copyright © 2007 Sage Publications.
- "Ethno-National Pop-Rock Music: Aesthetic Cosmopolitanism Made from within," *Cultural Sociology* 1(3): 317–41, Copyright © 2007 BSA Publications Ltd® and Sage Publications.
- "Pop-Rock Music as Expressive Isomorphism: Blurring the National, the Exotic and the Cosmopolitan in Popular Music," *American Behavioral Scientist* 55(5): 558–73, Copyright © 2011 Sage Publications.

— 1 —

THEORIES AND CONCEPTS

Miyuki Nakajima is a female singer-songwriter from Japan, who has enjoyed a successful and influential career since the 1970s. In 1979 she wrote and recorded the soft sentimental ballad "Ruju" ("Rouge"). In this song, about 90 seconds into the recording, an instrumental bridge (between verses) opens with a delicate electric guitar solo that soon soars to a dramatic height, to be joined by a full string orchestra before the vocals return. In 1992, the Hong Kong-based, Chinese female singer Faye Wong recorded her version of the song in Cantonese, for her album *Coming Home*. This version, called "Fragile Woman" ("Jung Ji Sau Soeng Dik Neoi Yan"), slightly dramatizes the string arrangement, but nevertheless retains the electric guitar part in the instrumental bridge. According to conventional narrative, the recording of "Fragile Woman" was the turning point in Faye Wong's career. Following its enormous success in Hong Kong (and later in mainland China and other countries), and with subsequent albums and performances, she became during the 1990s and into the new century, "the reigning diva of Chinese popular music" (Fung and Curtin 2002), and especially of Cantopop, the soft-sounding pop style associated with Hong Kong. Indeed, while unequivocally labeled "pop" singers by journalistic and academic discourse, this song, and many others by Faye Wong or Miyuki Nakajima, exemplifies the blurred line between "pop" and "rock." The soaring guitar solo is an emblematic sonic unit that symbolically represents the rock ballad, a song pattern that crystallized in the 1970s as a way to expose the supposedly softer side of hard rock bands. As much as they are sometimes perceived by fans and critics to be opposite categories, "pop" and "rock" are obviously linked together in their sonic textures and in their cultural histories. They form one musical and cultural category that can best be called *pop-rock music*.

1

Traveling from Anglo-American hard rock bands to East Asia (and to other parts of the world) and then between female pop singers in the region, the soaring electric guitar solo is but one element among plenty that epitomizes the multidirectional traffic of pop-rock music idioms across the globe, that is, not only from the UK and US to other parts of the world, but also between other countries and regions. Moreover, Faye Wong's career and stature as a pop musician that represents, not just for her devoted fans, a certain sense of Hong-Kongian or Chinese contemporary identity, a late modern sense of national cultural uniqueness, also epitomizes the widespread position achieved by pop-rock music in many countries. In contrast to its early perception as a major manifestation of cultural imperialism or Americanization, pop-rock styles and genres have gained by the turn of the century extensive legitimacy, both as a form of musical art and as a genuine expression of contemporary indigenous, national, or ethnic culture. This happened partially because of pop-rock's fusions with, and integration of, folklore and traditional elements. Consider, for example, this quote, by a notable Argentinean music critic and cultural commentator, who refers to stylistic developments in Argentinean rock of the 1990s:

> Argentinean rock, where in the 1970s you'd be thrown away from stage by sticks and stones for playing the charanguito [a small guitar-like indigenous instrument, made from the shell of the back of an armadillo], begins to integrate in a natural manner Latin American rhythms, Jamaican rhythms like reggae, and also [Argentinean] folklore and tango. There starts to be a type of rock that has no shame to incorporate other genres, and for me this is richness. It is a new entity. (Alfredo Rosso, in program 8 of the documentary series *Quizas Porque: Historia del Rock Nacional* [Maybe Because: History of National Rock], first broadcast in Argentina in November–December 2009)

Adds veteran folk-rocker León Gieco, in that same program:

> In the 2000s decade a certain fusion occurred between tango, folklore and rock. The folklore bands incorporated drum kits into their chacareras [an indigenous dance rhythm], and the rockers started to identify with folklore and inserted folklore elements.

With pop-rock evolving to become this "new entity," as Rosso calls it, Argentinean pop-rock has joined folklore and tango as a legitimate expression of *Argentinidad* (Argentineaness) in music, a stature it had firmly consolidated among its fans many years earlier, in the 1970s.

2

Argentinean rock and Cantopop are two cases that exemplify how the very sounds and aesthetic idiom of pop-rock music, as well as its cultural position and meanings within national or regional societies, embody a major process that has been taking place in late modern world culture. It is a process of intensified aesthetic proximity, overlap, and connectivity between nations and ethnicities or, at the very least, between prominent large sectors within them. It is a process in which the expressive forms and cultural practices used by nations at large, and by groupings within them, to signify and perform their sense of uniqueness, growingly comes to share large proportions of aesthetic common ground, to a point where the cultural uniqueness of each nation or ethnicity cannot but be understood as a unit within one complex entity, one variant in a set of quite similar – although never identical – cases. *Aesthetic cosmopolitanization* is a term that is best suited to depict this process in world culture. That is, as can be inferred from Beck (2006), the term cosmopolitanism refers, literally, to an already existing world polity, while the term cosmopolitanization refers to the gradual formation of such polity. Following this, *aesthetic cosmopolitanization* refers to the ongoing formation, in late modernity, of world culture as one complexly interconnected entity, in which social groupings of all types around the globe growingly share wide common grounds in their aesthetic perceptions, expressive forms, and cultural practices. *Aesthetic cosmopolitanism* refers, then, to the already existing singular world culture, the state of affairs reached following the above.

A sociological theorization of aesthetic cosmopolitanism that involves forays into certain streams of current sociological theory may serve, therefore, as a highly adequate tool for explaining the emergence, legitimation, and consolidation of world pop-rock music and its global thriving; and world pop-rock may serve as a perfect empirical case through which aesthetic cosmopolitanism can be characterized, elucidated, and explicated. Put differently, this book seeks to offer a certain marriage between some currents in contemporary sociological theory and pop-rock music. While it may not add up to a tight coherent theoretical whole, the book offers a set of interconnected theoretical approaches, each framing a different facet of pop-rock music as a world cultural phenomenon. Three questions underlie this study of world pop-rock music and aesthetic cosmopolitanism: why did pop-rock emerge to become such a prominent cultural form on a world scale?, how did pop-rock music achieve its status and legitimacy?, and what are the cultural consequences of this achievement?

3

More than its mere reflection, pop-rock music is portrayed in this book as a resource in the formation of aesthetic cosmopolitanism, in the re-figuration of world culture. Being primarily a complex web of meaningful sonorities, a set of "things" that have sonic-physical presence in the world, pop-rock styles and genres become objects of interactions, building blocks that afford individual and collective actors the arrangement and construction of life-worlds, of ways of being in the world. Being a prominent force in the very formation of aesthetic cosmopolitanism is derived from the status of pop-rock music as a signifier of a universal modernity in the field of popular music. That is, as a signifier of universal modernity, pop-rock music became a world model for making contemporary popular music, and thus geared musicians and audiences around the world into active interactions with its sounds and meanings. These interactions led to emergence and consolidation of national, ethnic, and local styles of pop-rock music, and thus to the growing connectivity, proximity, and overlap between popular music cultures around the world.

This opening chapter discusses some preliminary issues and especially the key concepts of "aesthetic cosmopolitanism" and "pop-rock." It sets the conceptual and theoretical framework for the chapters to come. The following section of this chapter offers a general explanatory framework, informed by sociological theory, to cultural globalization and aesthetic cosmopolitanism. The second part of the chapter delineates in some detail what exactly is meant by the term "pop-rock music," especially its particularity with respect to the almost identical, but more general notion of "popular music."

Aesthetic Cosmopolitanism: A Theoretical Framework

In her study of music videos by female pop singers in Mali, and the meanings attributed to these videos by (mostly) female spectators, Schultz (2001) notes the typical structure of these pop songs:

> Whereas the song's melody and rhythm are reminiscent of conventional Malian musical aesthetics, it is played with a combination of Malian and Western rock music instruments. The original melody and rhythm of the folk song are preserved and played by the Malian twenty-one-string instrument the *kora*, electrically reinforced drums (*djembe*), electric guitars (played like a *kora*), and a saxophone. (Schultz 2001: 358–9)

Based on her observations of routine spectatorship, she asserts that "as cultural *bricoleurs*," the Malian female pop singers "combine

4

'Malian' morality and aesthetics with cosmopolitan life orientation" (Schultz 2001: 366). In this way:

> The pop singers' success shows that the increasing international flows of commodities and media images, rather than supporting the dislocation of identities, create new meanings and moral orientations for consumers ... [It] enables Malians to claim membership of a consumer community that extends beyond the borders of the local yet is firmly rooted in an "authentic" Malian moral universe. (Schultz 2001: 367)

One of the videos analyzed in this study is of the song "Bi furu," by Oumou Sangaré, a song that "has been one of the most popular hits since it was first broadcast in 1992" (Schultz 2001: 363). Oumou Sangaré, it should be noted, has enjoyed success since the early 1990s all over Africa and in the West. In 2009, a BBC music review referred to her new album, *Seya*, as "the best thing since her marvellous 1991 debut *Moussoulou*" (Jon Lusk, February 23, 2009, bbc.co.uk/music/reviews/nbzf, accessed June 23, 2011), while the influential music historian and journalist Charlie Gillett has called *Seya* "a masterpiece" (*The Observer*, February 15, 2009).

This brief glimpse at Malian pop illustrates the mechanism of cultural globalization as reflected through the prism of pop-rock music. Cultural globalization, the worldwide dissemination of products, artifacts, and activities determined by creative work and carrying symbolic meanings (see Krätke 2003) can be envisaged as a three-way circuit. In it, cultural materials that originate in the West flow into non-Western countries, where they are perceived as models of modernity. Eager to take part in modern culture, yet reluctant to fully embrace the Western variant of modernity, artists and consumers alike in these other countries selectively adapt elements and components from these materials and merge them with indigenous traditional materials. This allows them to preserve a sense of local uniqueness, while at the same time to feel participants in recent developments of modern culture. In addition, some of the cultural products created in this way in non-Western countries flow to metropolitan countries, to be hailed as genuine, albeit "exotic," expressions of contemporary culture, and sometimes to exert some influence and inspiration on Western artists. All in all, the workings of this circuit usher world culture to a condition in which its different sub units, as much as they maintain uniqueness and distinction, display greater connectivity, overlap, and proximity than ever before or, in short, to a condition of aesthetic cosmopolitanism.

5

Characterizing Aesthetic Cosmopolitanism

At its core, then, the circuit of cultural globalization that produces aesthetic cosmopolitanism consists of quests for recognition, for a sense of parity, for participation and membership in what collective and individual actors around the world believe to be the innovative frontiers of creativity and artistic expression in modern culture. On the one hand, new types and patterns of expression in all forms of art and culture, implicitly or explicitly presented as models to be followed in order not to lag behind "the new and exciting" in modern culture, are constantly disseminated by leading forces in different art worlds through the global media, the cultural industries, and, to some extent, the education system. On the other hand, collective and individual actors at various national and local levels, believing in the value and meaning of these models, develop interests to become recognized participants in these frontiers, and seek to contribute their own variants of these types and patterns of expression to the global circulation.

When portrayed in this way, the theorization of cultural globalization engulfs both the notion of power that metropolitan centers of cultural production (most notably in the West) exert on peripheral ones, and the notion of multidirectional flow, including counter-hegemonic ones. Indeed, as Crane (2008) notes, theoretical approaches to cultural globalization have been characterized by a certain movement, a development from the cluster of approaches underlined by the idea of cultural/media imperialism, to approaches that stress transnational, multidirectional flows of cultural products and meanings, and the emergence of global communities and cultural networks. The cultural imperialism approach, associated with terms such as McDonaldization, Americanization, McDisneyzation and Coca-Colonization (Ritzer 1993; Ritzer and Liska 1997; Ritzer and Stillman 2003; Wagnleitner 1994), is essentially a thesis about domination "of America over Europe, of 'the West over the rest' of the world, of the core over the periphery, of the modern world over the fast-disappearing traditional one, of capitalism over more or less everything and everyone" (Tomlinson 1999: 80). Domination leads, according to this thesis, to world monoculture, that is, to cultural homogenization.

The other approaches share the thesis that cultural globalization does not eliminate cultural diversity, but rather transforms older notions of cultural variance into new ones. Cultural globalization is not only about flows of products and meanings from the West to other parts of the world, but also from East Asia, Africa, and Latin America to the West, or from Japan to East Asia (Iwabuchi 2002). In addition, the reception, interpretation, and use of cultural products are not identical across the world. People in different countries or social settings tend to decipher and use the same products – television dramas, fast food – in ways that appropriate them to their local culture (Katz and Liebes 1990; Watson 1997). Moreover, actors in art worlds across the globe create their own indigenous variants of modern cultural forms, sometimes presenting them as expressions of resistance to the Western, hegemonic ones. In these works, aesthetic idioms, stylistic elements and genre components from multiple national and ethnic sources are mixed and welded to serve the preferences and interests of local taste cultures and identity formations. Hybridity, creolization, complexity, mixture, fusion, and deterritorialization are key concepts in the approaches that stress multidirectional cultural flows and networks (Appadurai 1990; Garcia Canclini 1995; Hannerz 1992) as well as the glocalization of world culture (Robertson 1995). Taken together, however, all approaches share the understanding that late modern world culture is, in effect, one cultural space. That is, the traditional and modernist perception of world culture as composed of distinct, separate cultural units – be they national, ethnic, local or indigenous – has been replaced by a perception of world culture as one entity composed of numerous sub-units that interact between them in complex ways. All approaches acknowledge that the nature of ethnic, national, local, and indigenous cultural uniqueness has been transformed. The sense of cultural uniqueness shared by any given social entity on earth can no longer stand in real or perceived isolation from that of other entities. Complex forms of connectivity, relations of power, and currents of influence render all frames of cultural uniqueness as sub-units in a single world cultural web. In the words of Beck and Sznaider (2006), a sociological account of world culture must therefore abandon "methodological nationalism" in favor of a "methodological cosmopolitanism." That is, a methodology that partakes the idea of the world as one place, one society. In the case of culture, methodological cosmopolitanism translates to aesthetic cosmopolitanism as a concept that best reflects the existing global cultural reality of late modernity.

Works by Urry (1995), Szerszynski and Urry (2002, 2006) and Tomlinson (1999), have located aesthetic cosmopolitanism at the individual level, as a "cultural disposition involving an intellectual and aesthetic stance of 'openness' towards peoples, places and experiences from different cultures, especially those from different 'nations'" (Szerszinski and Urry 2002: 468), or as having taste for "the wider shores of cultural experience" (Tomlinson 1999: 202; see also Hannerz 1990). In this usage, aesthetic cosmopolitanism presumes, self-evidently, the existence of ethnic and national cultures as spaces of exclusive expressive content, as symbolic environments to which certain cultural products and art works inherently "belong." Thus, when individuals, as members of one national or ethnic culture, have a taste for cultural products or art works that unequivocally "belong" to a nation or ethnicity other than their own, they display aesthetic cosmopolitanism. If, on the other hand, individuals have a taste exclusively for cultural products and art works that conventionally "belong" to the ethnic or national entity of which they are members, they do not count as aesthetic cosmopolitans. Based on the modernist perception of world culture as composed of distinct, separate cultural units, this understanding of aesthetic cosmopolitanism does not fully cover the global cultural complexity of late modernity.

In late modernity, the disposition of overt openness toward "other" cultures is not just a matter of individual inclination, but rather a structural facet of national and ethnic cultures in general or, at the very least, of major sectors within them. It is not a whim of curiosity, but an institutionalized constraint. Practically any given national, ethnic, local, and indigenous culture displays openness to forms of expression and aesthetic idioms exterior to its own heritage – especially to those forms and idioms that gain global institutionalized status as the frontiers of creativity in late modernity.

Openness consists not only of straightforward consumption of imported cultural goods. It also includes explicit absorption, the indigenization and domestication, of exogenous stylistic elements, creative practices, techniques of expression, and other components into the production of local, ethnic, and national culture. Consequently, cultural products and art works that signify contemporary national or ethnic uniqueness come to consist of aesthetic elements knowingly borrowed and absorbed from sources exterior to the national culture which they signify. Art forms and stylistic elements deliberately drawn from sources exterior to indigenous traditions come to play significant roles in the representation and performance of national uniqueness, thereby leading national and ethnic cultures into greater connectivity and overlap between them. Aesthetic cosmopolitanism, in other words, takes place not only at the individual level, but mostly at the structural and collective level. The individual level might be viewed, in this regard, as a continuum that stretches from the most advertent and fully conscious aesthetic cosmopolitans – either as

8

cultural producers or as consumers – to the most passive and inadvertent consumers. In late modernity, "everybody is more or less cosmopolitan" (Hebdige 1990: 20).

Central to the emergence and consolidation of aesthetic cosmopolitanism is the institutionalization of certain forms of art, or rather, certain technologies of expression, as signifiers of a universal modernity, as manifestations of the proper way to create and express cultural uniqueness in late modernity. Foremost among these forms are film and television, or rather the art forms based on the technologies of "moving pictures." Another one is pop-rock music, or rather the musical art form based on sound manipulation by recording machines, electric and electronic instruments, and amplification. The technologies at the heart of these forms render them culturally neutral, as it were. They are hardly ever perceived as "belonging" to a specific national or ethnic heritage. On the other hand, for most national and ethnic cultures in the world, they have been also a sort of exogenous intrusion into local historical continuity. That is, they were hardly ever perceived as inherently stemming from local indigenous tradition. Thus, while these technologies of expression certainly brought into national cultures – when they were first introduced, at the very least – an element of "otherness," they have still been perceived by various collective and individual actors as a vehicle for modernizing national culture, and not necessarily as an imperial imposition. The worldwide proliferation of the art forms associated with these technologies of expression is a key element in the growing proximity and overlap between national and ethnic cultures, in the consolidation of aesthetic cosmopolitanism.

Theoretical Framework

Sociologically, the consolidation of aesthetic cosmopolitanism as the global cultural condition of late modernity should therefore be analyzed as the combined effect of two dynamics. One consists of the power that emanates from the functioning of certain art forms, stylistic trends, and aesthetic idioms as signifiers of modernity and contemporariness. The other consists of forces within national societies who work to absorb, implement, indigenize, and legitimize such forms, trends, and idioms into the fabric of contemporary ethnic or national uniqueness. The functioning of certain art forms, stylistic trends, and aesthetic idioms as signifiers of modernity and contemporariness can be conceptualized by considering them, following Fraser (2001), as manifestations of *institutionalized patterns of cultural*

9

value, while their effect as such patterns on national cultures is a process best described, in an extension of work by Meyer and others (Meyer 2000; Meyer et al. 1997), as *expressive isomorphism*. The work done by individual and collective actors in national settings to advance up-to-date variants of national and ethnic cultures according to models set by institutionalized patterns of cultural value – the work of agency – can be understood by applying and extending to the sphere of cultural globalization Bourdieu's notion of homology between the supply and demand sides of culture (1993a). From a related theoretical angle, and following DiMaggio (1987, 1992), aesthetic cosmopolitanism can be seen as stemming from the revamped classification of art forms, that corresponds to the growing heterogeneity and fragmentation of status groups in late modern national societies, to the "boundary work" carried out by such groups (Lamont and Fournier 1992; Lamont and Molnár 2002), especially those associated with the "new upper middle class" sectors and their pattern of omnivorous cultural consumption (Peterson and Kern 1996). While not amounting to a detailed coherent whole, the short elaboration of all the above that follows is offered as a general guiding framework for an understanding of aesthetic cosmopolitanism, and pop-rock music as part of it, along certain currents of sociological thought.

The quest for status, participation, and parity in modern world culture that lies at the core of aesthetic cosmopolitanism can be seen, then, as deriving from the proliferation of *institutionalized patterns of cultural value*:

> To view recognition as a matter of status is to examine institutionalized patterns of cultural value for their effects on the relative standing of social actors. If and when such patterns constitute actors as *peers*, capable of participating on a par with one another in social life, then we can speak of *reciprocal recognition* and *status equality*. When, in contrast, institutionalized patterns of cultural value constitute some actors as inferior, excluded, wholly other or simply invisible, hence as less than full partners in social interaction, then we should speak of *misrecognition* and *status subordination*. (Fraser 2001: 24)

Fraser further argues that in order to gain recognition and status, the institutionalized patterns of cultural value that relegate certain social actors to inferiority should change and be replaced by patterns that constitute these actors as equals. Another possible consequence of her assertion, however, is that social actors who are relegated to inferiority and exclusion by such patterns, and who nevertheless adhere to a belief in these values, will seek to adapt their ways of life, their

10

cultural practices and performances, to the dictates of such patterns. In the realms of art, creativity and cultural consumption, such patterns typically formulate hierarchies of worth and importance. They define which expressive forms, aesthetic idioms and stylistic elements are at any given moment the carriers of creative innovation, of "the new and exciting" in art and culture. These hierarchies relegate to a lower status on the scale of modernity those individuals and collective actors whose tastes hardly consist of works from the creative frontiers, actors whose sense of distinction and uniqueness is based on forms of art and on styles that lag behind recent stylistic trends.

Consequently, individual and collective actors who aspire to participate as equals in what they perceive as the cultural frontiers of modernity, tend to acquire tastes in, and adjust aesthetic sensibilities to, those forms, styles, and idioms hailed by the institutionalized patterns of cultural value. In other words, global institutionalized patterns of cultural value present and dictate to aspiring artists, creative workers, and cultural consumers around the world what are the art forms, the stylistic elements, and the aesthetic idioms that should be adopted in order to count as candidates for recognition, participation, and parity in the innovative frontiers of world culture.

Indeed, closely connected, and in fact directly derived from the global proliferation of institutionalized patterns of cultural value is the worldwide replication of art forms, the emergence and consolidation of certain forms of expression as models to be followed and implemented within national cultures. Adherence to beliefs in the cultural value of certain forms of expression prompts the replication of these forms in many different countries. A useful way to sociologically conceptualize the replication of such models is to extend John Meyer's theoretical framework about isomorphic processes in world society to the realm of expressive culture, and refer to the process as *expressive isomorphism*. Expressive isomorphism is, then, the process through which national uniqueness is standardized so that expressive culture of various different nations, or of prominent social sectors within them, comes to consist of similar – although not identical – expressive forms, stylistic elements, and aesthetic idioms. It is the process through which expressive cultural uniqueness is constructed by adopting, adapting, adjusting, incorporating, and legitimating creative technologies, stylistic elements, genres, and forms of art derived from world models. While in the past national cultural uniqueness was organized around the principle of striving toward totally different expressive forms and stylistic elements, with expressive isomorphism

11

it becomes organized around proximity, similitude, and overlap of art forms and stylistic elements between nations.

The notions of institutionalized patterns of cultural value and expressive isomorphism provide, jointly, a useful conceptual framework for a general sociological understanding of the power that emanates from the functioning of certain art forms, stylistic trends, and aesthetic idioms as signifiers of modernity and contemporariness. They provide a general answer to the question why actors in national cultures engage in production and consumption practices that lead to aesthetic cosmopolitanism. They do not explain, however, how these practices work – what their social logic is. An understanding of the agency of actors in this terrain, of the forces who work to absorb, implement, indigenize, and legitimate the cultural forms that lead to aesthetic cosmopolitanism, should turn to Bourdieu's analysis of the relationship between cultural production and consumption.

Bourdieu's understanding of the role of culture might be divided in two: a theory of distinction and cultural capital (Bourdieu 1984), and a theory of the fields of art (Bourdieu 1992, 1993a). The theory of distinction outlines the role of cultural capital in the production and maintenance of inequality, superiority, and prestige. The theory of the cultural field delineates the social dynamic of struggles and changes in fields of cultural production, whereby new forms and styles gain legitimacy and recognition, while the old ones either decline or retain their dominant, consecrated position. Bourdieu points to a certain homology, an unintended correspondence, between the struggles within art fields, that constantly invent and re-invent art genres and styles, and the emergence of class fractions and sub-fractions demanding recognition and legitimacy. That is, he points to the fact that the success of new genres and styles, in legitimizing themselves as respected positions in a given art field, serves the interests of rising class formations to construct their claim for social position, for power, around their self-definition as specific taste cultures and lifestyles. Or as he puts it:

> by obeying the logic of the objective competition between mutually exclusive positions within the field [of art], the various categories of producers tend to supply products adjusted to the expectations of the various positions in the field of power, but without any conscious striving for adjustment. (Bourdieu 1993a: 45)

Bourdieu's own work tends, however, to be limited to older types of class structure and cultural capital, based on traditional high art and its institutions. Except for some hints and occasional remarks, he hardly ever addresses the change in the status, position, and prestige of contemporary cultural forms known as "popular culture" (film, television, popular music). Referring to emerging styles and genres, or, one should speculate here, to new and emergent cultural forms, he does, however, assert that:

> Without ever being a direct reflection of them, the internal struggles [in the field of art] depend for their outcome on the correspondence they may have with the external struggles between the classes ... When newcomers ... bring with them dispositions and *prises de position* [i.e. genres, styles, cultural forms] which clash with the prevailing norms of production and the expectations of the field, they cannot succeed without the help of external changes. These may be ... deep-seated changes in the audience of consumers who, because of their affinity with the new producers, ensure the success of their products. (Bourdieu 1993a: 57–8)

Extending this logic to the case of aesthetic cosmopolitanism, its emergence and consolidation should be envisaged as resulting from the correspondence between cultural producers whose field-specific interests propel them to creative work with art forms, stylistic trends, and aesthetic idioms that signify modernity and contemporariness; and social groupings who, amid these same forms, tend to define their lifestyles and their sense of distinction around taste preferences for styles and aesthetic idioms that signify a stance of "being with the times."

On the supply side of culture, then, aesthetic cosmopolitanism stems from the emergence of artists, creative workers, and producers of meaning (critics, journalists, and academics) who develop an explorative interest in new and contemporary forms of art, stylistic trends, and aesthetic idioms as a way to participate in innovative expressive frontiers. This interest propels them to engage in the production of local variants of such forms, and in waging classificatory struggles for recognition and legitimation of these artistic works and products. These actors are in fact self-mobilized into occupying simultaneous positions in two fields of cultural production: the global field of the art form in question (for example, the field of film or of pop-rock music), and the field of the national culture in which they are situated. Aesthetic cosmopolitanism emerges as the socially produced consequence of the interplay between these two fields.

The working of this interplay, its social mechanism and cultural logic, can be analyzed by considering two elaborations on Bourdieu's analysis of cultural fields. The first comes from the work of Sewell

Jr. (2005), who criticizes Bourdieu's analysis of habitus because it "cannot explain change as arising from within the operation of structures" (p. 16). He then goes on to argue that the transformation of structures from within is possible thanks to five key characteristics of fields (or social structures), two of which are *the multiplicity of structures* and *the transposibility of schemas*. These two imply that individuals, as social agents, are always situated in more than one field, and routinely transpose elements from one field-specific habitus to their actions and practices in a different field. Artists and other cultural producers are no exception: they occupy positions in more than one field, each field with its own specific forms of capital and habitus, with its own hierarchies, structures, and schemas. The intersection of two (or more) fields of cultural production thus becomes a source for innovation and change. The work of agency, of producing cultural change, is performed through the transposition of specific types of habitus from one field to another. Aesthetic sensibilities, criteria of evaluation and creative patterns are some key elements transposed by cultural producers from one field to another, as part of the dynamics of innovation and surpassing of existing patterns that characterize all artistic fields.

A second elaboration comes from the work of Toynbee (2000), who applies a key concept of Bourdieu's field theory, that of "space of possibles" (or possibilities), to the work of musicians in the field of popular music. Examining Bourdieu's concept, which defines the creative trajectories available to an artist at a given moment, Toynbee goes on to develop a model he calls "the radius of creativity." His main point is that, within the given space of possibilities available to an artist in the field, there is always a certain likelihood that some possibilities will be preferred over others. This likelihood is a function of the artist's own dispositions, the position she or he occupies in the field, and the readily available creative means, as offered by the actual institutions within which the artist works. It is this likelihood that ultimately defines which creative possibility will be adopted, including stylistic innovation.

In the very act of becoming artists who work in contemporary forms of art, then, individuals in any country are self-mobilized into membership and actorhood in the global fields of these art forms. Such artists and other producers of culture find themselves in the intersection of two fields and with an expanded radius of creativity. The space of creative possibilities opened to them consists of both the general, global genres and stylistic trends of the art form in question, and the ethno-national heritage of which they are successors. This means, in practice, transposing schemas from the global fields to the national field and vice versa. The term "hybridization" is often used to describe the creative practices employed by cultural producers of the type just described, and it certainly depicts the nature of their techniques of creativity. In light of the above, however, it should be stressed that hybridization is not an arbitrary or whimsical creative practice, but rather an artistic practice structured by the social embeddedness of artists in the intersections of their respective global fields of cultural production with fields of national culture.

On the demand side of culture, the emergence and consolidation of aesthetic cosmopolitanism is closely associated with the rise and expansion of middle- and upper-middle-class fractions, especially groupings whose sense of lifestyle, of generational identity, of national or ethnic belonging – in short, their sense of distinction – becomes highly dependent on the cultural consumption of contemporary forms of art, stylistic trends, and aesthetic idioms. These are groupings who develop tastes for "the new and innovative" as a way of defining their sense of distinction along contemporariness and modernity, and thus also interests in having national variants of contemporary art forms, stylistic trends, and aesthetic idioms. They seek to have "their own" national or ethnic manifestations of those expressive forms that signify contemporariness and modernity. These groups have been labeled "the new middle classes" (Lash 1990) and "the new cultural intermediaries" (Featherstone 1991). In their consumption practices, these groups aim to shift their national cultures away from essentialist purism, towards openness, engagement with the expressive frontiers of world culture and diversity. Indeed, as some research has demonstrated, the aesthetic cosmopolitan aim goes hand in hand with the development of omnivorous tastes within and across cultural forms. As Kendall et al. (2009) assert, "cosmopolitan omnivorousness becomes a symbol of social status and moral worth" (p. 145). Thus, following work on omnivorous cultural consumption (Peterson and Kern 1996), and coupling it to Bourdieu's concepts, Coulangeon (2003) refers to this type of omnivorousness as "enlightened eclecticism," while Ollivier (2008) calls it "humanist openness" and elsewhere argues that conspicuous openness to cultural diversity has become a major ingredient in the behavior of the upper-middle classes, a way of demonstrating and performing distinction (Ollivier 2004).

Taken together, then, the work by artists and cultural producers in which exogenous and indigenous cultural elements interweave to modernize local and national cultures caters, not necessarily in an intentional or planned way, to the status and distinction interests of cosmopolitan omnivores, mostly of the so-called "new upper-middle classes." Jointly, these types of producers and consumers become the agents of aesthetic cosmopolitanism in national societies. In other words, and extending work by DiMaggio (1987) and Lamont and Molnár (2002), national adaptations and adjustments of globally circulating, supposedly neutral, contemporary forms of art that bring about changes in national systems of art, should be understood as corresponding to the emergence of new status groups, new collective actors, and the boundary work conducted by them within their national settings and amid parallel groups in other countries.

Finally, as hinted above, these actors may also be referred to as advert aesthetic cosmopolitans, especially when juxtaposed to the more passive, inadvertent type of aesthetic cosmopolitanism, in which the mixing of local or traditional expressive forms and elements with stylistic trends, cultural products, and expressive technologies associated with transnational cultural industries is performed through routine cultural consumption and production. Inadvertent aesthetic cosmopolitanism can be also referred to, following Billig (1995), as banal aesthetic cosmopolitanism, or as ordinary (Lamont and Aksartova 2002). Unlike the consciously minded advert aesthetic cosmopolitans, inadvertent cosmopolitans do not intentionally engage in nurturing their cosmopolitanism. They become banal, ordinary, and mundane cosmopolitans simply by consuming typical, ubiquitous products of the cultural industries.

Not necessarily a dichotomy, these two types of aesthetic cosmopolitanism stand rather as the poles of a continuum that stretches from the most active agency of aesthetic cosmopolitanism to its most passive. This point is best exemplified by the case of pop-rock music. Enthusiastic fans of pop-rock genres, ardent followers of new and recent stylistic trends, experts who discuss and spread pop-rock knowledge, and musicians who work creatively in pop-rock genres within their own national settings, are jointly the almost ideal type of advert aesthetic cosmopolitanism in any given national society. At the other end of the continuum stand passive listeners, whose routine exposure to the sounds of pop-rock music because of its ubiquity, its omnipresence in shops, soundtracks, or radio broadcasting, inadvertently dips them in aesthetic cosmopolitanism. Being a manifestation of aesthetic cosmopolitanism is exactly what sets pop-rock music apart from other forms of popular music. But this difference, as well as the hyphened form "pop-rock" that are preferred here over just "rock" or "pop," should be clarified and elucidated.

16

Rock, Pop, and Popular Music

The question about the difference or similarity between "rock," "pop," and popular music, especially as it pertains to the globally dominant Anglo-American context, seems to bother quite a few scholars and commentators of popular music. Two issues tend to be at the focus of attention in this context. One is the relationship between "rock" and "pop," and the other the place of "rock" within the larger category of popular music. The confusion about the terms "pop" and "rock" can be illustrated by several citations. Here, for example, is a quote from a scholarly oriented handbook of popular music:

> Rock'n'roll was created by the grafting together of the emotive and rhythmic elements of the blues, the folk elements of country & western music, and jazz forms such as boogie-woogie. Pop is seen to have emerged as a somewhat watered-down, blander version of this, associated with a more rhythmic style and smoother vocal harmony. (Shuker 1998: 226)

Roy Shuker echoes here a familiar distinction between "rock" as the more "authentic" or "artistic" section of popular music, and "pop" as the "lighter" and "entertainment" sector (see also Hesmondhalgh 1996). The following quote, from an album review by a leading New York popular music critic, represents a different view:

> Americans enticed by talk of "rock"-dance fusion should bear in mind the cultural deprivation of our siblings across the sea. Befuddled by the useless "rock"–"pop" distinction, they believe "rock" is something that happened in the '70s. The more inquisitive among them are aware of Pearl Jam and Nirvana, but if they've ever heard of Los Lobos or Hüsker Dü they probably think they're "pop." (Christgau 2000: 321)

For Christgau, there is no real difference between "pop" and "rock" – they are interchangeable. Sometimes "popular music," as an all-encompassing term, is preferred over the two. But "popular music" is not the same as "pop":

> While the use of the word "popular" in relation to the lighter forms of music goes back to the mid 19th century, the abbreviation "pop" was not in general use as a generic term until the 1950s when it was adopted as the umbrella name for a special kind of musical product aimed at the teenage market. (Gammond 1993: 457)

Gammond goes on, in this encyclopedic entry on "pop," to exemplify the term by referring mostly to the history of "rock." The issue, in

17

other words, is far from settled, and calls for some clarification about the use of the term "pop-rock" in this book. Two points will be illuminated in this regard, namely the use of the hyphenated form "pop-rock" and its complex relations to the general notion of "popular music."

In this book, "pop-rock" refers to music consciously created and produced by using amplification, electric and electronic instruments, sophisticated recording equipment (including samplers), by employing certain techniques of supposedly untrained vocal delivery, mostly those signifying immediacy of expression and spontaneity, and by filtering all these through sound editing, modification, and manipulation devices. For pop-rock musicians, these technologies of sonic expression are not just aids for enhancing or capturing sound produced by traditional acoustic instruments and the human voice, but rather creative tools for generating sonic textures that cannot be produced otherwise (Gracyk 1996; Wicke 1990). Pop-rock music is predominantly a creation of recording machinery in studios and elsewhere, destined primarily for phonograms (and their mutation as computer files). The use of this set of practices renders all styles of pop-rock participants in one sonic idiom, in one semiotic system. In addition, pop-rock is culturally organized around a stylistic genealogy and a historical narrative for which the emergence of the *rock'n'roll* style in the mid-1950s in the United States serves as a mythical moment of "birth" (Peterson 1990). The history of pop-rock tends to be narrated as an unfolding lineage of styles, for which "the eruption of *rock'n'roll*" (Garofalo 2005) serves as a starting point, marking thereby a symbolic divide between earlier periods and the "rock era." All styles of pop-rock are characterized in such narrations as developments, mutations, and expansions derived from the original style of *rock'n'roll* and from the successive styles that developed from it. Moreover, pop-rock styles and genres have been portrayed over the years as suppliers of aesthetic languages and packages of meaning around which consecutive generations of teenagers and young adults have defined their late modern sense of particularity, of distinction (Grossberg 1992). By the early twenty-first century, the stylistic genealogy of pop-rock includes forms, periods, fashions, trends, and fads of music known by names such as *hard rock, alternative rock, punk, progressive rock, power pop, soul, funk, disco, dance, house, techno, hip-hop, heavy metal, extreme metal, reggae, country rock, folk rock, psychedelic rock, singer-songwriters*, and, notably, *pop* – as well as many more. The set of creative practices around which pop-rock is organized, the cluster of sonic textures associated with

18

these practices, together with the perceptual scheme that organizes the historical narrative and stylistic lineage of pop-rock, may well be called the "pop-rock aesthetic." As a musico-cultural worldview, the pop-rock aesthetic is characterized by a constant incentive towards stylistic innovation, driven either by artistic exploration or commercial interests. The relentless innovation and proliferation of pop-rock styles are materialized through the growing sophistication of the creative technologies themselves, greater awareness and complex utilization of these technologies by musicians and producers, cross-fertilization between styles and periods, and by hybridity – the tendency to merge and mix pop-rock styles with any other type of music.

The meaning of "pop-rock" as described above, often by referring to it simply as *rock* music or as *rock & roll*, distills the cultural logic that underlies much of the discursive and institutional practices surrounding the music itself as it has evolved since the 1950s. In other words, the above portrayal of pop-rock reflects a cultural convention, prevalent to the point of being self-evident among critics, historians, commentators, and scholars of popular music. Take, for example, the book entitled *The Rock History Reader* (Cateforis 2006). The articles are divided into six sections, each devoted to one decade, from the 1950s to the 2000s. The first chapter is about Chuck Berry, and the last one about rap music. In between, among its 59 articles, there are chapters about Elvis Presley, the Beatles, Bob Dylan, punk, heavy metal, and alternative rock, but also about James Brown, reggae, Phil Spector, Motown, disco, and Madonna. Another exemplary book is *The Rolling Stone Illustrated History of Rock and Roll* (DeCurtis and Henke 1992), which, in addition to obvious chapters about musicians such as the Rolling Stones, Stevie Wonder, Neil Young, Led Zeppelin, and Bruce Springsteen, also devotes chapters to styles and phenomena such as doo-wop, Brill Building pop, girl groups, soul, bubblegum, funk, disco, reggae, rap, and global beat. These books are just two among many other encyclopedic projects, television series, and internet websites, that exemplify the cultural convention, the institutionalized practice that manifests itself not only discursively, but also in the organizational functioning of the music industry and the media. It is a practice that groups together into one category not only the whole range of styles and genres most obviously belonging to "rock music," but also its "blander" or "diluted" variants, those typically referred to as "pop," as well as styles associated with the African-American community or with electronic dance music. Indeed, as a study of critics' work in leading magazines has found, changes in the aesthetic classification system of critics substantiated the thesis of "declassification" or "pop-rockization" ... critics perceive and evaluate different genres with more similar evaluative criteria ... [they] also tend to perceive the category pair of "pop" and "rock" as less distinct. (van Venrooij 2009: 329)

Therefore, the hyphenated form "pop-rock," as an umbrella term, is preferred here because it clearly indicates the inclusion of the "lighter" forms of rock music in this category, as well as the actual practices in the field.

When examined globally (as will be done in this book), one cannot but assert that by the early twenty-first century, world culture is, to a large extent, calibrated to the sounds of pop-rock music. Rock ballads, electro-dance pop tunes and hip-hop hits fill up the background music in fashion stores, supermarkets and malls, car radios, TV commercials, internet websites, and many other channels all over the world. Electric and electronic sounds, pulsating beats, and guttural vocals have become trivial, ubiquitous components in popular music styles in almost every country. Pop-rock songs serve as soundtracks for films and television dramas, functioning as sonic signifiers of moods, periods, generations, and locations. Pop-rock styles and genres provide aesthetic idioms and bundles of meaning around which generational and lifestyle groupings, as well as ethnic factions and other prominent sectors within national societies define their sense of late modern identity. In other words, in the course of its several decades' history, pop-rock – or rather, the pop-rock aesthetic – has become omnipresent in many countries. The sweeping presence of pop-rock is sometimes reflected in the tendency to use the term "popular music" when in fact dealing, almost exclusively, with pop-rock music (Frith 1996; Longhurst 1995; Shuker 2001).

Pop-rock, however, is not a synonym for popular music. In countries where indigenous traditions of modern popular music preceded pop-rock music, and have persisted along with it, the whole range of pop-rock styles and genres is typically regarded as an art world and aesthetic realm distinct from other forms and aesthetic idioms of popular music. Thus, for example, an introduction to a collection of articles on pop-rock in Latin America clearly uses a definition along the parameters suggested here in order to refer to the type of musical cultures analyzed in the book. It refers to rock as

a template within which a variety of sounds and behaviors can be located and still be understood as a coherent category. Such a broad and flexible description thus accommodates all music that is mass-mediated, self consciously "contemporary," makes at least some use of electric or electronic instrumentation, is associated primarily (but not exclusively) with youth, and whose aesthetics are hybrid, that is, reflecting multiple cultural sources ... the idea of a rock template allows us to properly include musical forms such as funk and techno ... (Pacini Hernandez et al. 2004: 5)

As the quote above exemplifies, when considered beyond the Anglo-American milieu, and even when eventually naturalized and indigenized, the whole range of pop-rock styles and genres are jointly perceived as one exogenous, imported musico-cultural realm. Argentinean *tango*, Spanish *flamenco*, French *chanson*, Indian film music, Italian "bel canto" and operatic traditions, Brazilian *bossa nova* and *samba*, Japanese *enka*, and "the great tradition" of mid-century Arab music, as well as Carribean genres like *rumba*, *merengue*, or *salsa*, are all modern forms of popular music that have flourished before pop-rock became prevalent in their respective home countries, and kept on thriving even as local pop-rock became well established. Understood in this way, pop-rock clearly differs from the wider notion of popular music.

But, even within the dominant Anglo-American context, the practice of using the term "pop-rock" (or "rock") tends to include in it the music recorded by the likes of Britney Spears, Metallica, Public Enemy, Oasis, Joni Mitchell, Aphex Twin, Bob Marley, and the Who, while at the same time excluding names such as Dean Martin, Ethel Merman, Ray Conniff, Shirley Bassey, or Stephen Sondheim. The aesthetic and cultural logic underlying the pop-rock aesthetic allows us to include in it a diversity of styles and musicians that ranges from the most raucous work of bands such as the Velvet Underground or Nirvana, to the most formulaic work of the Archies or Avril Lavigne, from the most experimental work of Sonic Youth or Brian Eno, to the most pleasing work of Take That or Beyoncé – while excluding the likes of, say, Johnny Mathis, *The Sound of Music* soundtrack, or the works of Barbara Streisand.

Indeed, the term "popular music" covers a much wider scope of musical practice than pop-rock. Scholars from different disciplines, including ethnomusicology, musicology, and media and cultural studies, have spent much effort in attempting to characterize or define popular music (see thorough discussions in Manuel 1988; Middleton 1990; Shuker 2001), as well as attempting to clarify its variance of meaning in and across different languages (Jordán González and Smith 2011). Suffice to say that rather than designating a genre or style, the term refers to the socio-cultural setting in which music is produced and received. Popular music is thus typically positioned against two other incarnations of modern musical socio-cultural contexts. These are folk music and art music. Folk music is linked primarily with practices of music making associated with pre-modern or rural societies, oral traditions, and musical idioms that musicological knowledge often labels as "unsophisticated." Art music, on the other hand, has typically been associated with dominant and educated classes, notated forms of music, and complex musical structures. Against these two, popular music is usually characterized as the musical culture of modern urban societies:

> A term used widely in everyday discourse, generally to refer to types of music that are considered to be of lower value and complexity than art music, and to be readily accessible to large numbers of musically uneducated listeners rather than to an élite. It is, however, one of the most difficult terms to define precisely. This is partly because its meaning (and that of equivalent words in other languages) has shifted historically and often varies in different cultures; partly because its boundaries are hazy, with individual pieces or genres moving into or out of the category, or being located either inside or outside it by different observers; and partly because the broader historical usages of the word 'popular' have given it a semantic richness that resists reduction ... Even if 'popular' music is hard to define, and even if forms of popular music, in some sense of the term, can be found in most parts of the world over a lengthy historical period, in practice its most common references are to types of music characteristic of 'modern' and 'modernizing' societies – in Europe and North America from about 1800, and even more from about 1900, and in Latin America and 'Third World' countries since the 20th century, and even more strongly since World War II. (Middleton and Manuel 2010)

Pop-rock can be viewed, in this regard as a sub-category of popular music. While this view certainly depicts the relationship between the two categories to some extent, it does not fully explicate the complexity of this relationship. This complexity is manifested in the process that can be referred to as the "pop-rockization" of popular music. That is, the exponential growth of pop-rock styles themselves, the hybrid tendency within pop-rock music to merge and fuse pop-rock with other styles and genres, and the tendency of musicians and producers working in various genres of popular music to adopt and implement at least some creative practices associated with pop-rock, most notably the adoption of electric instrumentation, have contributed to a process whereby the pop-rock aesthetic became the dominant force in world popular music, marginalizing thereby other

,tyles and genres of popular music. As Laing succinctly asserted early ɔn:

> Pop music begins with rock & roll. The radical differences between rock and the popular music that preceded it produced radical changes in the structure of the whole musical field. The popular music ballad had then to adapt itself to survive under the hegemony of rock & roll. (Laing 1969: 63)

Pop-rock became quantitatively dominant by the sheer commercial success and number of productions, and it became qualitatively dominant by setting the standard modes of instrumentation and creativity, and by constantly providing the innovative stylistic frontiers, the "avant-garde," for popular music. The process of "pop-rockization" is, in a sense, the socio-cultural transformation addressed by and analyzed in this book. The emergence of pop-rock music, its consolidation and legitimating as a contemporary musical art, as a signifier of universal modernity, but also as a viable expression of late modern musical nationalism in many countries, are jointly the set of processes that make pop-rock a major manifestation of aesthetic cosmopolitanism.

Structure of the Book

It should be stressed, at this point, that this book does not aim to provide a general account of music and cultural globalization (for an excellent review of this issue, see Stokes 2004, 2007). Nor is this book about *world music*, a marketing term devised by music corporations in the 1980s as an all encompassing catchphrase for almost all non-Anglo-American popular music (Laing 2008), thus rendering all such music "exotic" or portraying it as the voice of the subaltern against Western dominance (Feld 2000; see Frith 2002 for a discussion of the discourse on world music). Examining pop-rock of the world as one art world, this book also avoids the use of the term "world beat." Anglo-American centric by its essence, the latter term is used exclusively for pop-rock originating in countries other than the US and the UK. These two terms reflect a perception of global pop-rock critically exposed by Taylor (1997) while discussing the work of Youssou N'Dour from Senegal and Angelique Kidjo from Benin. These two musicians

> view Western demands for authenticity as concomitant with demands that they and their countries remain premodern, or modern, while the

23

rest of the globe moves further toward a postindustrial, late capitalist, postmodern culture. N'Dour and Kidjo are concerned in becoming global citizens and do this by showing that their countries and their continent are neither backward nor premodern, that they can make cultural forms as (post)modern as the West's. (Taylor 1997: 143)

Focusing here on pop-rock music as a prime exponent of aesthetic cosmopolitanism, means that this book portrays it as one global field of cultural production, in which dominant Anglo-American as well as other national and ethnic variants of pop-rock interact in complex ways.

As stated above, the chapters in this book are organized along a set of interconnected currents in sociological theory, each framing a distinct dimension of world pop-rock music as a cultural phenomenon, and giving the chapters their different titles. The first step in explaining pop-rock's prominence as the prime musical manifestation of aesthetic cosmopolitanism is, simply, to assess its presence and proliferation in world culture, across a large number of countries. Chapter 2 is indeed devoted to delineating the scope of pop-rock music as a world phenomenon. In other words, it outlines the cultural phenomenon that is the core subject of this book. It draws a sort of cultural map of the stylistic range and historical narrative of pop-rock across the world, and reviews its multiple and diverse incarnations in a variety of countries. Employing the concept of *expressive isomorphism*, the chapter demonstrates the isomorphic proliferation of pop-rock music in the world. Presenting examples from different countries, the isomorphic presence of pop-rock is surveyed along several dimensions, including the domestic propagation of pop-rock styles and genres in countries around the world; the best-selling and most played musicians (on radio and television channels) as indicators of the sonic textures that dominate the musical public sphere; the discursive and institutional ways by which the presence of the music is given cultural meaning through schemes of periodization and classification; legitimation discourse, through which the domestication and indigenization of pop-rock styles and meanings are justified.

Following the assessment in chapter 2, chapter 3 traces the institutionalization of the cultural value of pop-rock music, its emergence in the core Anglo-American context as a world model for making contemporary popular music. The chapter portrays the consolidation of pop-rock as a field of cultural production, organized around a dominant aesthetic ideology and cyclic patterns of stylistic innovation and expansion. The chapter illustrates the working of the field by

24

reference to examples from the history of pop-rock music. It is argued that the field of pop-rock that emerged during the second half of the twentieth century has a hierarchical structure and logic of struggle quite similar to other artistic fields. Namely, it has dominant positions, consisting of consecrated canonic musicians and their works (The Beatles, Bob Dylan, Jimi Hendrix, The Rolling Stones, etc.), and corresponding production of meaning positions (i.e., critics, journalists, historians, etc.) that maintain the successfully imposed criteria of evaluation. The history of the field is exposed as a series of struggles by new entrants to gain the ultimate prize of becoming part of the canon. The ever developing and expanding field is constructed through a series of additions to the canon, each justified in its turn by power-holding producers of meaning as important stylistic innovations. The analysis of pop-rock in terms of field theory serves the purpose of demonstrating the ever expanding scope of the pop-rock aesthetic. The chapter shows how the relatively narrow aesthetic language of rock'n'roll has gradually grown and been legitimized, to include several decades later a wide array of styles, ranging from the most experimental electronic music to the most standardized variants of pop music.

Chapter 4 examines the logic and practices through which pop-rock genres and styles, and the pop-rock aesthetic at large, have been adopted, adjusted, and adapted by musicians and meaning production agencies in different parts of the world. Focusing on the production side – that is, the work of musicians and producers of meaning – the chapter looks at the diachronic process through which pop-rock music gained recognition, legitimacy, esteem, and dominance in national fields of popular music. The chapter examines the practices and strategies by which musicians and producers of meaning not only produced national, indigenized variants of pop-rock music, but also succeeded in legitimizing them in the contexts of musical nationalisms. At its core, the chapter develops a model of the process, portrayed here as a *longue durée* event and labeled *the musical historical event of pop-rock*, in the course of which the musical culture in many countries has gradually transformed from being based on quests for, and notions of, native exclusivity and folk purism, to being dominated by the aesthetic practices and worldview of pop-rock. The model consists of four major phases: early history, consecrated beginnings, consolidation and rise to dominance, and diversification and glorification. The working of this process is exemplified by the cases of pop-rock music in various countries, with special focus on Argentina and Israel. Throughout, the chapter focuses on the tension between the interest to participate in the stylistic frontiers of pop-rock as defined by mostly Anglo-American musicians and critics, and the will to maintain a sense of local and national uniqueness. Drawing on the aforementioned work of Sewell Jr. (2005), it looks at musicians and other practitioners as caught in the intersection of two fields of cultural production: the field of pop-rock and the field of national culture.

Chapter 5 deals with the reception side of global pop-rock, its consumption and fandom. It takes its lead from studies on collective phenomena typically associated with pop-rock fandom, such as scenes and subcultures, as well as consumption studies of popular music, in particular those which document omnivorousness. The chapter develops the notion of the *aesthetic cultures of pop-rock* as a way to link these approaches. It looks at pop-rock fandom as a continuum that stretches from "hardcore" participants in scenes and subcultures to casual listeners, and examines the changes and transformations in the participation of fans around the world in the taste and knowledge community of pop-rock, in its aesthetic cultures, in light of consumption practices that emerged with the Internet, most notably file sharing, forums, and blogs.

In the final step of this study, chapter 6 takes a phenomenological and a more pronounced interpretive turn. It focuses on the presence of pop-rock styles and genres, and especially on their typical sonic textures and vocabularies, in the musical soundscape of urban environments, and in individuals' bodies. Drawing on works about music and space and about music and the body, and employing a few notions from actor-network theory, the chapter argues that pop-rock styles and genres have ushered similar bodily experiences of music among generations of devoted fans and casual listeners around the world. Pop-rock sonic idioms have also become major building blocks of the sonic environment in urban settings across the world. With these two functions, pop-rock music has greatly contributed to growing proximity and overlap between countries and regions in the everyday experiences of identity and locality.

Methodological Note

This book is informed by two major lines of research. One consists of my own work on pop-rock in Israel, Argentina, and Spain (all the quotations originally published in Spanish or Hebrew are translated into English by myself), as well as on the discursive formation of

26

Anglo-American pop-rock. The other consists of extensive readings of scholarly literature about pop-rock music in countries around the world. The book does not, however, aim to provide encyclopedic knowledge about pop-rock music of the world. Although many cases and examples of such music from numerous countries are presented in the following pages, an abundance of additional cases are absent from the text.

The empirical aspects of the book are guided by an effort to detect the local experiences and perceptions of pop-rock music in various countries. The book, therefore, as noted above, tends to avoid informative, non-scholarly literature on "world music" or "world beat." Such literature is inclined at exoticizing non-Anglo-American pop-rock and to overemphasize those styles and genres of indigenous pop-rock that appeal to Western ears as "authentic" in an essentialist way. While these types of music are certainly treated and discussed in the book, they are nevertheless depicted as just examples among various incarnations of national pop-rock music around the world.

— 2 —

EXPRESSIVE ISOMORPHISM

In the summer of 2003, the Spanish popular music magazine *Efe eme* published the results of a critics' poll to select the "100 best albums of Spanish pop" ("Los 100 discos mejores del pop español"). The album that was voted into the number one spot was *Veneno*, released in 1977 by a band of the same name, and in fact carrying the name of its leading musician, Kiko Veneno (real name José María López Sanfeliu). Coming from Seville, Veneno consisted also of brothers Rafael and Raimundo Amador (who later went on to form Pata Negra, a band specializing in electric flamenco). The band created a musical mixture inspired equally by flamenco and Anglo-American pop-rock:

> Veneno sounded fresh. Kiko Veneno was transmitting the legacy of Bob Dylan and the California hippy through the sieve of those gypsies who were dying to play electric guitars. Rockeros aflamencados, flamencos rockerizados. It was impetuous music of the street, and it did not ask permission from London, nor from San Francisco – and not from Madrid or Barcelona – in order to exist in its own terms. (Diego A. Manrique, *Efe eme* no. 50, July–August 2003, p. 29)

This album received the same position in the critics list of the magazine *Rockdelux*, published in November 2004 as the "100 best Spanish albums of the 20th century" (los 100 mejores discos españoles del siglo XX). *Efe eme* and *Rockdelux* were not the only Spanish publications to carry such critics' polls. *MondoSonoro* published in November 2002 a list of the "best 25 albums in Spanish" (los 25 mejores discos en castellano), and yet another poll was carried in May 2010 by the Spanish edition of *Rolling Stone* magazine (los 50 mejores discos de la historia del rock español). An analysis of the combined lists have found that the presence of several albums by the 1980s band Radio Futura and by singer-songwriter Joan Manuel Serrat places these two as the most valorized musicians in Spanish pop-rock music (del Val et al. 2011). Another finding is that five of the ten most valorized musicians in the combined lists (Radio Futura, Gabinete Caligari, Nacha Pop, Alaska and Dinarama, Loquillo), are associated with the so-called "movida madrilena" (the Madrilian move) of the early 1980s, generally regarded by critics and scholars as a seminal moment in the history of popular music in Spain, in which pop-rock music's stature as a viable form of musical art was consolidated (Fouce 2006). It should be noted that, except for some notable representations of so-called "new Flamenco" (by Camaron, for example), no album of traditional flamenco, nor of any other traditional style of Spanish popular or folk music, was included in these lists.

During the 2010s, as these lists were being compiled by experts, the charts of the best-selling albums, most downloaded songs from web stores, and most played songs on Spanish radio stations have been dominated, next to Anglo-American names such as Rihanna or Coldplay, by the likes of El Canto del Loco, Alejandro Sanz, Amaral, Estopa, or La Oreja de Van Gogh. These commercially successful bands and musicians of the 2000s in Spain covered a repertoire of styles ranging from energetic, power pop (El Canto del Loco) to senti-mental, dramatized romantic ballads (Alejandro Sanz). Practically all of them exhibited aesthetic values and creative practices of pop-rock music. That is, studio production, electric instruments, and vocal techniques directly derived from pop-rock stylistic heritage. Being the most commercially successful songs and albums, this was also the music that dominated the public musical sphere, especially in urban environments (shopping centers, fashion stores, cafés, taxis, TV channels).

With its critics' polls and popularity charts taken together, the field of popular music in Spain as it existed in the 2000s serves as the almost perfect case for illustrating how pop-rock musical idioms and aesthetic worldview have been isomorphically replicated across a wide range of countries and socio-cultural settings worldwide. While pop-rock sonic textures and styles dominate the cultural public sphere, a discursive formation – constructed and maintained by pro-fessional specialists – provides a historical and interpretive scheme for mapping and making sense of the field. As local styles of pop-rock become ubiquitous and omnipresent, as their sonorities become the default, taken-for-granted forms of music that populate the airwaves, the experts and critics consecrate certain pop-rock musicians as the great talents whose recorded works have pioneered, inspired, and ushered in the new and – according to this narrative – exciting era of local/national music. The scheme of historical linearity and artistic hierarchy frames the socio-cultural meaning of the presence and development of pop-rock in Spain, portraying, in fact, the currently successful artists as descendents, albeit "commercialized" to some degree at the very least, of those early consecrated musicians. In other words, the field of popular music in Spain in the early twenty-first century displays, in a sort of taken-for-granted manner, a periodization of its own history and a classification of styles, that clearly distinguish pop-rock music from "pre-rock" and "non-rock." Ruling the sonic environment, it consists of a stylistic range that stretches from the experimental corners of alternative or indie rock to standardized electro-dance pop, and it has a firm interpretive scheme that contextualizes it within Spanish society and culture.

The Spanish field of popular music is not the only one to display an artistic hierarchy and a historical scheme of local popular music derived from the pop-rock aesthetic worldview, yet domesticated and indigenized to the point of being perceived as depictions of contemporary Spanish uniqueness. It is certainly not the only national setting whose sonic environment is dominated by pop-rock sounds. These major features, as well as others, can be found in many other national fields of popular music. Not every single feature of the field, however, is present in all national fields. There is variance and diversity in the functioning of pop-rock music in different national cases. Yet when examined together, across countries and periods, pop-rock emerges as a global musical culture isomorphically present in a large number of countries.

Pop-rock thus serves as a prime exponent of a process in late modern culture that can best be characterized as *expressive isomorphism* – a process whose end result is aesthetic cosmopolitanism. In other words, it serves to substantiate the argument that isomorphism of world culture takes shape not only in the realm of rational instrumental culture, as claimed by Meyer and his associates (Meyer et al. 1997), but also in the realm of expressive culture. This point deserves some elaboration. In their assessment of the structure of contemporary world society, Meyer and colleagues propose that "many features of the contemporary nation-state derive from worldwide models constructed and propagated through global cultural and associational processes" (Meyer et al. 1997: 144). These worldwide models include such notions that all nations should have modern

30

health care and all children should go to school. They go on to assert that "worldwide models define and legitimate agendas for local action, shaping the structure and policies of nation-states and other national and local actors in virtually all of the domains of rationalized social life" (Meyer et al. 1997: 145). Perceiving the cultural dimension of world society as "the cognitive and ontological models of reality that specify the nature, purposes, technology, sovereignty, control and resources of nation-states and other actors" (Meyer et al. 1997: 149), they understand this shaping of structure as isomorphic change, and they observe isomorphism in a variety of institutional fields across the world. Under this perception of culture, however, isomorphism is found only in the realm of rationalized instrumental culture. Meyer tends to be quite dismissive about the role of expressive culture in world society. Proposing that things like "variations in language, dress, food, traditions, landscapes, familial styles and so on" – and, one would presume, the arts – "are precisely the things that in the modern system do not matter, which means to say they have no direct, rational relation to instrumental actorhood" (Meyer 2000: 245), Meyer implies that culture in world society develops through a path of rational-instrumental similarity, based on world models, and expressive diversity, based mostly on local-national traditional patterns.

At once a critique and an extension of the propositions quoted above, the notion of expressive isomorphism asserts that expressive culture is also standardized to a large extent along world models. That is, expressive cultural uniqueness characteristic of late-modern actorhood, either for sectors within national societies or for nations at large, is also susceptible to isomorphism. A review of pop-rock's major features in a variety of national cases demonstrates the extent to which national fields of popular music are standardized and shaped along the parameters of pop-rock music. A survey of the manifestation of these features across a wide range of countries amounts to an assessment of the global presence of pop-rock music. It reveals that pop-rock is a world cultural phenomenon whose various local and national incarnations are threaded by isomorphic similarities and thus an embodiment of aesthetic cosmopolitanism. In other words, such an assessment points to stylistic, institutional and discursive patterns that surface in almost every national field of pop-rock, reflecting the extent of the cultural overlap and proximity between them.

In what follows, then, pop-rock's isomorphism, its world cultural presence and impact, is assessed by surveying the following parameters: domestic proliferation of pop-rock styles and genres; best-selling and most played musicians (on radio and television channels) as indicators of the sonic textures that dominate the musical public sphere; discursive and institutional ways by which the presence of the music is given cultural meaning through schemes of periodization and classification; and legitimation discourse, through which the domestication and indigenization of pop-rock styles and meanings are justified.

Pop-Rock Styles and Genres

The first and probably most significant measure of pop-rock's global presence is simply the pervasiveness of pop-rock styles and genres in the socio-cultural map of many different countries across the world. Documenting and analyzing the dynamics of popular music in China in the late 1990s, de Kloet (2010) describes the following scenes in Chinese pop-rock: *underground, heavy metal, hard core punk, hip-hop, folk-rock, pop-rock* (meaning here the softer, accessible style of rock music), *pop-punk,* and the so-called fashionable bands (mostly *electro-dance pop*). In addition, he looks into the widespread style – all over China – of *gangtai* pop, sometimes known as Cantopop or Mandapop, originating in Hong Kong and Taiwan. This mapping of Chinese pop-rock of the 1990s demonstrates the extent to which pop-rock styles and genres have been replicated in various local and national settings of popular music. Indeed, the history of pop-rock music since its symbolic emergence in the 1950s with rock'n'roll amounts to diversification and sub-division into a long line of styles. *Hard rock, alternative rock, urban (r&b) pop, hip-hop, metal, electronic dance music, reggae,* and *mainstream pop* are some salient labels that hint to the stylistic variety of pop-rock music over the years. Each of these contains various stylistic nuances that further multiply the variation.

As part of its isomorphic expansion worldwide, local variants and adaptations of many of these styles have emerged in many different countries, in modes ranging from sheer duplication to local adjustment and modification. Most obvious is the propagation of the pop-rock mainstream, whose salient incarnation consists of several typical phenomena. Two of them are the female superstar, often referred to as *diva* and subject of a "larger than life" glamorous aesthetic; and the rock *auteur*, a rock singer-songwriter voicing social and moral consciousness and frequently hailed as a national voice, sometimes even dubbed as the "local Bob Dylan." However, while local variants of these widely appealing, successful forms of pop-rock music often signify a universal sense of modernity, it is interesting to note also how specific pop-rock styles and genres have gained global currency as cultural tools for proclaiming alliance with transnational scenes or subcultures, yet at the same time asserting and reaffirming local identities in a variety of ways. One prominent way has been the use of pop-rock genres for asserting a critical stance towards authoritarian regimes or conservative national culture, and thus proclaiming a "new," updated, and counter-hegemonic variant of national culture. Youth from diverse social sectors – including intellectuals, bohemians, the middle class, the working class, migrants, ethnic, and regional minorities – came to find from the 1960s and 1970s in pop-rock styles the self-evident tools for expressing dissent and affirming alternative identities. Pop-rock practitioners of this type have often found themselves in the somewhat ambiguous position of being in between universal modernity and national uniqueness. Or, as Baulch (2002: 167) concludes from her ethnography on Bali's punk rock scene (dubbed *alternapunk*) of the mid-1990s (and echoing Turner 1969), "rather than opposition *or* compliance, the practice of alternapunk is more reminiscent of qualities . . . assigned to liminality." Prominent genres that have widely circulated in many countries along these parameters at different points in pop-rock's history are *progressive rock, punk, metal, electronic dance, hip-hop* and the cluster of styles that will be referred to here as *ethnic rock*.

Pop-Rock Divas

Although having some of its roots in the historical traditions of *bel canto* operatic singing and vocal popular song in general, the phenomenon of the pop-rock diva is not necessarily based on vocal capabilities. While some pop-rock divas do possess vocal skills of the type associated with non-amplified music, their stature is, however, organized around projections of dramatized and magnified visual images of femininity, coupled with a musical repertoire that encompasses diverse pop-rock styles – from hard rock or soft ballads, to electro-dance, soulful rhythm and blues, and more. By absorbing influences from a large pop-rock stylistic vocabulary and adjusting them to their own images, and through their often immense commercial success and popularity, pop-rock divas sometimes become symbolic figures not only of mainstream pop-rock in a given country, but of national identity as well.

Alla Pugacheva, from Russia, is one illustrative example of the pop-rock diva. "Harlequin," her 1976 hit, "established her fame as the

33

leading Russian pop diva, a reputation that survives into the present day" (Beumers 2005: 237). This song, a cabaret-like tune, was the first in a long row of hits that presented "a well-balanced combination of pop, rock, folk, and gypsy songs" (Partan 2007: 489). Her career survived well not only the political transition and the demise of the Soviet regime, but also the changes that took place in Russian popular music, as "pop music has gradually pushed aside the other genres that existed in Soviet *estrada*, making them unprofitable or unmarketable" (Partan 2007: 493). This new, post-1990 form of pop, "represents a strange Russian-Western twist, where money and access to the new music video industry, with its skillful producers of music and special effects, play a critical role. Melody, which was once an essential foundation of Russian and Soviet lyrical songs, has been replaced by rhythmic electronic disco beats" (Partan 2007: 493). Pugacheva, however, has "skillfully used some of the [new] methods ... in order to stay marketable and in tune with changing trends" (Partan 2007: 494). Consequently, "although the heyday of her career was clearly the 1970s, Pugacheva continues to make the headlines, whether it is with her marriage to the much younger pop singer Filipp Kirkorov, or the launch of a shoe and fashion label, or the participation in 1997 in the Eurovision Song Contest (Beumers 2005: 238).

Another case of a national female diva is Greece's Anna Vissi, whose career also began in the early 1970s. Her tendency to frequently change visual images, many of which revolve around erotic vocabularies, and her intensive use of electro-dance rhythms and textures (synthesizers, samplers, electronic percussion), propelled the media to dub her "the Greek Madonna" (after the American female musician). Nevertheless, attempting to gain legitimacy as a Greek authentic musician for the local as well as for the international market, her music also incorporates elements associated with traditional Greek music. Her music and career thus radiates a sort of double-edged meaning:

> Her CD single "Call Me" [English lyrics], which was distributed in the United States in 2005, put emphasis on the modern-Greek otherness of Anna Vissi, featuring certain music signifiers and "authenticating" references to her "Greekness." The "oriental-sounding" whirling strings and backing vocals were by and large based on a succession of semitones and augmented seconds, thus acting as ingredients of the "exotic" and "ethnic" modern Greek sound. The Greek-rock remix of the same song, which in Greek is entitled 'Eísai' ["You Are," Greek lyrics], was performed live by Anna Vissi during the MAD-Music-Video-Awards

show in Athens in June 2004. Electric guitars, synthesizers, drums, sequencers and samplers prevailed in a musical idiom largely dependent on the stylistic features of Western rock music. In other words, Vissi here promoted the "Madonna" part of her "Greek-Madonna" persona. The "oriental" musical elements were minimized and used as mere reminders of the initial "ethnic-pop" version of the song "Eísai." In this case, Vissi, a prestigious star from the centre of the national music industry, seems to take the opportunity to experiment flexibly with diverse musical styles. She is allegedly freed from the need of cultural "authenticity," because she is arguably expected to renovate and spice up once conservative and inward-looking Greek popular-music styles. (Polychronakis, 2007: 513)

Additional illustrative examples of the pop diva phenomenon include, for example, Laura Pausini, the Italian performer whose superstar position has gone beyond her homeland to Latin America, and Faye Wong, the "empress of cantopop," whose

incorporation of both mainstream and non-mainstream songs and musical elements into her repertoire led her to be referred to in the Chinese music industry press in 1994 as *Faye Chu Lau Tze Yam*, a term meaning "the voice of Faye's mainstream," but also "the voices of the non-mainstream" in spoken Cantonese, which could also be translated as "Fayestream." This indicates that she could almost be said to occupy her own category in the Chinese pop music spectrum, and she has continued to combine mainstream pop songs with more "alternative," even avant-garde oriented tracks throughout her career. (Mitchell 2007: 2)

Rock Auteurs

With Bob Dylan serving as a prototype, the figure of the pop-rock *auteur* stands in the pop-rock aesthetic as the ultimate individual rock musician. Most typically a male (although many prominent female *auteurs* also occupy significant positions in the pop-rock canon), the pop-rock *auteur* is an individual who composes, writes, sings, plays, and occasionally also produces his music. In addition, in the case of the most acclaimed *auteurs*, the lyrics are often considered to be carriers of poetic, moral, political, and other "serious" meanings. By mastering all aspects of the creative process of pop-rock music, the pop-rock *auteur* stands within the pop-rock aesthetic world as the total musician in pop-rock, an individual whose work is often presented as the decisive testimony to artistic creativity in pop-rock music. While the typical rock *auteur* is usually an individual who recruits different backing musicians for his various projects, some *auteurs* are better known for being the leaders of bands (Ray Davies of the Kinks is one prominent example), or for having a permanent band working with them through most of their career (Neil Young and Crazy Horse, Bruce Springsteen and the E Street Band). Following the model set by Dylan, Springsteen, Young, and others, local pop-rock *auteurs* have been hailed in many countries as pioneers and heralds of domestic pop-rock music, and in some notable occasions as artists whose oeuvre represents prominent ideological and cultural sectors, or indeed the nation at large.

One such musician is Zimbabwe's Thomas Mapfumo. His career from the 1970s to the 1990s saw him move from being a young pop musician performing in various styles (rock, soul, light jazz), to indigenous-based electric music, which prominently features the electric mbira-guitar – that is, an electric guitar sound that imitates the sonic textures of the mbira, an indigenous instrument (sometimes referred to as "thumb piano") often used in the traditional music of the Shona people from Zimbabwe (Turino 2000). Mapfumo's artistic explorations have paralleled, and in fact converged with the struggle for liberation that culminated with independence in 1980. The lyrics of his songs came to express national sentiments and the fight for political freedom. Throughout his work, Mapfumo clearly adapted indigenous patterns of traditional music to the conventions of pop-rock music. While he "maintains the characteristic polyphonic textures of indigenous Shona music, he carefully arranges the music so that clarity of parts prevails rather than the dense overlays and spontaneous dynamics and variations of indigenous performance . . . Mapfumo has standardized and shaped indigenous Shona music for cosmopolitan consumption at home and abroad" (Turino 2000: 346). By his own account, Mapfumo proclaims himself to be "one who inherited, improved and perfected" traditional mbira music, "and managed to present it by modern electrical instruments, and made it to be liked by more people in these hightech times" (interview with the Zimbabwean journal *Moto*, 1990; quoted in Turino 2000: 346).

Sweden's Ulf Lundell is another personification of the rock *auteur*. Lars Lilliestam's history of Swedish rock, *Svensk rock: Musik, lyrik, historik* (1998) already pointed to connections between Lundell's lyrics and certain themes in Swedish folk music. This is reiterated by Lindberg (2007):

Lundell writes in a double tradition: that of the "authenticity rock" of Dylan or Springsteen, and that of the Swedish *visa* – an important ingredient of the national song treasure. There are interesting links between the indigenous tradition of the *visa* and rock lyrics written in Swedish . . . Lundell often voices a working-class solidarity filtered through the youth revolt of the 1960s. A closed-down mine here invokes the loss of "the people's home" . . . It is Springsteen adapted to Swedish conditions . . . The Sweden of Lundell's dreams is the outcome of successful nego-tiations between the need for community and the need for Bohemian freedom. (Lindberg 2007: 352–4)

Pop-rock *auteurs*, then, are most typically individuals whose music is taken to symbolize and represent the artistic seriousness of pop-rock music and its creative authenticity. They are therefore highly eligible, in the eyes of critics, to become pop-rock's manifestations of national culture. Thus Yehudit Ravitz from Israel is described as

one of the most prominent female rock artists in Israel. Her composi-tions and singing had a significant part in creating the "Israeli sound" of the late 1970s and early 1980s, and especially that of our female singer-songwriters. (Yoav Kutner, *Mooma*, mooma.mako.co.il/artist. asp?ArtistId=1302; accessed September 2011)

And in Italy many rock *auteurs* have sought the label of *cantautori* and to be accepted into the realm of *canzone d'autore*, because, after the 1960s, the term *cantautore* "no longer designated simply a singer who is also a songwriter but the singer and the songwriter of a different song – something that by its very distinguished existence could redefine (and circumscribe) the boundaries of 'commercial' or a more obviously 'light' music" (Santoro 2002: 116). Later on, *canzone d'autore* was consolidated as a "separate realm (from market and industry constraints and rules), and one involving the symbolic classification and framing of it as a form of culture that, even if 'popular' and 'mass mediated,' has 'high' artistic value" (Santoro 2002: 120).

Progressive Rock

The cluster of styles known among pop-rock cognoscenti as *progres-sive* or *art rock*, emerged in the early 1970s – and then lasted well into the 1980s – as a prime mode for expressing and advancing artistic consciousness about pop-rock music, mostly among upper-middle-class youth (Holm-Hudson 2002; Macan 1997). In some former Soviet bloc countries in Eastern Europe, it also came to express cri-tique and resistance towards authoritarian regimes (Mitchell 1996; Szemere 2001). This was also the case in some Latin American countries. Merging elements of local folk music and rock to create long complex pieces of music, exhibiting compositional prowess, virtuosic capability in the playing of musical instruments, and poetical sophistication in the lyrics, bands like Arco Iris or Serú Girán (Argentina) and Los Jaivas (Chile) used the genre to create nuanced, poetically intricate criticism of the regimes in their respective countries. Gonzalez (2012) refers to them as the "primitive vanguard" of Latin American pop-rock. Other notable national scenes of progressive rock in countries other than the US and the UK include Italy, which saw the blooming of the genre during the 1970s, led by bands such as Premiata Forneria Marconi (PFM), Le Orme and Area; and France, which also saw some noteworthy progressive rock bands like Atoll, Pulsar, and especially Magma and Ange. Magma's music has been described as "not rock, not jazz, not even jazz rock, but all of them at once, also with some influences from Bartok and Stravinsky" (Brierre et al. 2000: 73), while Ange's first album, *Caricatures*, was characterized as "a mélange of long musical pieces, in a progressive style à la King Crimson/Genesis" (Brierre et al. 2000: 64). Spain's variant of 1970s progressive rock included the cluster of bands that are sometimes referred to as *rock andaluz*. It included bands like Triana, Guadalquivir, Alameda, and Medina Azahara, among others, who weaved elements of flamenco into their otherwise typical performances of progressive rock. Germany also witnessed a scene of progressive bands with the likes of Can, Tangerine Dream and Kraftwerk, whose avant-garde stance and use of electronics made them highly influential for years to come on global pop-rock music at large; and so did Japan, with art rock bands like Happy End, and especially Yellow Magic Orchestra.

Punk and Metal

Punk as well as *heavy* and *extreme metal* are two additional prominent examples of the isomorphic proliferation of pop-rock genres. Although the two genres are sometimes portrayed as antagonistic to each other, they do share the aesthetic stance of taking the sound of the electric guitar band to extremes. In the case of *punk*, this is done by reducing it to minimalism, repetitiveness and primitivism (Laing 1986), and in the case of *metal* by magnifying it to baroque dimensions of indulgence and drama (Kahn-Harris 2007; Walser 1993; Weinstein 2000). Despite their occasionally opposing aesthetic attitudes, stylistic trends like *grunge* or *thrash metal* have nevertheless been welcomed by critics and fans as successful fusions of *punk* and metal. In either case, domestic scenes of both genres have emerged widely since the 1970s in different countries and regions, mostly accompanied with oppositional ideological and aesthetic stance.

From its origins in the 1970s either in New York or London, the genre of punk has diversified stylistically and polarized. By the 1990s, it has been used on one extreme to express left-wing anarchism and Dadaist aesthetics, like in the cases of punk in Indonesia (Pickles 2007) or Spain and Mexico (O'Connor 2004). On the other extreme, it came to be strongly associated with "white power" racism in various European countries (Cotter 1999). Punk, however, was not necessarily aligned with extreme politics in all countries where it emerged. In South Korea, for example, it often expresses "a sense of social responsibility . . . couched in terms that invoke a sense of nationalism" (Epstein 2000: 22). Furthermore,

> when Korean punk invokes the term "our nation" – and chooses to do so in English rather than using Korean *uri nara* – it becomes neither simply a patriotic expression nor an ironic comment on Korean nationalism: rather punks appropriate Korean discourse . . . in order to re-create the Korean nation, to create a new place for Korean youth to stand, one in which they can feel comfortable. (Epstein 2000: 27)

This new place seems to be one of mainly cultural opposition to other forms of popular music deemed "mainstream" within punk ranks. "Korean punk and other forms of underground music belong in this sense to an aesthetic counter culture" (Epstein 2000: 23) – that is, not necessarily a socio-political one.

Even more than punk, the global scene of *extreme metal* (sometimes also known as *thrash* or *death metal*), that emerged in the 1990s in the wake of *heavy metal* (itself a worldwide genre), has become in the twenty-first century one of the most widespread forms of pop-rock music (Wallach et al. 2011). Local scenes of extreme metal are found in, among other countries, Nepal (Greene 2001), Bali (Baulch 2007) as well as in Scandinavia and Israel (Kahn-Harris 2007). Given the aesthetic idiom of extreme metal, which renders bands' sound all over the world quite similar (while at the same time it verges, to some ears, on sheer noise), extreme metal – more than any other pop-rock style – is often marginalized and excluded from any accepted notion of national music. In Brazil, the extreme metal scene overcame this obstacle through Sepultura, a band that gained much international acclaim and commercial success, even beyond the circle of extreme metal fandom. While retaining the characteristic idiom of extreme metal, the band's work growingly tended toward

experiments with unexpected tempo variations inspired in Brazilian/
Afrodiasporic polyrhythms. This would lead to the "explosion of
sounds" heard on [the album] *Roots* [1996], where the band enlisted
collaboration from Brazilian multipercussionist Carlinhos Brown and
relied on recordings from the Amazonian Xavantes, collected by the
band during a visit to their reservation. (Avelar 2003: 338)

Thus, "when they reached worldwide success and became an international band, the defenders of national purity did not have much
time to condemn them, as Sepultura effected a political and musical
rediscovery of Brazil in the cross-genre experiments of *Roots*" (Avelar
2003: 333).

Although their radical aesthetics are not quite similar, punk and
extreme metal do share a conscious attitude of transgression. The
target of transgression, however, seems to vary according to country
and cultural context. One plausible interpretation for both styles
argues that they provide "locally specific forms of escape from a
wider, all encompassing 'modernity,' rather than from any one of
modernity's specific manifestations," allowing fans "to voice their
frustration at the alienation and disempowerment produced by
modernity" (Kahn-Harris 2007: 157, 159).

Electronic Dance Music

Electronic music, with its mixture of highbrow traditions, new technological development and new popular culture styles, is probably the
musical field that more than any other genre has challenged questions
of authenticity, authorship and localness. Its preference for sounds and
rhythms rather than words and speech ... are all complex aspects in
rearranging the dialectic between the local dimension of electronic
music and its globalization. (Magaudda 2003: 537)

These lines accurately depict not only the difficulty in pinpointing
any indigenous source of electronic dance music, but also hint at the
global pervasiveness of this music and its wide perception as expressing global modernity – a point that propelled musicians in countries
across the world into working within these stylistic trends. In this
regard, Magaudda points to one creative practice employed by Italian
producers of electronic dance in the 1970s. Namely, after recording
the tracks in Italy, they would go to New York studios in order to
add a layer of English vocals to the tracks, hiring for this purpose
black singers in order to render the music "soulful." This practice
was intended to conceal the "Italianicity" of the music, in order to

raise its appeal to international markets. Indeed, national sources of dance tracks became ever more indistinguishable as the sequence of styles that commenced with *disco* in the 1970s evolved in subsequent decades into a plethora of stylistic labels such as *techno*, *house* and its derivatives (acid house, jazz acid), *drum'n'bass* and *trance*, many of which came to consist of tracks without vocals. Isomorphic expansion of electronic music and its localization in national context revolved, then, not necessarily around music production but also around creating local scenes of clubs and raves. In the 1990s, places like Ibiza (Spain) or Goa (India) became world renowned locations of electronic dance club culture and raves. In fact, having a lively local electronic dance music scene consisting of parties in clubs became almost obligatory for any "global city" worthy of its name. Thus, as part of being the Indian capital of high-tech industry, Bangalore has seen the blooming of a party scene (Saldanha 2002), while Berlin, after reunification, regained an aura of cosmopolitanism by becoming a world center of *techno* music (Richard and Kruger 1998). And in Israel, after the country was swept by *trance* parties in forests and desert valleys throughout the 1990s (Schmidt 2012), Tel Aviv became a dance culture haven whose clubs follow every stylistic nuance of electronic music (Shor 2008).

Hip-Hop

One genre of pop-rock that has been overwhelmingly adopted worldwide is hip-hop. Originating, according to conventional narrative, from urban African-American culture in the South Bronx and Harlem districts of New York (Rose 1994), hip-hop became by the 1990s a genre associated globally with the voice of youth from marginalized social sectors (Osumare 2007). Either by adopting it to assert identity, or as a way of sympathizing with "blackness," hip-hop became one of the most widely spread forms of pop-rock music (van Venrooij 2009). Also common is the hybridization of hip-hop with reggae, another pop-rock genre that signifies "blackness" and marginality. Hip-hop cultures have been documented and analyzed in a wide range of countries: Japan (Condry 2006), East Africa (Kenya, Tanzania; see Njogu and Maupeu 2007), Israel (Shabtay 2003), Arab countries (Kahf 2007), Brazil (Pardue 2004), Turkey (Solomon 2005), France (Darling-Wolf 2008), Germany (Bennett 1999), Burma (Keeler 2009), Bulgaria, Holland, Basque country, Korea, New Zealand (Maori hip-hop), and more (Mitchell 2001). In most countries, hip-hop's stylistic development followed a trajectory that took it from

41

mere copying of American rappers to indigenization. This was, for example, the case for hip-hop in African countries:

> In Tanzania and Senegal, for instance, budding musicians copied American popular musicians, taking their lyrics and tunes and translating them into local languages (Kiswahili and Wolof, respectively). Hip-hop artists Xuman of Pee Froiss and Aziz Ndiaye, for instance, confirm that hip-hop in Dakar, Senegal, started within the frame of American hip-hop following the styles of performance they saw of popular rappers. Xuman says "in the beginning I started by copying American rappers – big chains, rhyming in English, [and] talking about stuff that I really did not understand. When you talk of hip hop culture [in Senegal] we did get a lot of influence from the US." Aziz remembers when he together with Didier Awadi were copying Kurtis Blow, Grandmaster Flash, and Grandmaster Melle Mel. In Dar es Salaam, Tanzania, budding musicians and other entrepreneurs also used the beats and styles of American hip-hop songs and inserted their own lyrics in Kiswahili. In 1991, for instance, Swaleh J compiled an album titled Swahili rap, which used Vanilla Ice's song "Ice Ice Baby" with Kiswahili lyrics. In South Africa ... an indigenous form of rap music called Kwaito played a key role "as a key site for the indigenization of American gangster images and their associated musical idioms." Despite this direct correlation with American hip-hop in the initial stages, African hip-hop has undergone significant indigenization and today the majority of hip-hop artists articulate a kind of music that is very much reflective of local musical styles and sensibilities. In Senegal, where the majority of hip-hop artists are Muslim, for instance, their lyrics and imagery are guided by the local style of music called Mbalax as well as by normative social decorum dictated by their faith. (Ntarangwi 2010: 1319–20)

More than just indigenization, some of hip-hop's local adaptations claim to have equal roots in native culture. This is the case in Italy, where a wave of so-called hip-hop "posses," that emerged in the 1990s from the politically oriented social centers around the country, made rap music using regional dialects (Mitchell, 1996). Indeed as Santoro and Solaroli (2007) point out, Italian hip-hop should be seen on the one hand as a

> historically mediated field of artistic production, composed of an original, distinctive set of social practices through which *hip-hop* members can define their identity as representatives of an international cultural movement, rather than as a specific, subversive, local subculture. (Santoro and Solaroli 2007: 473)

Yet, on the other hand, rapping in regional dialects, as well as some other creative and institutional practices, tend to blur in some notable cases the line between hip-hop and the artistically presitgious category of *canzone d'autore*:

> Even if Italian rappers usually do not consider themselves direct heirs of *cantautori*, the *cantautori* represent an implicit reference point of both their poetics and politics . . . the local appropriation of rap, its indigenisation and subsequent reterritorialisation, has been mediated in Italy by the strongly legitimised culture of the *canzone d'autore*. While on the one hand most Italian rappers often openly dismiss *canzone d'autore* and *cantautori* as (at least some of) their possible cultural sources, at the same time, on the other hand, this connection comes to be almost inevitable in the minds of critics and listeners. (Santoro and Solaroli 2007: 482)

Ethnic Rock/New Folk

Given the quest for legitimacy as national music, and the perceived cleavage between pop-rock and folklore, it is of particular interest in the isomorphic process of pop-rock to note the emergence of styles that attempt to dilute the sharp division between folklore or traditional forms of popular music and pop-rock styles. This is done primarily through styles that can be grouped under the label of "ethnic pop-rock." This is a generic term that refers to hybrid forms of pop-rock that consciously merge rock elements with indigenous styles. Unlike styles like punk or electronic dance music, which may sound similar in different countries, ethnic rock has unique sonic textures in each country or region. For example, ethnic rock from the Balkans (Croatia, Serbia, Bulgaria), with its incorporation of gypsy and other indigenous elements (see Rasmussen 2002), is clearly different from Latin American ethnic rock, with its Andean textures and rhythms (Salas Zuniga 2000) or from a form of Chinese rock that has a Northwestern tinge. As an idea, however, or as an artistic notion, ethnic rock clearly owes its inspiration to the space of possibilities indicated in the work of musicians like Bob Dylan, Richard Thompson and, most importantly, Bob Marley (Toynbee 2007). Being at the same time "rock" as well as "ethnic," ethnic rock may be used on occasion to evoke meanings of national uniqueness and adherence to heritage, while on other occasions it can signify modernity and cosmopolitanism. In addition to the already discussed work of Zimbabwe's Thomas Mapfumo or the 1970s flamenco-tinged progressive rock from Andalucía, other notable genres of ethnic pop-rock include Latin American fusions of pop-rock with Andean folklore and local traditions of popular music:

What is happening is the appropriation of the Latin American musical tradition but not necessarily its destruction or disappearance. These groups adopt musical structures and themes from traditional and popular music to transform and renew these traditions. There are two bands in Latin America today that are making this transformation part of their musical style. Colombia's Aterciopelados and Mexico's Café Tacuba transform Latin American music tradition through rock and punk. Originating from punk, both groups have moved into playing with and absorbing popular and traditional forms into their musical language. In this way these groups adopted the contentious stance of punk to transform traditional genres of music in Latin America. It is a popular musical form that neither forgets Latin America's rich popular and folk traditions nor adapts them passively. These groups adopt and adapt mambo, bolero, cumbia, and carrilera, but they do so critically. (Esterrich and Murillo 2000: 33)

Turkey is another country in which an influential style of ethnic pop-rock emerged in the 1970s:

This pop-folk fusion, dubbed Anadolu Rock (Anatolian Rock), drew less from popular forms of the Mediterranean and more from Euro-American popular music, particularly rock and roll. This was a kind of east-west synthesis . . ., a mixture of Euro-American popular forms, particularly rock and roll with Turkish music, played on a mixture of western (electric guitar, bass, trap set, moog) and Turkish (bağlama, dümbelek, davul) instruments. Erkin Koray, Cem Karaca, Barış Manço, and Moğollar, Apaşlar, and Kardaşlar were some of the performers and groups who made their mark during the late 1960s and well into the 1970s. The term Anadolu Rock was first used by the group Moğollar, an influential instrumental group that backed singers such as Selda Bağacan and Cem Karaca. The electric guitar, evident in early popular musical genres in Turkey, in the hands of musicians such as Erkin Koray, took a more central role in Anadolu Rock. Anadolu Rock reached its height of popularity in the mid-1970s and was eventually eclipsed in popularity by Arabesk, but many popular musicians continue to reference, if not perform, this music today. Anatolian rock, as a genre, lies at the crossroads between the popularization of folk music and the Europeanization of Turkish music. (Karahasanolu and Skoog 2009: 60–1)

Beyond the obvious cases of ethnic pop-rock, the expansion of the pop-rock aesthetic has its imprint even in music regarded strictly as "folk." One such example is provided by Los Nocheros, a very successful band from Argentina, where it has been classified as "folklore." Its variant of folklore nevertheless differs from what has traditionally been subsumed under this tag. The band uses electric bass and a

44

drum kit, and its sound occasionally features electric guitars as well. Lyrics hardly ever engage in nationalistic or nostalgic appraisals of gauchos and peasants, but rather tend to be about romantic love. In terms of image, band members very early in their career disposed of traditional apparel like the poncho, and their appearance on posters and videos has all the characteristics of typical pop stars. The band won the annual Gardel prize several times. However, in an attempt to distinguish such musicians from the still proliferating performers that sound and look like classic folklore, the Gradel prize organizers formed a new category of "new folklore."

Another example comes from Japan, where the traditional folk style known as *tsugaru shamisen* (both the name of a genre and its major instrument) became highly popular in the 1990s, beyond its customary audience. Although partially keeping loyal to the traditional song repertoire of the genre, musicians like Kinoshita Shin'ichi, Agatsuma Hiromitsu or the Yoshida Brothers broke away from traditional modes of playing the instrument. They incorporated techniques, postures, and stage images from the world of pop music, as well as stylistic elements from rock:

> The new stars of Tsugaru shamisen are also composers and arrangers, freely blending old and new sounds on their records. Yet they have not turned their backs on the past, and it is possible that if they did, they would not be considered Tsugaru shamisen musicians at all. If they experiment too much, they risk losing their older audience, but if they are not "pop" enough they also risk losing younger fans. (Peluse 2005: 69)

Indeed, it seems that the assertion that these Japanese folk musicians "combine innovative techniques with reverence to the past, producing music that constantly shifts between the categories of 'traditional,' 'folk' and 'pop'" (Peluse 2005: 58) is applicable to other cases as well – like the "new folk music" from China (best represented by the Twelve Girls Band) or the "newly-composed folk music" of former Yugoslavia (Rasmussen 2002).

With Yugoslavia in mind, this section cannot end without mentioning Bijelo Dugme, the band that enjoyed massive popularity all over former Yugoslavia between 1974 and 1989. Moving between *progressive* and *hard rock*, the band's aural signature culminated in the 1980s with a pop-rock ethnic sound that took its influences from Macedonian, Bosnian, Serbian, Croatian, and Balkan-Roma folk music. "They were the first band to blend Western and local musical forms in Yugoslavia, and became arguably the biggest Yugoslav band of all time – it has been suggested more than once that they were the Yugoslav equivalent of the Beatles" (Pauker 2006: 75). Bijelo Dugme "drew unabashedly on ethnic melodies and succeeded, in the process, in giving a 'Yugoslav' stamp to rock music" (Ramet 1999: 96).

Dominance of the Musical Public Sphere

Whatever the political, social, and cultural meanings attributed to them by their practitioners – audiences and musicians alike – the above styles, as well as many others, expand globally in an isomorphic manner to create similar soundscapes and aesthetic environments. Indeed, another most salient indicator of pop-rock's pervasiveness is the presence of its sonic textures and idioms in the cultural public sphere, and thus its immense influence on the affective nature of the cultural environment. Bearing in mind mostly narrative forms of popular culture (primarily television dramas), the cultural public sphere in late modernity is characterized as

> the various channels and circuits of mass-popular culture and enter-tainment, the routinely mediated aesthetic and emotional reflections on how we live and imagine the good life. The concept of a cultural public sphere refers to the articulation of politics, public and personal, as a contested terrain through affective (aesthetic and emotional) modes of communication ... The cultural public sphere provides vehicles for thought and feeling, for imagination and disputatious argument. (McGuigan 2005: 435)

While the lyrics of songs may occasionally provide a platform for articulations of ideas and concepts, in the case of pop-rock it is mostly the sonority of musical styles that plays a major role in the cultural public sphere. The very presence of certain musical sounds in public places sets their cultural tone, designs their emotional ambiance, and thus makes a cultural political statement about the affective nature of public places, mostly in urban settings. The musical soundscape, in this regard, is a contested area, where musical idioms, with their different sonorities, struggle over the affective nature and cultural orientation of public places, as in the case of *musica mizrahit* (oriental pop) in Israel in the 1980s (Regev 1986). The omnipresence of pop-rock styles and genres in the cultural public sphere, with their typical electric, electronic, and amplified sonorities, is a prominent marker of the aesthetic cosmopolitanization of urban environments.

The dominance of pop-rock styles in the public cultural sphere is best substantiated through a survey of the musicians and styles that occupy the leading slots in the charts of the best-selling and most played music in various national and regional settings. Lists and charts of best-selling singles and albums, more then just being measures of commercial success and popularity, are indicators of the sonic environment in a given country. The musical sounds that fill the air in shops and malls, played as background in bars and cafés, used in advertisements, and played on the radio or television channels, typically comprise the most downloaded songs, or tracks taken from best-selling albums. Best-selling music, in other words, is the music that sets the sonic cultural tone of urban settings, of the public cultural sphere. In the first decade of the twenty-first century, this was overwhelmingly pop-rock music, and in many countries this dominance started some 20 years earlier. This point is illustrated here by the cases of Japan, Israel, and Brazil.

In the 2000s, the charts of the best-selling music by domestic artists in Japan were dominated by female performers like Ayumi Hamasaki, Yumi Matsutoya, Hikaru Utada, Seiko Matsuda, Namie Amuro, Akina Nakamari, and Miyuki Nakajima (based on the charts published by Oricon, oriconcharts.livejournal.com). These female performers, with their various takes on pop music, were, according to Mōri, the last phase in "the golden age of J-pop" (basically the 1990s and the 2000s) before the decline of CD sales following the surge of the download market. J-pop, according to Mōri, is "'Japanese' pop made in Japan by Japanese musicians for a Japanese audience." He goes on to assert that

> throughout the 1990s, the term J-pop was gradually adopted to represent all kinds of Japanese pop music for young people. It started to cover *visual-kei* rock bands, more authentic Japanese rock bands, female pop singers, techno dance music, popular hip hop groups and even Japanese male idol groups. (Mōri 2009: 476)

According to reports by the Recording Industry Association of Japan, the consolidation of J-pop as an all encompassing term for domestic pop-rock coincided with enormous growth in the total production value of recorded music in Japan, which means, in other words, that starting in the early 1990s, pop-rock styles have been the most played, broadcast, and listened to sounds of music in Japan.

In Israel, according to the lists of ACUM (the authors and musicians association that monitors copyright and royalties), the most played domestic musicians on all radio channels in the country, and the ones toping the best-seller lists in the 2000s, include musicians

47

such as Rita, Berry Sakharof, Shlomo Artzi, Idan Reichel's Project, Shlomi Shabat, Sarit Hadad, and Eyal Golan. The last two names are of special interest, as their presence in the list represents a certain victory of *musica mizrahit* in its struggle for recognition and legitimacy (Horowitz 2010). However, the move of these two as well as many other *musica mizrahit* performers into the so-called "mainstream" of Israeli pop resulted, partially, from diluting the Arab and Middle Eastern colors of the music in favor of more pronounced patterns of Anglo-American pop-rock (Kaplan 2011, 2012).

Brazil is yet another country where, contrary to some stereotyped images of Brazilian music, pop-rock has been dominating the musical soundscape for decades:

> Anyone visiting Brazil today in search of an idealised 'Brazilian Sound' might, at first, be disappointed with the popular music scene. The visitor will soon realise that established musical styles such as bossa nova and MPB (*Música Popular Brazileira* [Brazilian Popular Music]), with their well-defined roles within the Brazilian social and political scene of the 1960s, 1970s, and early 1980s, have lost their immediate appeal with some contemporary audiences, and especially with Brazilian urban youth. In the 1990s, Brazilian radio and TV are saturated with a variety of new local genres that borrow heavily from international musical styles of all kinds and use state-of-the-art electronic apparatus. Hybrid terms such as *samba-rock, samba-reggae, mangue-beat, afro-beat, for-rock* (a contraction of forró and rock), *sertaneja-country, samba-rap,* and *pop-nejo* (a contraction of pop and *sertanejo*), are just a few examples of the marketing labels which are loosely applied to the current infusion of international music in the local musical scene. (Magaldi 1999: 309)

It should be stressed that the presence of pop-rock sonorities in the cultural public sphere is not a matter of smooth evolution, but rather the result of conscious cultural initiatives and struggles. This is made clear when looking at the early moments of electrification, that is, the adoption of the pop-rock electric ensemble as a standard format for performing music. Indeed, the ubiquity of pop-rock sonorities in the public cultural sphere, something which in fact means the omnipresence of musical idioms emitted from electric and electronic instruments, might be understood as just another case of global diffusion of modern technology. However, ever since pop-rock music has been institutionalized in the cultural field as the art form *par excellence* for which electric guitars and electric/electronic keyboard instruments serve as the major mode of expression, it is practically inevitable that almost any incorporation of such instruments by musicians anywhere in the world will be influenced by the techniques of playing, sonic vocabulary, or musical phrases formulated and established within pop-rock genres by prominent instrumentalists. Put differently, as a cultural practice (rather than sheer technological ability), playing of electric guitars and electronic keyboards displays itself as embedded within genres and styles. It arrives in semiotic units, loaded with meanings, connotations, and socio-cultural contexts. Taking up the playing of such instruments is therefore typically done as a conscious move of embracing influences and inspiration from genres and styles associated with certain techniques and sonic textures, or from pop-rock at large.

To be sure, the electric guitar is probably the most iconic instrument of pop-rock. Although American urban blues musicians like Muddy Waters or B.B. King were among its early prominent players, by the 1960s and 1970s it became the iconic instrument of pop-rock music. Guitarists like Jimi Hendrix, Jimmy Page and Eric Clapton, to name the most obvious, are conventionally regarded as those who have explored the expressive possibilities of the instrument, formulated and defined its sonic textures. With their playing, and that of many others, the connotations of different electric guitar textures have been firmly established as symbols of various pop-rock genres (Gracyk 1996; Waksman 1999; Wicke 1990). Consequently, adoption of electric guitars by musicians in different parts of the world gained the symbolic meaning of joining the ranks of the pop-rock aesthetic. Thus, for example, in two famous incidents that took place during televised Brazilian music festivals in 1967 and 1968, musicians Caetano Veloso and Gilberto Gil came on stage backed by electric bands and performed original songs that incorporated influences from Anglo-American pop-rock of the period – especially Dylan, Hendrix and The Beatles. The performances stirred a public controversy about *Brazilidade* (Brazilianness) in music because "at the time," as Dunn (2001: 65) notes, "the electric guitar was still regarded by many cultural nationalists as a sign of cultural 'alienation.'" Against this view, "Veloso and Gil proposed a 'universal sound' that claimed participation in an international modernity" (Dunn 2001: 69).

And in South Korea, tracing the gradual shift of popular music in the late 1960s away from acoustic orchestration, Pil Ho Kim and Hyunjoon Shin note that

with the new sound and repertoire came a new term for bands like Shin's [referring to musician Shin Joong Hyun]. What had been called vocal groups turned into "group sounds" as the electric guitar became

49

as important as the human voice in their music. Whereas the vocal group was a transitional form between the jazz-style combo band and the rock band, the group sound was identical to the latter (Kim and Shin 2010: 214).

Electric and electronic keyboards, especially synthesizers, also became strongly associated with pop-rock styles in the 1970s. Their incorporation, along with electric guitars, into the indigenous Trinidadian style of calypso is described in the following way:

> Calypso style has changed under the impact of modernization and technology . . . The adoption of the electric guitar and bass in the early 1970s changed the sound of the ensemble, and by 1980 most groups incorporated synthesizers as well . . . Around 1977 the term "soca" for "soul-calypso" was coined . . . to describe the energetic, disco-influenced style of commercial calypso party music coming to vogue. (Manuel 1988: 82)

In other words, the electrification of calypso is clearly identified with influences from pop-rock genres like soul and disco.

Becoming a symbol of "international modernity," and consequently the default mode of instrumentation, the taken-for-granted components of backing and recording musical ensembles in countless productions all over the world is probably one of the most significant ways through which pop-rock creative practices became isomorphically reproduced. Decoupled from their original stylistic contexts, electronic keyboards and electric guitars became in the last decades of the twentieth century signifiers of musical modernity for an ever growing number of musicians around the world, rendering the sounds of electric and electronic instruments ubiquitous and omnipresent.

Legitimation Discourse

Pop-rock music as a cultural phenomenon originates from the US and UK, and its canonic artists as well as most commercially successful ones are also from those countries. In order to justify their musical practices vis-à-vis discourses of national purism, practitioners of pop-rock therefore tend to produce justification discourses, as a way of gaining legitimacy and to get their musical works accepted into national cultural capital, that is, as ingredients in the "repertory of practices, tastes, sensibilities, elements of knowledge and canons of art forms and art works . . . that define 'natural' membership in a given national culture" (Regev 2000: 226). These discourses are typically organized around notions of hybridity and selective adaptations. Musicians and critics write and talk about national styles of pop-rock as being hybrid products, in which pop-rock influences are mixed with native traditions. Pop-rock is talked about as being "indigenized." They also emphasize the selective application of such influences. Dangdut, for example, is an Indonesian pop-rock style with strong Islamic flavors.

> Rhoma Irama, the master of the dangdut style . . . exploded onto the pop charts with a gradually changing, somewhat more rock-oriented, electrified and highly danceable dangdut style . . . Rhoma added electric guitars, synthesizer and a drum set to more traditional instruments in a conscious attempt to substitute a truly Indonesian music for the Western rock he had abandoned. As he explained in 1988: "we sieve what comes from the West, we don't just swallow. We take what's good and throw out the rest." (Lockard 1998: 95)

A similar sentiment is expressed by Shalom Hanoch, probably Israel's prominent rock *auteur* and ideologist, when explaining the Israeliness of his music and his refusal to sound "oriental":

> Here, a [national] culture is still being created. Anyone who says that he knows what Israeli culture should be like is simply a fool. This belongs to history. Time will tell. Anything that is being done in this country is Israeli until further notice . . . The more that people will stop discussing it, and everyone will do what he feels like, the more we shall gain from the process of fusions between styles. As for myself, I do rock as an artistic experience. This is my mode of creativity. I feel right with it. It fits me. I love rock. In fact, I have done everything. I wrote many quiet songs. In rock you go through the whole range of feelings. There is everything in rock. I don't like the attempt to be ethnic very much. It is good for folklore. I don't do folklore. I am engaged in contemporary creation. I deal with my life today. I don't search for roots in this regard. My roots are within me. I don't have to justify anything. I don't have to add oriental flavor for people to know that I am from the Middle East. If people would take rock more directly, the meaning of rock, not as a musical style, but as a conception – because this is what rock is for me, a conception, and a form of expression – then everything can get into rock. In the world, oriental music has long been incorporated into rock. Israel cannot invent anything new here. (Interview in *Reshet Gimmel*, the pop-rock radio channel of the Israel Broadcasting Authority 1988)

By gaining legitimacy and indigenizing it, pop-rock music becomes in one way or another "national" music. This point is manifested most clearly in the cases of Argentina and Brazil, where *rock nacional* is a standard label for classifying locally produced pop-rock. As such, pop-rock in fact transforms musical nationalism and with it existing perceptions of national identity and culture.

> French rappers do, however, assertively define their own hybrid identity as French . . . In claiming their "Frenchness," rappers, who represent a diverse multiethnic community, are pushing for a redefinition of what it means to be French . . . Ultimately, despite much resistance, French rappers' assertions of "Frenchness" are locally consented to. The works of many . . . have received some of France's most prestigious music awards. (Darling-Wolf 2008: 199)

Indeed, if hip-hop represents and expresses "Frenchness," or if rock fulfills similar functions for "Indonesian-ness," "Israeliness," "Brazilian-ness" and "Argentineaness," then these are no longer the musical nationalisms expressed by *chanson*, *gamelan*, *shirey eretz yisrael*, *samba*, or *tango*, respectively. Indigenized pop-rock stands as a transformed, aesthetic cosmopolitan form of musical nationalism.

Ritual Classification: Tradition vs. Pop-Rock

Borrowing from DiMaggio (1987), and echoing Bourdieu, ritual classification of art is understood here as a socio-cultural mechanism of categorizing and organizing forms of art, genres and styles in a way that accentuates, emphasizes, and enhances differences between them. Such classification works to dramatize and strongly demarcate distinctions between social sectors or lifestyle groupings, whose taste preferences are associated with certain cultural forms. In most countries, electrification of musical ensembles, in general, and the conscious joining of the pop-rock aesthetic, in particular, almost directly resulted in revamped musical classification systems that reflected changing attitudes, approaches, and ideologies toward identity and uniqueness. In the classification systems that emerged in the wake of the emergence and legitimation of pop-rock music, forms of popular and folk music that preceded pop-rock have often been regrouped into one category of indigenous and traditional music, most often associated with social sectors supportive of purist notions of local music, and in sharp contrast to pop-rock.

Traditional forms of national popular and folk music in many countries are usually subdivided into several genres and styles, according to region, ethnicity, and other social and cultural variables. Moreover, it is widely admitted that many such styles are the product of syncretism and cross-influences, including Western ones (in the case of non-Western countries; see Nettl 1985). However, with the emergence of pop-rock, these styles tend to be grouped into one category typically defined in terms of cultural purism, indigenous heritage and nativism. National pop-rock, on the other hand, is hardly ever perceived as a smooth development of and transition from earlier forms of national music. That is, the emergence and institutionalization of national pop-rock genres is typically embedded in discursive and institutional practices that clearly set it apart from the music presented as pertaining to indigenous or native traditions. In other words, an isomorphic ritual classification of music emerges, which groups "traditional" styles of music on the one hand, and "pop-rock" on the other. In addition, this division is sometimes experienced by local actors as a friction between the two categories.

Thus, for example, the Arab music world is sharply divided between music of the "golden age" (1930s–1970s) and the Arabpop phenomenon that has emerged since the 1980s. Although originally incorporating influences from European music, the music recorded by the likes of Umm Kulthoum, Mohammed Abdel Wahab, Abdel-Halim Hafez, and Farid el Atrach came to signify high art and Arab uniqueness. When, in the 1990s, Arabpop singers started to record songs by these canonic artists in electronic, danceable arrangements, it evoked some enraged responses:

> Is it right for a modern person to take phrases from the music introduction to one of the songs of Umm Kulthoum and turn it to a dance rhythm which moves the young people of today in nightclubs? . . . There is a trend to take the classics and modernize them, which has some people furious and others excited, but which is in general a deformation of our heritage. (Ibrahim al Aris; quoted in Hammond 2005: 153)

Likewise, French music culture is clearly divided between the *chanson* tradition, as epitomized by the likes of Edith Piaf, Jacques Brel, George Brassens, and Charles Trenet (as well as some latter day musicians), and pop-rock culture. Initially called *yéyé*, French pop-rock first gained prominence in the early 1960s with Johnny Hallyday (real name Jean-Philippe Smet) and in later decades evolved and diversified, reaching certain peaks with the duos Rita Mitsouko in the 1980s and Air in the 2000s, as well as with other electronic musicians and French rap. However, for all their success and popularity, French pop-rock artists, even when granted some legitimacy as representing national culture, are always classified as different when juxtaposed to the canonic artists of chanson and their successors (Looseley 2003a,

2003b). In Israel, the category of *shirey eretz yisrael*, (songs of the land of Israel), includes not just the invented folk music associated with rural life (highly influenced by Russian folk music; see Hirshberg 1995), but also other early forms, inspired among other sources by French chanson, mid twentieth-century cabaret music, and popular song in general. It is generally regarded as clearly different from Israeli rock (Calderon 2009; Regev and Seroussi 2004). Similar divisions can be found around Africa and Latin America, where categories like "Afropop" and "rock en español" are used to signal a fracture between pop-rock and folklore or indigenous music.

Somewhat similar in its cultural logic to *rock en español* is the case of East Asian pop-rock of the 1990s and 2000s. Although not sharing the same language like Latin American pop-rock, ritual classification of Asian pop-rock emerged as a category of music that serves to assess a sense of late modern East Asian identity shared in countries such as South Korea, Japan, Taiwan, Hong Kong, and Thailand, as well as the interest of the music industry in each country to export its products to other countries in the region (Chua 2004). Terms such as K-pop and J-pop thus came into currency, not only for domestic audiences in their respective countries of South Korea and Japan, but also for designating the origin of rock bands and pop idols that enjoyed massive success across the region (Shin 2009a, 2009b; Siriyuvasak and Shin 2007), and clearly classifying them as different from traditional and folk genres.

Ritual Periodization: The "Birth of Rock"

Classification is typically coupled with periodization, anchoring the division in a mythic moment of eruption or "birth" of national pop-rock. Following the incorporation of pop-rock, the historical narrative of popular music in many countries came to be organized around a "great divide" between the pre-rock and the rock eras. This divide, in fact, points to a moment after which local popular music has been gradually taken over by the pop-rock aesthetic. These narratives often point to a mythic moment of the "birth" of national rock music, or its "coming together" after early periods of scattered beginnings:

In 1992, world rock is 40 years old and Argentinean rock 25. We take as reference the explosion, in 1952, of *rock and roll* in the USA, and the recording in our country, in 1967, of "La Balsa," hymn of the "shipwrecked" . . . This is not an arbitrary composition. On the contrary, it is a verifiable point of reference that beyond the musical chronology includes a series of generational phenomena. (Grinberg 1993: 4)

This quote from a leading rock critic in Argentina is not dissimilar to the one coming from a prominent Chinese critic, Wang Xiaofeng. Writing about the performance of the song "I Have Nothing" by Cui Jian, in the One Hundred Pop Stars concert at Beijing Worker's Stadium on May 10, 1986, he declares that "a new chapter in the history of Chinese popular music has begun" (quoted in Jones 1992: 94). That concert was "the first of its kind and another indication of the full official recognition of *liuxing/tongsu* music [the soft-rock genre influenced by music from Hong Kong and Taiwan]. It is because of these two events that 1986 is considered the year of the birth of mainland pop" (Baranovitch 2003: 18).

Less symbolically pronounced, but nevertheless regarded as a key dividing moment, is the so-called "group sound" fad in Japan, usually considered as the cradle of local pop-rock:

The Ventures' 1965 Japanese concert tour set off the *ereki bûmu*, or the electric boom, and thereafter electric guitars in ensembles became the standard format by which pop music was produced . . . Many Japanese began imitating the Ventures' and the Beatles' styles and creating *ereki* (electric) sound. (Stevens 2008: 43)

The ensuing trend "contributed to the musical sensibility of young Japanese with music that emphasized beat and vocal harmony," while "some talented former members turned to what were called art-rock and psychedelic music" (Mitsui 2005: 143).

Other ritual periodizations of the same character can be found in the attribution of the emergence of rock in Russia to the bands associated with the Leningrad Rock Club in the early 1980s (Cushman 1995; Steinholt 2005; Stites 1992) or the works of the so-called "elite" of Israeli rock in the early 1970s (Regev and Seroussi 2004). Ritual periodization is one element in the construction of histories of national pop-rock. It serves to portray the musicians associated with it and their works as the "classic" period of national pop-rock (a point further developed in chapter 4).

* * *

The isomorphic similarities surveyed in this chapter clearly follow a certain pattern, a cultural logic that serves as a model to be followed. This model is comprised, essentially, by the history and dynamics of

Anglo-American pop-rock, which has been functioning as a leading dominant force in pop-rock music. Perceived from an early stage as the musical expression of neutral modernity, supposedly devoid of national or ethnic connotation, it became the object of worshipping around the world, a musical art to be followed and embraced. This point is nicely captured in the following story about The Beatles monument that stands at the heart of Ulaan Baatar:

> "We finished that monument in October 2008," explained Dolgion Balchinjav, instantly recognizable to Mongolian rock music lovers by his trademark silk neck scarf. Dolgion is producer and judge of Mongolia's answer to Idol [i.e. the TV talent competition show] . . . and a Beatles fan from way back. Built by locally renowned sculpture Den Barsboldt, the guitar-shaped brick wall represents the division Dolgion and his urban peers felt from the West during rock'n'roll's golden age. The side facing west, which supports the friezes of John and company, always seems to be in the sun, while the other side towards the east is in perpetual shade. There is a figure of a long haired young man who sits alone playing his guitar, lonely and cut off from the rest of the world. While Beatle-mania raged and most of the planet basked in the light of free love and peace during the 60s and 70s, Mongolia was isolated. "All we heard at that time was communist ideology. Many people knew the Beatles and liked them, but we couldn't listen to them . . . We used to listen to LPs smuggled into Mongolia, mostly by the children of diplomats who had been living abroad wherever their parents had been posted. It was risky though, to be a fan of the Beatles in those days, we had to listen in hiding and turn the volume down in case the neighbours heard. By building this monument we wanted to show to the rest of the world that Mongolia is not just horses and Chinggis Khan," Dolgion explained. "We have a modern urban culture too, and that isn't just something we've found in the last few years; just like the West we go back to the 60s, we know and love the Beatles, Clapton and the Stones just as much as the rest of the world" (*Mongolia Views*, 11 March 2010, mongoliaviews.com, accessed March 28, 2012).

Before further exploring additional facets in the working of national pop-rock, then, the following chapter examines the dominant dynamics of pop-rock, as they have been molded in Anglo-American pop-rock and becoming, in the process, a world model.

— 3 —

A FIELD OF CULTURAL
PRODUCTION

In 1986, in its third volume, the journal *Critical Studies in Mass Communication* (later to be known as *Critical Studies in Media Communication*) published a symposium about the "end" of rock. The lead article by Lawrence Grossberg, entitled "Is There Rock after Punk?" was followed by critical responses from Simon Frith, Greil Marcus and Stephen L. Nugent (Grossberg 1986; Frith 1986; Marcus 1986; Nugent 1986). The reason for conducting this symposium was the apparent decline of punk rock as a viable creative force in pop-rock music. In the aftermath of its 1976–8 heydays, punk rock seemed to have become as institutionalized as any previous pop-rock style it originally rebelled against. This coming of age of punk rock symbolized to fans and critics a loss of critical edge for all pop-rock music. That is, if punk – widely perceived as a cultural phenomenon that came to invigorate the critical power of rock, supposedly lost somewhere in the early to mid-1970s – is itself losing such power, than this is probably the end, or the "death" of rock altogether. Although not all participants in the symposium fully shared this view, the publication of the debate reflected the ambivalent character of much early pop-rock scholarship, namely, a sort of undecided self-image about its mission, between on the one hand advancing assertive interpretations of pop-rock music, which ultimately amount to quasi appraisals of the music and its meanings, and on the other hand neutral, "value free" observations and analyses of the music in its socio-cultural context. This ambivalence stemmed directly from the neo-Gramscian theoretical approach that framed much of pop-rock scholarship in its early stages. Halfway between evaluative assertions and sharp interpretations, the neo-Gramscian perspective led much of pop-rock scholarship into readings of the musical culture along the axis of hegemony vs. resistance. Some pop-rock scholarship was in this regard not too removed from fans' notion of "sell-out" (see Chapple and Garofalo 1977), and the cultural proliferation of pop-rock in the 1980s could not but be interpreted as co-optation and incorporation into hegemonic culture:

> I am now quite sure that the rock era is over . . . Rock was a last romantic attempt to preserve ways of music making . . . that had been made obsolete by technology and capital. The energy and excitement of the music indicated, in the end, the desperation of the attempt . . . Nowadays, rock anthems are used to sell banks and cars . . . There are two ways to read this situation. Either what is being packaged now is no longer rock. Or else rock's "new" commercial function proves that it was actually no different from any other leisure product all along. (Frith 1988: 1)

The contrast between "autonomy" and "commercialism," then, seems to have stood at the heart of early pop-rock scholarship.

The relationships between these two notions, however, when viewed from a different perspective, are not those of contradiction, but rather of mutual dependence, where the first functions for the other as an exploratory mechanism and supplier of new aesthetic grounds, while the latter functions for the first as the impetus to never sit still creatively, to constantly look for unexplored expressive ground. "Autonomy" and "commercialism" are two sides on an axis of creativity that infuse each other in a dynamic of expansion which is typical of almost any art form in modernity. The cyclic dynamism generates the accumulation of styles and periods which is the history of any field of cultural production.

However, even when viewed from this different theoretical perspective, namely Bourdieusian sociology of art and culture, punk was indeed a significant landmark in the socio-cultural trajectory of pop-rock, not so much because it was supposedly the last authentic eruption of critique in this musical culture, but because it was the first time that the classificatory struggle around the cultural value of pop-rock was waged against already existing, dominant styles of pop-rock. Until the arrival of punk, struggling for cultural and artistic legitimacy was waged primarily against dominant forces in the broader cultural field, and it was marked by certain linearity and coherence within pop-rock. The revolt of punk, in 1977–8, against the styles of pop-rock that had already succeeded in establishing cultural legitimacy, and then the success of punk itself in gaining such legitimacy around 1980, meant that pop-rock had grown to become a full-fledged field of cultural production, in Bourdieu's meaning of the term (Bourdieu 1993a). By being initially heretical against the established positions of pop-rock, and by consequently becoming itself an established position, punk has rounded up a cycle, initiated by the revolt of rock'n'roll against earlier forms of popular and art music. If 1950s and 1960s pop-rock was initially a heretical break with other forms of (popular) music, then punk's successful claim to being a new avant-garde demonstrated that by the 1970s pop-rock had already become a consecrated avant-garde. The consecration of punk and the canonization of some of its works and musicians therefore signaled that pop-rock had evolved into a field of cultural production for itself. It had crystallized as a new structure, similar to numerous other artistic fields in modern culture, characterized by a perpetual, cyclical contest for consecration between power holders and their challengers.

Taking, then, 1955 as the mythologized "beginning" of pop-rock, the next 25 years should be seen as the formative years that led to its consolidation as field of cultural production around 1980. In constituting itself as a cultural field, pop-rock created its own canon, its own mechanisms of consecration, and its own dynamics of stylistic innovation. And, just like in similar artistic fields such as film or television drama, the field of pop-rock became almost immediately an international one. Musicians and fans around the world embraced a belief in the stature of its canonical works, and developed local variants of consecration and innovation, most often highly inspired and influenced by those taking place in the dominant Anglo-American positions of the field. Moreover, when Anglo-American mechanisms of consecration and appraisal began at a certain point to discuss, review, and generally refer to styles and musicians from countries beyond the English-speaking world, these mechanisms became reference points for pop-rock musicians the world over. In this chapter, then, the trajectory of pop-rock, its mode of change and expansion to become a globally leading creative realm in popular music, especially as it took place in its leading model locations of the US and UK, is traced and portrayed as a field of cultural production, an arena of struggles for legitimacy, recognition, and artistic esteem.

Working of the Field

Saying that pop-rock is a field of cultural production means that it is a space of hierarchical relations, whose dominant positions consist of consecrated canonic musicians and works, and of corresponding production of meaning positions that maintain the successfully imposed criteria of evaluation and who monitor the entrance into the canon of new (or old) musicians. Being a field of cultural production means that pop-rock is a cultural realm constantly in flux, with constantly emerging styles and musicians seeking artistic recognition and prestige. Being a field of cultural production also means that the struggles for recognition and esteem are also struggles for preserving or challenging the dominant criteria of evaluation. These criteria, in any case, are based on an ideology of art that is nothing but an adaptation, an adjustment to the specific aesthetic nature and creative practices of pop-rock of the general ideology of autonomous art.

Variously referred to as "the theory of art-as-such" (Abrams 1989), "the theory of the superior reality of art and of autonomous genius" (Williams 1963), or "the ideology of the aesthetic" (Eagleton 1990), the ideology of autonomous art – a preferred title borrowed from Wolff (1987) – is a set of requirements and expectations from cultural products and from their producers, widely believed to be the essential traits a cultural form should have in order to be legitimately considered as genuine art. These traits can be succinctly summarized by saying that, in order to be counted as candidates for artistic legitimacy, cultural forms and products are required and expected to have their specific formal-aesthetic idiom, some sort of original narrative or expressive meaning, creative human entities that are the intentional origins of specific works, and a good measure of autonomy from market and other utterly utilitarian considerations in the creative process. Crystallized in early modernity, and receiving its classic formulation in Kant's *Critique of Judgment*, the ideology of autonomous art is the essential worldview of modern aesthetics, and it has been serving as the major cultural tool for constructing and justifying the canon of art works and artists in all fields of art. Thus, while erecting and maintaining the musical canon, the parameters and requirements of this ideology in the realm of music have traditionally denied artistic recognition from popular music, most famously so in the work of Adorno (1941), whose influential text in this regard was published before the advent of pop-rock, but also much later in the work of a cultural critic like Allan Bloom (1987) or, institutionally, in the widespread absence of pop-rock, well into the twenty-first century, from the academic curriculum of university music departments in most countries. In order to wage its struggle against this rejection, to formulate its own variant of the ideology of autonomous art, and indeed to construct a permutation of this ideology that will fit its sense of aesthetic specificity and thus consolidate its own cultural boundaries as a musical art, pop-rock has created its very own mechanisms of interpretation and evaluation. It constructed its own authoritative institutions of criticism to perform judgments based on this ideology, where critics enact pop-rock's aesthetic ideology in order to point to the actual works (albums, songs) and musicians that stand as poor manifestations or prime achievements of its aesthetic worldview. Therefore, before delineating the contours of pop-rock's aesthetic ideology and the dominant evaluative criteria derived from it, the major practitioners and the podia where the evaluations and judgments are executed are outlined below.

Production of Meaning

Given that works of art exist as symbolic objects only if they are known and recognized, i.e. socially instituted as works of art and received by spectators capable of knowing and recognizing them as such, the sociology of art and literature has to take as its object not only the material production but also the symbolic production of the work, i.e. the production of the value of the work, or, which amounts to the same thing, of belief in the value of the work. It therefore has to consider as contributing to production not only the direct producers of the work in its materiality (artist, writer, etc.) but also the producers of the meaning and value of the work ... the whole set of agents whose combined efforts produce consumers capable of knowing and recognizing the work of art as such. (Bourdieu 1993a: 37)

In other words, for pop-rock to function as a form of art, for its practitioners – be they fans or musicians – to have a vocabulary of concepts and adjectives, reasoning logics, and justifications to explain pop-rock's aesthetic qualities, it must have a discursive institution in which music – past masters as well as brand new works – is constantly discussed, scrutinized, appraised, explained, and interpreted. Such an institution of rock criticism took its initial form in the early days of pop-rock through magazines like *Rolling Stone*, *Creem*, *Melody Maker* or *New Musical Express* (*NME*), music sections like the one in New York's local weekly newspaper *The Village Voice*, and many other short lasting publications.

Popular music scholarship has rarely focused on this institution of pop-rock as an object of research. One notable exception is the work of Lindberg et al. (2005), which not only analyzes the emergence of pop-rock criticism, but also reveals its crucial contribution to establishing a widespread belief in the cultural value and aesthetic uniqueness of pop-rock music. Referring to the first generation of

61

pop-rock critics that emerged in the leading publications, they assert that it "seems that a transatlantic 'clergy' of critics whose shared standards and dialects form a hegemonic discourse had taken shape by 1972–1973" (Lindberg et al. 2005: 198). In their early work, these critics in fact invented a jargon, a style, a textual space, that laid the ground for almost all future writing on pop-rock. They provided to their readers – that is, the community of individuals for whom pop-rock music was becoming a crucial taste preference and a defining element of their lifestyle – the necessary vocabulary for articulating and expressing the meaning of the music, its qualities, and its difference from other forms of music.

The writing of critics such as Jon Landau, Greil Marcus, Robert Christgau, Dave Marsh, and Lester Bangs in the US press, as well as that of Nick Kent or Charles Shaar Murray in the UK, was certainly diverse and far from identical. They even had contradictory views on specific works or on some aspects of pop-rock culture. But jointly, however,

> [t]hey shared the optimism and the vision of pioneers convinced that not only was rock a "legitimate" art form, but one that voiced the contemporary cultural situation much better than any other . . . All of them saw writing on rock as a necessary part of the rock culture as a whole – they all felt a need to improve the quality of the music (and the writing) . . . Adapting aesthetic criteria from other fields in varying degrees, they all think that an important part of their job is to distinguish good rock music from bad rock music. Their ideal of rock combines quality with popular appeal, they all attack "undeserved" popularity without mercy, and all of them lend strong support to some acts that really never made it. (Lindberg et al. 2005: 189)

By the 1980s and into the 1990s, the production of meaning mechanism of pop-rock expanded and diversified. While older magazines kept circulating and some of the critics mentioned above became highly influential elders of pop-rock knowledge, many new magazines appeared, focusing on specific styles or demographic segments of the increasingly fragmented audience for pop-rock. First appearing in the 1980s, *Spin* and *Q*, for example, were general pop-rock magazines that catered to a slightly younger generation, one whose preferences focused on musicians and styles that emerged in the wake of punk. *The Source* and *Vibe*, on the other hand, emerged as major platforms for rhythm and blues and especially hip-hop reviews and coverage. *Kerrang!* and *Terrorizer* became important podia for articulating and spreading the specific knowledge of and about heavy and extreme metal, while *Mixmag* and *DJ Mag* fulfill parallel functions for the stylistic universe of electronic dance music. Yet another highly specialized magazine is *The Wire*, focusing on various forms of experimental music. Finally, covering since the 1990s what had become, by then, "classic" rock, *Mojo* magazine emerged as a platform for re-telling, in a detailed manner inferred from hindsight, past chapters of pop-rock music. This short list of magazines far from exhausts the number and range of magazines published in the Anglo-American core of pop-rock music. But it does represent the diversification and fragmentation not only of the music itself, but also of the discourse that surrounds it.

Magazines, however, are not the only channel through which production of meaning takes place for pop-rock music. As far as the printed press is considered, the sections and columns in major daily newspapers are an additional and significant presence, projecting in some cases – like *The New York Times* or *The Guardian* – an aura of cultural respectability and legitimacy to pop-rock and its meanings. Indeed, the very coverage of pop-rock in elite newspapers, not only in the US and the UK, but also in France, Germany, and the Netherlands (Schmutz et al. 2010), as well as a shift toward evaluation of pop-rock in terms derived from high art discourse (van Venrooij and Schmutz 2010), have greatly contributed to the legitimation of pop-rock as a contemporary form of musical art.

As pop-rock diversified and fragmented, as its repertoire of works, periods, and styles has been accumulating, some of its leading experts have found it increasingly important to produce authoritative histories and guides. As early as the 1970s, but especially in the 1990s, a steady flow of books started to appear, some of them authored or edited by established, authoritative journalists, in which the knowledge of and about pop-rock was offered in various guises. Chronological histories, encyclopedias or lexicons and album guides were the leading formats. One early, highly influential guide was *Stranded: Rock and Roll for a Desert Island* (Marcus 1979). Notable examples of other formats include *The Rolling Stone Illustrated History of Rock and Roll* (DeCurtis and Henke 1992), *The New Rolling Stone Encyclopedia of Rock and Roll* (Romanowski and George-Warren 1995) and *The Encyclopedia of Popular Music* (Larkin 1995).

Beyond the written word, pop-rock knowledge has obviously spread and diffused in sound and vision through broadcasting channels. In addition to regular radio formats and programs of various types, as well as television shows, production of special documentary projects was starting to take shape as of the late 1970s, in which the history of pop-rock was brought to audiences. One such example in radio was the 25-episode BBC Radio 1 series "25 Years of Rock," aired for the first time in 1979–80, and then repeated with five additional segments in 1984 as "30 Years of Rock." In television, one pioneering series was Tony Palmer's *All You Need is Love* (1976) that covered all of popular music – not just pop-rock. It was, however, the BBC's 10-part series *Dancing in the Street* (1995) that produced an authoritative documentary of pop-rock history along narrative lines similar to those in the printed histories and encyclopedias.

Histories of pop-rock, either in books, encyclopedias or on film, are essentially lengthy annotated lists of names and titles, that is, lists of musicians and albums, as well as names given to periods and styles, all accompanied with descriptive and explanatory, lengthy or short texts. In these meaning producing products, the universe of pop-rock is composed of musical biographies, albums, and their clustering into styles. It is composed, primarily, of the names and titles included in the encyclopedias, history books, and films. In other words, in a certain sense these products are mechanisms of selection. Inclusion in such texts, not to say being devoted a lengthy entry or full chapter, signals that the given musician, band, album, or style holds an important and significant place in pop-rock's cultural body – or at least, it is an element of that body that deserves being remembered. In this way, these texts delineate the contours of pop-rock, its boundaries and internal hierarchies or, in short, its canon.

Compiling "best of" lists is one practice, much favored by pop-rock critics and fans, which takes boundary and hierarchization work to a mechanical extreme. Most common are the "best albums of the year" lists, compiled annually by magazines (Schmutz 2005). In addition, magazines and books occasionally come up with wider lists that summarize a decade, a given style, or indeed "best of all time" album lists. Analyzing 38 "best album of all time" lists, published in pop-rock magazines and columns from 1985 to 2004, and compiling a "meta-list" of 30 albums that stand as the definitive pop-rock canon, von Appen and Doehring (2006) found unanimous stability in the canon. Comprised overwhelmingly of albums by male guitar bands, and recorded, for their most part (20 of the 30 albums) between 1965 and 1979, the meta-list of 30 pop-rock canonic albums contains more than one album by just three names: The Beatles, Bob Dylan, and The Rolling Stones. Other names prominently and repeatedly featured in such lists with more than one album include Jimi Hendrix, Neil Young, The Velvet Underground, and Stevie Wonder.

If printed materials of meaning production have exponentially grown and diversified over the years, then with the Internet the process became a flood of countless websites taking all sorts of forms. Web formats of printed magazines, independent web magazines, Internet radio stations, blogs, chats, and forums, as well as extensive encyclopedic websites have emerged in the twenty-first century to spread pop-rock knowledge, its meanings, and its stylistic history. With many of them integrating verbal text with music and video, pop-rock websites have greatly advanced immediacy of knowledge and opinion about new music, and at the same time greatly facilitated acquaintance with and preservation of past styles and musicians (see more on this point in chapter 5). One website that stands as almost the ultimate source of knowledge and meaning production about Anglo-American pop-rock (and to some extent pop-rock from additional countries) is *allmusic* (originally *AMG – All Music Guide*). Providing a wealth of data about the music, and combining it with lengthy evaluative reviews of albums and songs, the website is also an exemplary portrayal of how labels and tags are used in abundance for naming genres, styles, and sub-styles of pop-rock.

All of these platforms, while not necessarily fully conscious or reflexive about it, do employ and enact in their texts, and especially in their evaluations, an aesthetic worldview about pop-rock music. Hardly a fully coherent or systematic body, an aesthetic ideology of pop-rock can nevertheless be extracted from these platforms, as it is the essential logic around which the working of the field is organized.

Pop-Rock's Ideology of Art

Combining an examination of evaluative practices among fans and critics with his own analysis and observations, Simon Frith has provided over the years the most extended and coherent construction of a pop-rock aesthetic, one that takes into consideration both the music and its socio-cultural context. In his seminal early work (*Sound Effects*, 1981), Frith argued that pop-rock's aesthetic ideology combines a "folk" claim about being the collective representation of youth with a romantic artistic claim about being the expression of creative sensibility. This argument, however, did not provide an answer to the question of evaluation. Namely, how is pop-rock music judged aesthetically, what is the logic that underlies evaluations of songs and albums? In an initial step to tackle such questions, Frith examined the social functions of popular music, concluding that these are "in the creation of identity, in the management of feelings, in the organization of time. Each of these functions depends, in turn, on our experience of music as something which can be possessed" (Frith 1987: 144). The factors that enable pop-rock to fulfill these functions were fully developed by Frith in *Performing Rites* (1996). Tastes, or evaluations, are based on the affective work of three major elements of popular music. The first is rhythm as bodily experience, because "a steady tempo and an interestingly patterned beat ... enable listeners without instrumental expertise to respond 'actively,' to experience music as a bodily as well as a mental matter ... In the end, music is 'sexy' not because it makes us move, but because (through that movement) it makes us feel; make us feel (like sex itself) intensely present" (Frith 1996: 143–4). The second element is rhythm as experience of time:

> Music is not, by its nature, rational or analytic; it offers us not argument but experience, and for a moment – for moments – that experience involves *ideal time*, an ideal defined by the integration of what is routinely kept separate – the individual and the social, the mind and the body, change and stillness, the different and the same, the already past and the still to come, desire and fulfillment. Music *is* in this respect like sex, and rhythm is crucial to this – rhythm not as 'releasing' physical urges but as expanding the time in which we can, as it were, *live in the present tense*. (Frith 1996: 157; emphasis in original)

Finally, the third element consists of the voice as experience of personality, because

> [i]n taking on the singer's personality we are, in a sense, putting on a vocal costume, enacting the role that they are playing for ourselves. But a singer's act in this respect is complex. There is, first of all, the character presented as the protagonist of the song, its singer and narrator, the implied person controlling the plot, with an attitude and tone of voice; but there may also be a "quoted" character, the person whom the song is about ... On top of this there is the character of the singer as star, what we know about them, or are led to believe about them through their packaging and publicity, and then, further, an understanding of the singer as a person, what we like to imagine they are really like, what is revealed, in the end, by their voice. (Frith 1996: pp. 198–9)

As penetrating and accurate as they are, Frith's assertions are of a phenomenological nature, and hardly relate to sounds, to the specific sonic idioms of pop-rock music that carry and produce the experiences. In fact, some elements of his aesthetic observation may apply to any type of music. Indeed, a musicological supplement to Frith's work can be found in Moore's examination of rock's "primary text" (2001), while an aesthetic-philosophical examination of pop-rock's sonic specificity is offered in the work of Gracyk (1996), for whom pop-rock's essential difference from other forms of musical art resides in its ontology and the "thickness" of the recorded work. That is, in pop-rock, the musical work is the end product of the recording work, the packaging of various instrumental and vocal performances into one whole piece, inscribed on phonograms. A pop-rock musical work cannot be reduced to its notation. Knowing Bruce Springsteen's album *Born to Run*, for example, as printed and released in 1975, means being familiar with all the aural layers and sonic elements of the recording. Any true analysis and detailed evaluation of the album can be accomplished only upon listening to it on a music-playing device that emits all the sonic intricacies of the recording.

The sociological question that remains unaccounted for, however, in these characterizations of the aesthetic specificity of pop-rock, is how evaluation takes form in practice, in the actual judgmental work of critics, who produce the explanations and justifications as to why certain songs or albums are more successful than others in invoking the experiences Frith describes, or in being better incarnations of pop-rock's aural "thickness." These evaluations are, in their turn, the ones that supply to listeners and to the field at large the terms, concepts, and vocabularies that compose the prevailing aesthetic discourse of pop-rock.

A scrutiny of some prominent critical writing about pop-rock reveals that underneath the jargon, it certainly adheres to the parameters of autonomous art, albeit in an adjusted mode, made to fit the creative practices and the sonic textures of pop-rock styles. While not fully articulated into a coherent aesthetic perspective, the discursive universe of pop-rock criticism has in fact developed, implicitly, a permutation of the ideology of autonomous art from which producers of meaning derive the criteria of evaluation and in fact impose it on the field – at least as far as artistic consecration is concerned. This, for example, is an excerpt from a review of an album that enjoys broad critical consensus about being one of pop-rock's greatest works:

Exile on Main Street is the Rolling Stones at their most dense and impenetrable ... the Stones group everything together in one solid mass, providing a tangled jungle through which you have to move toward the meat of the material. Only occasionally does an instrument or voice break through to the surface, and even then it seems subordinate to the ongoing mix, and without the impact that a break in the sound should logically have ... because Jagger's voice has been dropped to the level of just another instrument, burying him even more than usual, he has been freed from any restrictions the lyrics might have once imposed ... he's been left with something akin to pure singing, utilizing only his uncanny sense of style to carry him home from there. His performances here are among the finest he's graced us with in a long time, a virtual drama which amply proves to me that there's no other vocalist who can touch him, note for garbled note . . . With Keith, however, except for a couple of spectacular chording exhibitions and some lethal openings, his instrumental wizardry is practically nowhere to be seen, unless you happen to look particularly hard behind . . . It hurts the album, as the bone earring has often provided the marker on which the Stones rise or fall. Happily, though, *Exile On Main Street* has the Rolling Stones sounding like a full-fledged five-into-one band . . . a tight focus on basic components of the Stones' sound as we've always known it, knock-down rock and roll stemming from blues, backed with a pervading feeling of blackness that the Stones have seldom failed to handle well. (Lenny Kaye, *Rolling Stone*, 6 July 1972)

As much as this review was written at a time when pop-rock criticism was still in an exploratory phase, searching for a discursive identity, it encapsulates the aesthetic ideology of pop-rock that will become the dominant measure of artistic quality in the field. The major parameters of pop-rock's ideology of autonomous art are present here: distinctive form, typical meaning, specific notion of authorship, and implied perception of autonomy.

Aesthetic form

Five key elements compose the expressive means most typically used in order to convey emotion, moods, and meaning in pop-rock. They are sonic textures of electric instruments, complexity and sophistication of studio work, techniques of vocal delivery, rhythmic drive, and the song's lyrics. Not all of them are used in every pop-rock song, but any combination of them that does exist in a given performance forms the basis for judgment and evaluation. The above quote clearly refers to the vocals, the tight production in the studio, the sonority of the electric guitar, and also to the rhythmic pattern (omitted from the quote). Songs and musical works are evaluated according to the expertise, virtuosity, innovativeness, and originality found in the use and presence of these means in a given work. Thus, the artistic esteem conferred on many consecrated albums and songs is linked to all or some of these practices: virtuosic playing on the electric and electronic instruments manifested in them, the seamless complex construction of sounds into one coherent package, the emotional commitment radiating from vocals, poetic or narrative quality of the lyrics, and occasional other elements. All of these might be given as "evidence" for deserved appraisals of given musical works.

Meaning

On their own, the above elements might sometimes be seen as manifestations of nothing but sheer technical ability. For a song or an
entire album to be judged as a good one, the expressive elements are
supposed to be carriers, foremost, of some credible emotional statement, a specific mood. Lyrics, when judged to be complementing the
affective meaning through their narrative or poetical qualities, bring
added value. The emphasis on mood and emotion rather than on any
cerebral meaning was succinctly defined early on by Jon Landau's
words that "rock and roll has to be body music, before it can be
head music, or it will wind up being neither" (Landau 1972: 134).
The moods and affective meanings typically expected to radiate from
pop-rock are either those of rage, anger, frustration, bleakness, and
despair (which could be interpreted as the "rock" aspect), or those
of fun, extreme joy, pleasure, and bliss (which might be interpreted
as the "pop" aspect). Jointly, they represent the two extreme poles
of pop-rock's image of rebellion. On the one hand, upright resentment and critique, on the other hand hedonism and no regard to
conventional morality. The sway between the two is captured in
the following excerpt that delineates how synthesizer music has
been accepted and legitimized after its initial explorations within
progressive rock:

> Synth-pop went through two distinct phases. The first was all about
> dehumanization chic. That didn't mean the music was emotionless (the
> standard accusation of the synthphobic rocker), but that the emotions
> were bleak: isolation, urban anomie, feeling cold and hollow inside,
> paranoia . . . The second phase of synth-pop reacted against the first.
> Electronic sounds now suggested jaunty optimism and the gregarious-
> ness of the dance floor, they evoked a bright, clean future just round the
> corner . . . And the subject matter for songs mostly reverted to tradi-
> tional pop territory: love and romance, escapism and aspiration. (Simon
> Reynolds, *The Guardian*, October 10, 2009)

Creative entity and authorship

A third major element in pop-rock's aesthetic ideology is its specific
form of authorship – meaning authorship as a cultural concept rather
than a legal one. Given the technological complexity underlying its
typical sonorities, the collective nature of the production process and
therefore the multiple tasks that may be regarded as being of a crucial
creative nature, authorship in pop-rock is expected to consist of performances of at least some of these tasks. One analogy that comes
to mind in this regard is film, where in the wake of so-called *auteur*

theory, film directors have been firmly established as the major creative authors. Looking for the *auteur* in pop-rock, Landau's words in the early days of pop-rock criticism again supply an essential aesthetic ideological statement:

> The concern has always been with the search for the author in rock music, the search for the source behind the music . . . the criterion for art in rock is the capacity of the musician to create a personal, almost private, universe and to express it fully. A point of view can be delineated through a combination of means. In some cases the vision is created through instruments alone in a way that can never be completely defined and never should be. In others the lyrics and music provide alternate or ultimately joint ways of expressing the same accessible ideas and feelings – as in the music of Bob Dylan. (Landau 1972: 14–15)

Indeed, Bob Dylan is probably not only the most critically acclaimed pop-rock *auteur* in the history of the field in terms of form, content, and quality of his music, but also the prime model to express the multi-tasking expected from such *auteurs*. Composing, writing lyrics, playing an (electric or electronic) instrument, singing, and in some cases doing also studio production work – these are the tasks a rock *auteur* worthy of her or his name is supposed to master. While pop-rock singer-songwriters did not invent the format – it can be traced to various traditions of folk and popular music, most notably French *chanson* – in pop-rock it received extra dimensions because of the technological skills involved in playing electric instruments and studio recording. Chuck Berry in the early days of rock'n'roll, and then Neil Young, Lou Reed, Stevie Wonder, Elvis Costello, and P.J. Harvey are some of the most highly regarded embodiments of this format of authorship.

The pop-rock band, or group, is another central mode of authorship in pop-rock. The centrality of the band concept in pop-rock, its institutional character in the context of this musical culture, stems directly from its functioning as a collective unit of authorship. Bands are expected to be self-contained creative entities, in which band members share between them the various creative tasks, thus allowing the crediting of authorship to the band as a whole. The deeply perceived importance of the band as a creative unit is reflected in the tendency of some individual pop-rock authors to work with a permanent band. This is the case with Bruce Springsteen, for example, most of whose albums have been recorded with the E-Street Band. In other cases, bands are in fact a sort of vehicle for the work of mostly

70

one leading author, as in the cases of Ray Davies (The Kinks), Pete Townshend (The Who), Chrissie Hynde (Pretenders) or Jeff Tweedy (Wilco). The importance of the band format is closely linked to the recognition that pop-rock is primarily an art of recording, of performance in the studio. Every note or sound nuance captured on record and eternalized as an element of the completed work is in fact an authorial contribution. This is also the reason why pop-rock bands, as collective entities, are supposed to be in creative control even when enlisting musicians who are not officially band members. One notable example in this regard is Steely Dan, which started as a full band but was later reduced to a duo that recruited different musicians for each song and album:

> Fagen and Becker were still pushing studio equipment to its utmost limits and *Aja* was said to have been remixed 13 times in the five months preceding its release. Equally the Dan seemed intent on employing every West Coast musician of quality in their search for perfection. When the album finally broke surface it boasted seven guitarists, six drummers, an equal number of keyboardmen, plus innumerous other sound-stokers including a sax squad. (Fred Dellar, *Vox*, December 1990)

Indeed, at its essential aesthetic core, pop-rock music is the art of making records, of capturing performances and weaving them into neatly built, intricate sonic wholes:

> The song maker, in the workshop of the studio with any conceivable sound as his raw material, can lift his own or other performances out of time to be repeated and revised, speeded up or slowed down, enhanced or distorted, weaved in with any number of separate recorded performances and sounds, using the tape recorder and its more sophisticated extensions as an aid to composition ... In a sense this is the best of all worlds, combining the aural opportunities of performance with the eventual permanence of creation, combining features of both "folk" and "art." Like folk and primitive musics (in which it has its roots), rock music has as its basis the art of performance, and therefore improvises and experiments with all kinds of vocal and instrumental sound. Like notated art musics, rock song on record is ultimately a lasting creation, a made "thing." (Clarke 1983: 201)

This is one of the major reasons The Beatles are so highly regarded in the annals of pop-rock history, occupying the most sacred position in its canon:

> The Beatles are the first rock band for whom recording came first ... The Beatles' work came to be conceived with the studio in mind – all

71

the production values a mixing board had to offer were used to serve the ideas conveyed in their music. A Beatle record is more than just a collection of songs, it is a performance for tape. (Riley 1987: 266)

The attribution of authorship to recorded sounds is also manifested when singers who rarely write their own materials are credited as major artists in the history of pop-rock. The vocal performances, as captured and eternalized on record, are seen as an authorial source of the music, no less than the composers or lyrics writers. This is especially the case with the stature of Elvis Presley in the pop-rock canon.

Autonomy

Pop-rock scholarship has been plagued by the issue of autonomy for many years, when trying to come to terms with the apparent paradox of the musicians being creative artists and producers of commercial goods at one at the same time. However, as already hinted above, it is only when acting from within the ideological, romantic perspective of autonomous art that the issue of autonomy – or authenticity, as it is most often referred to in the context of pop-rock – becomes a problem. At its extreme ideal-typical form, the notion of autonomy in art relates to a situation in which creativity is performed regardless of practical, utilitarian, or any other not purely aesthetic consideration. In the case of pop-rock's aesthetic ideology this means, most importantly, autonomy from commercial interests and market demands. However, as we learn from Bourdieu, even the most avant-garde, experimental art, by catering to the distinction and boundary interests of the tiniest shred of status groups, still has a social utilitarian function beyond sheer aesthetic experience. This is all the more so when dealing with artistic creation that caters to wider sectors and which is in need of firm economic existence, not to mention profitability.

Pop-rock music, especially, is hardly ever created under pure aesthetic circumstances. Being by its very nature an essential part of the cultural industries, pop-rock music cannot really be "noncommercial" in any pure or total meaning of the term. The aesthetic ideological question, then, faced by critical discourse when it comes to evaluate the autonomy and authenticity of the music, is how to accommodate the creative practices of pop-rock within the cultural industrial web which is its natural habitat. That is, how to define and find the contours of autonomy within the commercial practices.

One strategy is to simply disregard the industrial context and refer to the qualities of the music. Thus, most conventional accounts of the careers of major consecrated musicians like The Beatles, The Rolling

72

Stones, Bob Dylan, and Jimi Hendrix are told as an unfolding narrative of aesthetic developments and changes, with the commercial aspect mentioned primarily for signaling success. In other words, autonomy is taken here practically for granted, as if the industrial context is nothing more than an organizational home for creation of music and evolution of musicians. In some cases, however, much emphasis is placed over the fight of musicians for artistic freedom within the industry. Most famous in this regard are the cases of Marvin Gaye and Stevie Wonder. These two musicians recorded during the 1960s many successful hits for the Tamla Motown company, all in line with the company's sonic formula of pop-soul music. However, by the turn of the decade, both artists started to develop expressive interests beyond this formula, seeking new stylistic ground and authorial freedom. The initial refusal of the company to allow this was well publicized by the artists, especially after they won the fight and recorded their highly acclaimed albums of the 1970s. For Marvin Gaye, these were the albums *What's Going On* (1971) and *Let's Get it On* (1973), while for Stevie Wonder, these were *Talking Book* (1972), *Innervisions* (1973), *Fulfillingness' First Finale* (1974), *Songs in the Key of Life* (1976), and *Hotter than July* (1980) – a series of albums that firmly placed him at the top of the "best albums" lists for years to come, and which commenced with the album *Music of My Mind* (1971):

> This has been hailed as Stevie Wonder's final "coming of age", but I think this album is more important and will certainly have more important repercussions than that. To me this album represents the "coming of age" of black soul music. A growth that started with Curtis Mayfield, was extended by Isaac Hayes, and has now reached fruition in the hands of Stevie Wonder. It is that important a landmark in contemporary music . . . To Wonder this is a personal triumph. Not only in conveying his music to the listener, not only in no longer being thought of as simply a clever little black kid who swung through a song with apparent effortlessness. It's a triumph comparable to Marvin Gaye's break with Motown tradition for *What's Going On* so that he could go out alone and do what had laid innate in him for so many years. But in Stevie's case the break with Motown's confining musical structures and his own image was perhaps more desperate . . . sorting things out with the company, Wonder was finally allowed to explore outside his former limitations and to display a more brilliant dazzling side of his music than ever had a chance to emerge . . . the result of this musical carte blanche is an album of explosive genius and unshackled self-expression . . . Wonder plays everything – piano, drums, harmonica, organ, clavichord, clavinet, Arp and Moog synthesizer . . . Also producing, singing,

weaving all the intriguing vocal patterns behind his own [in addition to composing and writing the lyrics, of course]. (Penny Valentine, *Sounds*, 4 December 1971)

Another exemplary case in this vein is the much written and talked about hiatus in the recording career of Bruce Springsteen between 1975 and 1978, caused by his insistence on artistic freedom that led him to a court battle against the record company. This way of evaluation interprets autonomy as something that exists at the heart of the industry despite and against its profit interests. It is carved out, paradoxically in a sense, by musicians whose commercial success allows them to fight for and negotiate artistic freedom.

Another mode of pointing to pop-rock's autonomous creativity goes through the traditional romantic way, by simply putting strong emphasis on bands and musicians working in the avant-garde and experimental corners of the field, in whatever style. Autonomy here is, indeed, portrayed along the classic logic of artistic fields, namely "the economic world reversed." Critics tend to praise musicians and bands for pioneering and being faithful to an aesthetic vision. Commercial failure and being known to only a handful of devoted fans are virtues, portrayed as proof of artistic integrity and authenticity. The Velvet Underground stands here as the ultimate example:

It was the group's lot to be ahead of, or at least out of step with, their time. The mid- to late '60s was an era of explosive growth and experimentation in rock, but the Velvets' innovations – which blended the energy of rock with the sonic adventurism of the avant-garde, and introduced a new degree of social realism and sexual kinkiness into rock lyrics – were too abrasive for the mainstream to handle. During their time, the group experienced little commercial success; though they were hugely appreciated by a cult audience and some critics, the larger public treated them with indifference or, occasionally, scorn. The Velvets' music was too important to languish in obscurity, though; their cult only grew larger and larger in the years following their demise, and continued to mushroom through the years. By the 1980s, they were acknowledged not just as one of the most important rock bands of the '60s, but one of the best of all time, and one whose immense significance cannot be measured by their relatively modest sales. (Richie Unterberger, *All-Music*, allmusic.com/artist/the-velvet-underground-p5733/biography, accessed February 2012)

Another strategy is to look at the toying with pop-rock conventions, stylistic patterns, and formulas as a form of creativity and authenticity by itself. This is a tactic taken especially in the appraisal of works classified as "pop" rather than "rock," as in the cases of bands like ABBA or the Pet Shop Boys. Autonomy here is correlated with the authorial notion of pop craftsmanship.

> The Pet Shop Boys belong in a British role . . . a lineage of pop laureates . . . They're commentators, not dramatizers – mature, arch, and crafty . . . It's that odd twist that makes the group's 80s hits so easy to love, and so hard to dislike: They're too unassuming to be bothered by. The music may be clattering hi-NRG synth-pop, and full of high drama, but Tennant's thin, moneyed voice and cheeky play-acting cut against it: He's not a spotlight-hog, just a lone schemer in an expensive suit. It's these hits . . . [that] are their touchstone contributions to the history of pop music. You don't need to be told that they're fantastic, any more than you need to be told that *Thriller* is fantastic. These songs are, in a way, the urtext of dance-pop: The alternately ecstatic and ominous lilt of "Suburbia"; the strangely mellow, down tempo Latin freestyle on "Domino Dancing"; or the incredibly sly, stylish sing-speak on "Left to My Own Devices". (Nitsuh Abebe, *Pitchfork*, October 6, 2006; pitchfork.com/reviews/albums/9487-popart-the-hits)

* * *

In their essence, then, pop-rock magazines, books, encyclopedias, websites and other platforms of interpretation and meaning production are engaged in practicing the aesthetic ideology of pop-rock. They point to the meanings of music, identify its authorial sources, delineate the expressive means employed by the authors to convey meaning, and magnify the autonomous aspect of creativity. In the way they evaluate, review, interpret, and discuss music and musicians, these practices ultimately give shape to the history and structure of the field.

Mechanisms of Change and Innovation

Fields of cultural production are characterized by constant fluidity and change as well as accumulation and expansion of styles and genres. The logic of innovation, of coming up not simply with new works or products, but with new forms of expression, new modes of experience, is an essential trait of any modern artistic field. The result is a chronological linearity of accumulation and expansion which is the history of the field. This, however, raises the question about the practices of innovation and change, and the logic behind the influx of new works into the space of a field, in terms of their new forms of expression. In pop-rock, these can be divided into a logic of exploration similar to notions of the avant-garde in other artistic fields, and a logic of elaborations and adjustments of such explorations into aesthetic formulas, stemming from commercial interest in new product. The two are not totally different, especially in the sense that avant-garde practices often take place at the very center of the cultural industries. They are treated here separately in order to distinguish between their perceived impacts on the field.

Avant-Gardism

Stylistic inventiveness in pop-rock has traditionally been linked to the notion of "breaking new aesthetic grounds" of sonic textures and affective meanings, of creating new expressive possibilities and musical languages. Avant-gardism may take various forms within pop-rock. The most common and salient is the exploration of new sonic textures offered by technological developments in musical instruments, sound generating machines, and studio technology or, in short, advances in technologies of expressive means. Many of the new styles and pioneering works that emerged in the history of pop-rock have been attributed, directly or implicitly, to successful creative use of new or available technologies for manipulating or generating sound. Foremost among these are electric guitars. The cult of worshiping that surrounds figures like Jimi Hendrix, Eric Clapton, Jimmy Page, Jeff Beck, Duane Allman, and many other guitarists, stems directly from perceiving them, quite unanimously, as individuals who explored and formulated the sonic textures of pop-rock's major instrument. Some of these formulations became, in the hands of countless guitarists around the world, standard and conventional sounds of pop-rock music. The work of the names above is hailed, in other words, for pioneering and expanding the sonic and affective repertoire of pop-rock. In a similar vein, individuals like Brian Eno, Ryuichi Sakamoto or Jean-Michel Jarre, as well as bands like Kraftwerk and Tangerine Dream are hailed by critics as those who pioneered the use of electronic keyboards. Brian Eno also holds parallel acclaim, along with people like Phil Spector, Brian Wilson and The Beatles (with George Martin, their producer), for inventiveness in the recording studio, that is, for exploring and demonstrating the creative possibilities of recording technologies in constructing intricate and complex layers of sound (Jones 1992; Théberge 1997).

Another common mode of exploration is that of stylistic eclecticism, in which pop-rock modes of expression are applied to genres

76

and styles beyond those already associated with pop-rock. Indeed, stylistic eclecticism is probably an aesthetic strategy that in a way defines pop-rock creativity. By most accounts (Frith 1981; Wicke 1990), pop-rock came into being in the 1950s by fusing elements of blues, country music, and popular song under the umbrella of electrification and studio craftsmanship. From that moment on, much of pop-rock stylistic growth took shape by further applying and re-applying in new ways pop-rock aesthetic idioms to more genres. Two notable examples in the first 25 formative years of pop-rock include the application of pop-rock to compositional practices associated with classical music and jazz, resulting in the style known as *progressive* or *art rock* (Holm-Hudson 2002; Macan 1997; Martin 1998); and the fusion of pop-rock aesthetic practices with rhythms and melodies of various folk traditions, leading to the style known as *folk rock*. As noted in chapter 2, in countries other than the US and the UK, this aesthetic practice was essential in the emergence of local, ethnic, and national styles of pop-rock. It afforded the creative and aesthetic framework for creating ethnic and nationally specific genres of pop-rock. In their turn, stylistic elements taken from such non-Anglo-American styles have influenced the work of major musicians, most famously in the case of African stylistic elements influencing the work of Talking Heads and Paul Simon.

Indeed, a third major tactic of aesthetic innovation takes the form of fusion, influence and cross-fertilization between pop-rock styles. Some notable examples include the interchange between rock, soul, and jazz to create *funk* in the 1970s; the merging of *disco* and *alternative rock* by various musicians during the 1980s (the band New Order should be mentioned here); the fusion of *punk* and *heavy metal* into *grunge* in the early 1990s; and the hybrid of guitar-based rock with electronics explored by various musicians in the 2000s, like the highly regarded band Radiohead. A telling example of the intricacies involved in the cross-fertilization between pop-rock styles along its history is provided in the following quote, about the influence of the German band Kraftwerk who "started out as experimentalists in the grand Krautrock tradition, classically trained musicians in revolt against the old ways," before becoming famous for their "meticulous hypnotic grooves":

Scratch a techno whizkid or studio engineer, and nine times out of 10 you'll find a Kraftwerk fan (the tenth will be too busy sampling them to respond). And it's not only in the big studios that their influence is felt; in bedrooms and back rooms all over the globe, autodidact musicians are massively in their debt. Most amazing of all, it's undoubtedly true that without this whitest of white groups, the history of black music in America would have been completely different. When Afrika Bambaataa took Kraftwerk's "Trans-Europe Express" and "Numbers" and combined them to form "Planet Rock", he set in train (sic) a movement which, as the rappers say, just don't stop: not only was this effectively the birth of hip hop culture, but in Detroit young black kids like Derrick May, Juan Atkins, Kevin Saunderson and Carl Craig fed on Kraftwerk's hypnotic rhythms and developed what later became known as techno. In Britain, meanwhile, late-'70s industrialists such as The Human League and Cabaret Voltaire built on Kraftwerk's breakthroughs, taking the sequenced-synthesizer sound to the furthest reaches of, respectively, pop's heartland and rock's avant-garde. (Andy Gill, *Mojo*, April 1997)

Indeed, as can be inferred from the above, avant-gardism in pop-rock does not take place necessarily in some marginal, purely experimental corner of the field. It may well occur at the heart of the field.

Commercialism

While the aesthetic tactics described in the previous section tend to be perceived by critics as stemming from musicians' genuine creativity and search for expressive innovation, another mode of change and development is most often related to the profit seeking and marketing interests of the music industry. "Commercialism" is, in this regard, a practice of mimicking, copying, or selectively adapting aesthetic practices that have been proven successful either in terms of sales or artistic value, and their transformation into formulas. Interest to replicate commercial success, belief that the audience at large likes the "new sounds," and consumption industries' raison d'être to perpetually come up with new products, are the typical motives behind the practice of commercialism. The cultural dynamic of commercialism is by no means unique to popular music. But it has been a major force in this field since the 1950s, contributing dramatically to the expansion of pop-rock. Famous early examples of this pattern are the so-called *teen idol* singers of the late 1950s in the US, portrayed by their promoters as *rock'n'roll* singers, that is, as the equivalents of Elvis Presley, Chuck Berry, and Buddy Holly. Other examples include bands like The Monkees, formed by the industry in the wake of The Beatles' success and other pop-rock bands of the mid 1960s; and many of the "new wave" bands launched in the wake of punk in the late 1970s. Commercialism culminated in the

1990s with so-called "boy bands" and "girl bands," most of which were brainchildren of marketing professionals in the music industry. Not really a new phenomenon in pop-rock's history, but stylistically characterized at this point in their mixing of elements from electronic dance music, hip-hop, r&b, and, in general, a wide range of pop-rock styles, vocal bands like Spice Girls, All Saints, En Vogue, Destiny's Child, TLC, New Kids on the Block, N'Sync, Take That, Backstreet Boys, Boyzone, and many others not only enjoyed huge international success, they also marked the definite consolidation of aesthetic innovations originally conceived and formulated within the framework of avant-gardism. An even firmer confirmation of the extent to which the aesthetic idioms of pop-rock became the conventional, default, and widespread form of popular music came in the 2000s with the so-called "reality" television "idol" and "star" competition shows.

Two additional important cases of commercialism are the infiltration of pop-rock aesthetic elements into other forms of popular music, like *orchestrated vocal pop* or *easy listening*, and the sliding of some successful pop-rock artists into a stylistic context sometimes dubbed *adult oriented ballads* or *soft rock*. They are important because the permeation of electric and electronic instrumentation identified with, and formulated in, strict pop-rock contexts into styles and genres traditionally thought of as aesthetically opposed to pop-rock, and the gliding of pop-rock artists toward an affective realm quite removed from those of rage or hedonism, have jointly blurred the difference between pop-rock and other forms of popular music. This is, indeed, the point where "pop-rockization" of popular music takes one of its most blatant forms. Standout examples of the first phenomenon are the soundtracks composed and arranged by Ennio Morricone to Sergio Leone's trilogy of "spaghetti" Westerns, *A Fistful of Dollars* (1964), *For a Few Dollars More* (1965), and *The Good, The Bad and the Ugly* (1966). Beloved by some pop-rock critics for their use of electric guitar parts and sound effects, the success of these soundtracks, including the chart success of Hugo Montenegro's cover of the latter, nevertheless signaled a certain alignment between pop-rock and orchestral *easy listening*. Significant examples of the second phenomenon include parts of, or the entire career of, artists such as The Carpenters, Chicago, Bread, Dionne Warwick, Billy Joel, Elton John, or Lionel Richie:

It is said that Lionel Richie's previous solo album, *Can't Slow Down*, sold an unthinkable 15 million copies . . . no wonder the so-called "maestro of mellow" has taken three years to produce a follow-up . . .

79

it's difficult to believe now that his one-time band, The Commodores, used to play brawling Southern funk. *Dancing on the Ceiling* is son of *Can't Slow Down*, and proud of it. It's an immaculately-tooled set of songs which frequently verge on the corny, but Richie's gift is the capacity to know exactly where sentiment, emotion and mush collide. His songs seem to breed in the mind, making you think you've known them for years. (Adam Sweeting, *Q*, October 1986)

The case of the Eurovision Song Contest is also exemplary and highly relevant for the current context. Except for one significant exception ("Waterloo" by ABBA, 1974) and a few other songs, the overwhelming majority of songs performed in this contest until the late 1970s were in the *popular song* tradition of fully orchestrated performances. During the 1980s the share of performances modeled after the pop-rock band format gradually increased, becoming by the 1990s the dominant pattern, with contest winners like the electronic dance of the Israeli entry "Diva" (1998, performed by Dana International), and the hard/heavy metal of the Finnish entry "Hard Rock Hallelujah" (2006, performed by Lordi).

As much as practices of "commercialism" are often treated with a certain disdain within the aesthetic ideology of pop-rock, they nevertheless contribute various stylistic phenomena to the field – at the very least in terms of sheer volume of aesthetic range – that significantly add to the overall expressive spectrum of pop-rock.

The Spiral of Expansion

Ever since Peterson and Berger's (1975) seminal study, the linkage between musical diversity and the structure of the music industry has been a focus of pop-rock research. While some works are framed by issues stemming from organizational theory in sociology, namely the impact of organizational concentration and centralized production (Dowd 2004), others – echoing the neo-Gramscian perspective – are underlined by the theme of independence vs. large corporate control (Hesmondhalgh 1996; Negus 1992). Practically all studies find a cyclic pattern in which musical creativity sways between periods of increased and decreased diversity. The two lines of research, however, converge in the finding that, by the 1980s and 1990s, the accelerated pace of these cycles came to overwhelmingly exist, in one way or another, under the auspices of the major transnational music corporations. Extending an organizational studies' open system account, Dowd argues that:

During the era of decentralized production, the majors sought dominance by exploiting their respective rosters of established performers and by quashing the success of independents. This resulted in a fragile dominance that was eventually ruptured by the emergence of rhythm and blues and rock and roll in the mainstream market. Having learned their lesson, the majors shifted to a production logic that was increasingly decentralized. They pursued a widening roster of established *and* unknown performers, and they pursued alliances with an increasing number of independents. Consequently, the majors were well situated to absorb a succession of musical styles that ranged from punk to hip hop. Not surprisingly, musical diversity rose from 1955 onward, even in the midst of heightened concentration ... musical diversity rose as new performers and firms brought an expanded range of musical material into the mainstream market – as decentralized production allowed majors to co-opt the raw prototypes of emergent styles and to exploit further the elaborated treatments of established styles. (Dowd 2004: 1444–5)

In Hesmondhalgh's (2007) account, the move of the major corporations from centralized to decentralized production should be seen in the socio-political context of neo-liberal regimes, whose policies propelled a shift in the cultural industries from what he calls the "complex professional" era to the "marketization" era.

In either case, the point inferred from studies of the industry is that diversity and innovative creativity are directly influenced by the structure of the music industry and its modes of operation. A cultural sociology perspective, however, will put this assumption "on its head," arguing that artistic innovation and growing diversity in terms of style and genre should be seen as generated primarily by the social context of their existence in modernity, namely, the growing fragmentation of modern societies and the intensified boundary work of lifestyle groupings for recognition and distinction. The cultural industries should be seen in this regard as channels, as containers, in which some of this boundary work takes place and is given shape. While such organizations certainly have their own profit interests, in the long run – as seen in the total history of artistic fields – they are engaged in adjusting themselves to the changing modes of creativity and diversification, and not in initiating or leading them:

The structural and functional homology between the space of authors and the space of consumers (and of critics) and the correspondence between the social structure of spaces of production and the mental structures which authors, critics and consumers apply to products is at the root of the coincidence that is established between the different categories of works offered and the expectations of different categories of the public. Indeed it is a coincidence so miraculous that it may appear as the product of a deliberate adjustment of the supply to the demand. While cynical calculation is obviously not absent, particularly at the 'commercial' pole, it is neither necessary nor sufficient in order to produce the harmony observed between producers and consumers of cultural goods. (Bourdieu 1992: 162)

Put differently, new styles and genres, products and trends should be understood in terms of supply for a social market, in which existing and new social groupings are constantly in demand for cultural products in order to maintain and construct their sense of difference, of distinction.

Indeed, as was explored early on by Hirsch (1972) for the cultural industries in general, and then elaborated for the case of the pop-rock industry (Negus 1992), the music industry has functioned primarily as a hub for cultural intermediaries, organization professionals whose work consisted of adjusting supply to demand tendencies and vice versa, matching emerging stylistic innovations and rising taste patterns. In pop-rock, these are music professionals recruited from relevant taste cultures, who in their work practices blur the distinctions between consumption and production, personal taste and professional judgement, as well as artist, administrator, and audience (Negus 1996: 63). The gist of these practices can be found in the workings of so-called "labels," that is, small firms or large corporations' subsidiaries specializing in specific genres and styles. In them, organizational culture itself is practically identical to the molding of genres into clearly defined and easily identifiable musical idioms (Negus 1999).

In addition, innovation and diversification, as creative practices, are always performed in relation to already existing styles and genres. They are reactions to, and developments of, existing patterns of expression that define the space of possible creative explorations. In other words, in order to understand the cultural meaning of the cyclic sway between avant-gardism and commercialism, one should look at the overall history of the field and to the cumulative continuity of styles:

[T]hat pop music self-consciously combines continuity with change ... is illustrated perfectly by the fact that yet another wave of "minor" labels has in the 1980s come to challenge the domination of the established record companies, just as earlier waves did through the introduction of rock & roll during the fifties, rock during the mid-sixties and punk during the late seventies (Hatch and Millward 1987: 7)

At any given moment, then, the field of pop-rock consists not only of the styles and aesthetic tendencies perceived as "new," but also of the entire repertoire of styles and periods that constitute its history. It is a repertoire whose elements are present as reference points for new musicians, as taste ingredients for older audiences or young discoverers, and as canon for everyone involved. Consecutive cycles of independence and co-optation, of increased and reduced diversity, of repeated avant-gardism and commercialism, leave behind them a trail that is best described, metaphorically, as an expanding spiral. The accumulated styles, periods, trends, and other phenomena gathered along the trail are the ever present details of the history of the field, constantly radiating influence and inspiration to new or repeated modes of expression.

Structure of the Field

Fields of artistic production, as analyzed by Bourdieu, are typically based on "two fundamental and quite different oppositions; firstly, the opposition between the sub-field of restricted production and the sub-field of large-scale production ... and, secondly, the opposition, within the sub-field of restricted production, between the consecrated avant-garde and the avant-garde, the established figures and the newcomers" (Bourdieu 1993a: 53). This assertion, however, holds only partially for the case of the field of pop-rock music. This is because, as outlined above, the sub-field of large-scale production is often a supplier of newcomers, well received by the producers of meaning as innovators along avant-garde patterns. Furthermore, the major division in the field of pop-rock is not the one between large-scale and restricted production, but rather the division into generic sub-fields. The field of pop-rock is therefore better understood as a space consisting of several stylistic sub-fields, scattered around a central sub-field – often referred to as *mainstream*. Each of these generic sub-fields is characterized by its own opposition between an innovative, autonomous orientation that caters to relatively small groups of devoted fans, and a large-scale market orientation. Occasionally, as in some instances within the sub-fields of hip-hop and electronica, as a tactic of challenging the dominant aesthetic ideology of the field, critics and musicians in the autonomous poles of sub-fields tend to proclaim the genre as being "non-pop-rock." However, as much as each stylistic sub-field has its own canonical repertoire, the ultimate stake around which the dynamics of the field at large are organized is recognition and prestige in the central sub-field, that is, in the mainstream. As Käryä (2006) points out, the pop-rock canon might be divided into alternative canons, meaning thereby canons reflecting the aesthetics of specific genres; and a mainstream canon, consisting of works that gained acclaim across the entire field. The dynamic of change and innovation is expressed for each sub-field in the practice of labeling, of tagging. Small changes in sonic idiom, new configurations in the use of instruments and the incorporation of stylistic influences, resulting in nuanced variants of a given style, almost always lead to tagging these as a new sub-sub-style. The field has witnessed over the years various genres, and therefore sub-fields, that came and went, genres that were prominently present for a short period and then declined into marginality. Other genres have remained for longer periods, evolving through various trajectories (see Lena and Peterson 2008) and consolidating as major sub-fields. In addition, it should be remembered, the practice of cross-fertilization between styles means that innovative creativity in each sub-field might result from interactions between them. As of the 2010s, the major stylistic sub-fields of pop-rock music are the following:

- *Hip-Hop and R&B*: These two styles might as well be treated separately, where R&B is a musical genre performed mostly on conventional instruments and a strong commitment to melody and ballads, while hip-hop is closely associated with sampling, turntablism and rapping of lyrics. Classifying these two as one sub-field obviously reflects the widely accepted notion that they are both "black" music, and that both styles express in various ways the experience of "blackness" on both sides of the Atlantic (Gilroy 1993). In addition, the two are closely linked in their stylistic genealogy, and especially through the creative practice of sampling, in which hip-hop musicians tend to cite, mix, and re-work excerpts from R&B songs (Lena 2004). The opposition in this sub-field between purist aesthetic creativity and market orientation is articulated through terms such as *hardcore* and *alternative hip-hop*, where the first relates to purism and commitment to the core features of the style, while the latter refers to fusions and experiments with various influences. For R&B, uncompromising creative attitudes are designated by labels such as *deep-funk* and *deep-soul*.

84

- *Electronica*: Where stylistic labels are concerned, the sub-field of electronic music has been a supplier since the 1990s of an untraceable line of tags for constantly evolving stylistic nuances. *House, techno, ambient, drum'n'bass, jungle, trance*, and *trip-hop* have been some of the leading tags in this category. Divided and multiplied through many hyphenated labels, they are employed by critics to map the stylistic universe of electronic pop-rock since the 1990s. Ranging from instrumental tracks destined for the dance floor to the most abstract aural layers of sonic effects and textures, and employing a diversity of creative techniques that stretch from playing on electronic keyboards to audio collages of samples and electronically generated sounds, the stylistic universe of electronic music has immensely diversified and fragmented in the 2000s. Obviously, there is constantly an opposition between works perceived as investigations into the realm of meter and beat, or into the possibilities of aural sculpture, and those judged by dominant meaning producers as simply aimed at crowds in dance clubs (McLeod 2001).
- *Metal*: Evolving from the sonic ground explored in the 1970s by bands such as Led Zeppelin and Black Sabbath, *metal* music had grown by the turn of the century into an amalgam of styles that critics refer to by names such as *black, death, doom, thrash, speed, progressive*, and *goth*, some of which are sometimes grouped into *extreme metal* – mostly in order to distinguish these latter-day styles from the *heavy metal* sounds of the 1970s and 1980s (Kahn-Harris 2007; Walser 1993; Weinstein 2000). Screaming, yelling, howling, and shrieking vocals, often rendering the lyrics unintelligible, characterize much of extreme metal, in addition to heavily fuzzy distorted electric guitars. Still, while some bands tend to recycle stylistic formulas in a way that makes them accessible to wider publics, other bands use the framework of the style in order to further research and develop notions of sound and noise, speed, complex syncopation, and varied instrumentation. Bands of the latter type are grouped under labels like *experimental* or *avant-garde metal*.
- *Alternative/Indie*: The sub-field of *alternative* or *indie* is the self-proclaimed space of explorative autonomous creativity in pop-rock (Bannister 2006; Fonarow 2006). Having its roots in the 1960s work of bands such as the Velevet Underground and the Stooges, but also in *psychedelic* pop-rock (early Pink Floyd, Jimi Hendrix), *alternative* pop-rock is quite unanimously regarded by the major production of meaning mechanisms of the field as

85

the definite realm of avant-garde in pop-rock, where the most mythologized variant of the aesthetic ideology is practiced and believed in. Consisting overwhelmingly of guitar bands, it included at various points in time genres and styles such as *punk*, *grunge* and *alternative singer-songwriters*, but also musicians associated with *progressive rock*, and even *metal* and *electronics*. As a catch-phrase, *alternative pop-rock* stands for music perceived within the field's dominant discourse as its past and present creative frontiers. However, as much as the sub-field of alternative pop-rock is generally considered to be a space of mostly autonomous creativity, some of the bands and musicians working under this tag – especially those criticized for merely recycling aesthetic formulas associated with leading styles – are often devalued as carrying no original or innovative message, as being "sold-out" to cultural industries' profit interests.

- *The central sub-field*: Fueled and fed by aesthetic explorations performed in the various sub-fields, either in the form of musicians that move into wider market success, or in the form of stylistic elements infiltrating into the work of musicians not strictly working in one particular sub-field, the central sub-field consists of the works and musicians most widely known to all participants in the field at large, works that speak aesthetic idioms that borrow from all sub-fields (and from some additional sources). It consists of past musicians and styles that have gained the status of "classics," either for artistic excellence, for being much publicized phenomena of some sort, or for sheer market success. This is the domain of the main artistic hierarchy of the field, topped by those consecrated as the great artists of pop-rock, and bottomed by phenomenal market successes deemed artistically worthless by critical discourse. As noted above, the central sub-field parallels the sphere of music production and consumption often referred to as *mainstream*. In terms of its functioning in the social market of cultural goods, it is a domain "that brings together large numbers of people from diverse social groups and across large geographical areas in common affiliation to a musical style," and, furthermore, it is "best conceived as a process rather than a category ... [as] *mainstreaming*" (Toynbee 2002: 150). The central sub-field, in other words, is the arena in which stylistic explorations originating in generic sub-fields or elsewhere are made accessible to larger publics. It is the cultural location where the definitive canon of pop-rock is consecrated.

National (Sub-)Fields of Pop-Rock Music

With the isomorphism of genres, periodization, and other phenomena, national fields of pop-rock are replications of the field at large
as described so far. That is, they are spaces of musical production,
set within the cultural sphere of national societies, in which most, if
not all the generic sub-fields of pop-rock exist and interact in modes
parallel to those of the global, Anglo-American dominant field. One
major difference is the prominent presence, in addition to the other
generic sub-fields, of local, ethnically flavored indigenous genres
that amount to supplemental sub-fields. Thus in Israel, the national
field of pop-rock in the 2000s has consisted of a prominent central
sub-field, and then alternative, electronic, and, to some extent, metal
and hip-hop sub-fields. It also included, in addition, the prominent
sub-field of oriental pop (a.k.a. *musica mizrahit*), whose impact on
the central sub-field became a major development in the country's
musical culture during this decade (Kaplan 2011, 2012). Another
characteristic of national fields is a tendency to occasionally produce
their own variants of global stylistic patterns. These then amount to
indigenous phenomena, associated with local uniqueness. This is the
case of the boy bands, girl bands, and in general the teen pop idols
that thrived in the 1990s and 2000s in South Korea (K-pop) and
Japan (J-pop).

Yet at the very same time, each of the national generic sub-fields in
its own right, as well as national fields of pop-rock in their entirety,
are also participants in the global field. That is, national *hip-hop* or
electronica musicians, for example, next to their linkage to the native
context, are also participants in their respective global generic sub-
fields. One notable example is *metal* music. *Metal* bands from a wide
range of countries actively participate, and are sometimes recognized
and successful in the global field of *metal* (Wallach et al. 2011). In
fact, based on data accessible on the metal-archives.com website, a
masters thesis conducted in 2011 has found that in 1980, the number
of *metal* bands that ever existed stood at 3,200. Most of these bands
were active in countries of Western Europe and North America. By
2010 the figure rose to approximately 75,000 *metal* bands that were
founded through the years in some 131 countries across the world
(Mayer 2011).

Another example consists of the electronic musicians that emerged
in France in the 1990s. The musical output and surge to artistic
respectability and cultural legitimacy of bands and individuals such as
Daft Punk, Air, Alex Gopher or Etienne de Crecy are clearly situated

and explained within the French national field of pop-rock (Birgy 2003). Yet their work can also be understood as stemming from the dynamics of the global sub-field of electronics. In addition, however, the international success and critical acclaim of Air and Daft Punk firmly place them not only in the sub-field of electronics, but also in a highly regarded position in the central sub-field. That is, they are in fact counted as part of pop-rock's general canon, and thus as a French contribution to the canon. This point exemplifies the functioning of the French field of pop-rock in its entirety as a sub-field within the global one. In other words, each national field of pop-rock, as a whole, can be envisaged as a sub-field of the field at large, one that occasionally contributes works or stylistic influences to the dominant central sub-field.

Another example of this last point can be found in the cases of Mexican pop-rock, Spanish pop-rock, or, indeed, the language-based transnational field of *rock en español*. Next to the influence exerted on them by stylistic innovations from Anglo-American pop-rock, bands and musicians originating in these fields have occasionally enjoyed recognition and success in the global field. As early as 1966, the Spanish band Los Bravos enjoyed worldwide success with the English sung hit "Black is Black." In the 1990s, the Mexican band Café Tacuba was warmly welcomed by US pop-rock critics, and in the 2000s Colombian musicians such as Juanes and Shakira became household names in the global central sub-field of pop-rock.

It should be stressed, however, that reciprocity of influence between the fields is scarce. The global field of pop-rock is dominated, in all sub-fields, by Anglo-American music production and, most importantly, by Anglo-American production of meaning mechanisms and evaluative criteria. For the purpose of being consecrated as significant contributions to the musical art form of pop-rock as a whole, musicians and bands from any part of the globe have to pass the approval of Anglo-American critics and reviewers, the so-called "megaphone effect" (Bloch and Lemish 2003). They are the prism through which global recognition and artistic acclaim are ultimately granted to pop-rock music produced anywhere in the world.

Musicians, critics, and other actors in national fields of pop-rock are therefore constantly engaged in nurturing their self-image as equal participants in the modern musical art of pop-rock. In the case of contributing locally produced music to the global field, this may sometimes amount to a matter of national pride, like in the case of Russia's delegates to the Eurovision Song Contest in 2003, the duo t.A.T.u.:

Since the fall of the Soviet Union, the one-sided dominance of western Europe and the United States has become not only a source of resistance but also resentment, arising largely out of the conviction that while Russians possess tremendous creativity they have not yet mastered the skill of translating those energies into commercially viable global commodities. The selection of t.A.T.u. for participation in Eurovision 2003 loudly proclaimed . . . that this was no longer the case . . . [It was] an appealing act, infused with propulsive pop rhythms and clean vocal harmonies. (Heller 2007: 115)

But the most common and obvious practices for manifesting the sense of being part of global pop-rock, of involvement in it, revolve around the introduction of albums and songs, musicians and bands, genres and stylistic trends into the national contexts. Thus, local concerts and festivals featuring leading Anglo-American musicians, or radio and television shows that bring the latest, but also the classics of Anglo-American pop-rock, have been common in many countries since the 1960s. One important expression of the sense of being fully involved participants in the global field is found in national production of meaning mechanisms. Journalists, critics, radio editors, and others have been introducing, presenting and explicating, within their own national contexts, the artistic ideology of pop-rock, including its historical narratives. This has been done not as a report about phenomena that occur elsewhere, but in a manner of active evaluations and judgments of pop-rock works:

To celebrate the alleged fiftieth birthday of rock music, the largest daily paper in Finland, *Helsingin Sanomat* (*HS*), has since February 2004 been publishing short columns about the "central" phenomena of rock music. The columns are published twice a week (predominantly in the Monday and Thursday editions; they are also compiled on *HS*'s website), and in them a few authors (mainly the paper's own staff member rock aficionados) put forward "important" recordings by year – indeed only one recording per annum. Thus in 1954 Bill Haley was "a step ahead" with "Rock Around the Clock", in 1963 *The Freewheelin' Bob Dylan* "shook up rock with his lyrics", and in 1967 "the high priest of psychedelic rock", Jimi Hendrix, took rock "to a wild and unexpected direction." (Käryä 2006: 3)

Pop-rock's historical narrative, artistic ideology, and canonical world have been consistently introduced into the realm of national cultural contexts since the moment of their inception. Taken almost for granted as a culturally neutral modern artistic phenomenon, the introduction of pop-rock knowledge into local cultures paralleled, in the eyes of its practitioners, the spreading of the message of modern painting, film culture, or world literature. The series of Finnish columns reported by Käryä are but one example of similar journalistic endeavors taken in many other countries.

Entwined as they have been from the very early stage of the 1960s in the Anglo-American dominated field of pop-rock, and developing an eagerness to become worthy, recognized participants, it is no wonder that 40 years later national fields of pop-rock became isomorphically similar, and that pop-rock has grown and expanded into one global field. The cultural dynamic that has been underlying the evolution, expansion and rise to dominance of pop-rock in the realm of musical nationalism, however, still needs to be clarified.

— 4 —

LONG-TERM EVENT OF POP-ROCKIZATION

Andrés Calamaro is an Argentinean musician whose career evolved and flourished from the 1980s onward. His album *La Lengua Popular* was released in 2007. This is an excerpt from a review of that album:

> *La Lengua Popular* marks the full return of the composer, in an album that sits comfortably next to *Alta Suciedad* in his discography. These songs will be heard everywhere. On standard pop radio stations and on mp3 players, in football stadiums and in dance clubs, in taxis and buses, and yes, in our homes . . . These are twelve songs with no padding, all good, all distinct, hundred percent Calamaro . . . The new album functions then almost as a summary of the road travelled so far by Andrés, with cumbian rhythms that recall his alliance with Bersuit, the phase with Javier Limón, the Dylanesque influence, the Mexican one, the rock à la Los Rodríguez, and others . . . which are purely Calamarian, the style cloned to triteness by bands and soloists in recent years. (Claudio Kleiman, *Rolling Stone Argentina*, September 1, 2007)

Earlier in the decade, and referring to the collaboration (mentioned in the review above) between Calamaro and the band Bersuit Vergarabat, the daily *La Nación* wrote that

> in the last ten years Andrés Calamaro has been added, on the strength of a thousand and one songs, to the 'holy trinity of Argentine rock soloists' (Luis Alberto Spinetta, Charly García and Fito Páez). For this, Bersuit and Calamaro are already synonyms of Argentina, or rather, of *Argentinidad* [Argentineaness]. (*La Nación*, November 22, 2004)

These quotes firmly place Calamaro within a long history of pop-rock music in Argentina. They put him next to Spinetta and García, widely considered the mythical founders of rock in Argentina in the late 1960s and early 1970s, and they refer to his stylistic diversity, which incorporates into the rock idiom various Latin American styles. Indeed, as much as he is inspired and influenced by Latin American genres, Calamaro is unequivocally perceived as a rock musician. The aforementioned album, *La Lengua Popular*, won in 2008 the annual Gardel award in the "best album by a rock artist" category.

The Gardel award was inaugurated in 1999, and its format and categories mirror those of Anglo-American awards like the Grammies and the BRITs. That is, although named after the famous early twentieth-century musician Carlos Gardel (known mostly for his recordings of classic tangos), and indeed granting annual awards to tango as well as folklore musicians, its major thrust and public profile as a ceremony lies in its pop-rock categories. These categories very well reflect the extent to which the field of pop-rock in Argentina is embedded in the stylistic trends of world pop-rock. In 2010, for example, the leading nominations were in categories such as "best album by female pop musician," "best album by male pop musician," "best album by pop group," "best album by rock artists," "best album by rock group," "best alternative pop-rock album," and "best electronica album." Another indication of the embeddedness of Argentinean pop-rock in the global field is the influential presence of the national edition of *Rolling Stone* magazine, from which the first quote above has been taken. As already discussed in the previous chapter, the magazine is broadly considered among popular music critics, historians, and scholars as the most influential journalistic platform of pop-rock music since 1967 (Lindberg et al. 2005). In the 2000s, *Rolling Stone* magazine has stretched beyond its US/UK core, and established local editions in a variety of countries (including Germany, Spain, France, China, Brazil, Indonesia, Russia). The Argentinean edition is published in Spanish, and it offers a mixture of translated articles and reviews from the American issue with articles, news, and reviews of Argentinean pop-rock. It thus presents to its readers the art world of pop-rock music as a cultural space in which Anglo-American and Argentinean musicians reside in parity, as equal participants.

For all its accentuated *Argentinidad*, then, Calamaro's career, as well as the music he makes, has been implicitly structured along patterns and models set by leading forces of the global field of pop-rock music. His career, moreover, has had in addition an explicit international facet, one that stems from Calamaro's residence in Spain during the 1990s. The album *Sin Documentos* (1993) by the band he led in this country, Los Rodríguez, and two albums he recorded under his own name during this period, *Alta Suciedad* (1997) and *Honestidad*

Brutal (1999), are often counted among the best albums in the history of pop-rock in Spain (see, for example, issue no. 50, July/August 2003, of the Spanish rock magazine *Efe Eme*). Calamaro's career, in other words, is transatlantic, and his music sometimes stands as an expression not only of *Argentinidad*, but rather of Latin rock, or *rock en español*, terms that designate the pop-rock of Latin America and Spain together.

The appraisal of Calamaro's career and music, and in fact of *rock nacional*, as synonymous with *Argentinidad*, might seem quite trivial in early twenty-first century. So also does their embeddedness in, and close connectivity with, the sonic textures, aesthetic idioms, and the institutions of global pop-rock. This was, however, hardly trivial some 30 or 40 years earlier. Upon its initial arrival to Argentina, or to any other country in the world, pop-rock music, as epitomized most prominently by Elvis Presley and The Beatles, was considered as totally contradicting any conventional notion of musical nationalism and cultural uniqueness. It took several decades of cultural struggle, waged in national fields of cultural production by musicians, critics, media and music industry professionals, before pop-rock accomplished the status of national legitimacy. Gaining recognition for pop-rock music as a legitimate expression of national uniqueness amounted to the transformation of such uniqueness, as expressed in music, into a condition of aesthetic cosmopolitanism. This deep transformation of musical nationalism, of which Argentinean *rock nacional* is but one example, is conceptualized here, following Sewell Jr.'s (2005) analysis of the meaning and function of events in history, and DeNora's (2003) notion of "the musical event," as a *historical musical event*. Before discussing its specificities, these two concepts should be briefly elaborated.

Events

A historical event, according to Sewell Jr. (2005) is "(1) a ramified sequence of occurrences that (2) is recognized as notable by contemporaries, and that (3) results in a durable transformation of structures" (p. 228). That is, unlike other occurrences and happenings, events "have long-lasting effects on the subsequent history of social relations" (Sewell Jr. 2005: 271). Sewell Jr. clearly adheres to the notion that events are composed of "brief and intense sequences" (Sewell Jr. 2005: 271), meaning thereby a time period of a few years at the most. It seems, nevertheless, that his definition of events is highly adequate also to the transformation of musical nationalism along the pop-rock aesthetic, despite the fact that this process lasted in some countries for several decades. An understanding of the transformation of musical nationalism as an "event," or better still as a long-term event, is justified when considering the other component in Sewell Jr.'s definition, the notion of "structure."

Unlike other usages of "structure" in sociology, anthropology, and history, especially in the context of Marxist and structuralist approaches in which the concept refers to single whole societies, Sewell Jr.'s understanding emphasizes the plurality of "structures" within any social formation:

> [C]ultural structures should not be seen as corresponding to distinct "societies" . . . but rather as corresponding to spheres or arenas of social practice of varying scope that intertwine, overlap and interpenetrate in space and time. This would mean that for any given geographical or social unit, the relevant structures would always be plural rather than singular. (Sewell Jr. 2005: 206)

This perception of structure is very close to Bourdieu's notion of "fields," where each field is an arena of practices organized around a dominant scheme of things, a field-specific habitus that dictates and determines the perceptions, the interests, and the actions of agents in each field.

An "event," then, is a sequence of occurrences that has long-lasting effects on a given field, and therefore on the practices and experiences in the corresponding realm of culture for the larger social unit in which the field is set. It brings about a transformation of the field, of its habitus, and consequently a transformation of the ways a particular realm of culture is practiced in a given social formation. An event in the fields of medicine, of law, of religion, will have long-lasting effects on the practices and experiences in each of these spheres.

The field of popular music is one particular structure in this sense. An event in the field of popular music would mean, therefore, a transformation of its structure, of its habitus. It would mean a transformation of the aesthetic idioms and sonic textures of music, of the evaluative criteria for appreciating music, of the creative modes for making music, of the ways music is experienced. The process through which pop-rock music was introduced, legitimized, and eventually gained dominance in the realm of musical culture in many countries has all the characteristics of an event. Although it was not brief, it certainly brought about a transformation of musical culture in almost every country in which it occurred. Moreover, although dating its exact start and end points is a complicated task, the historical event of pop-rock can nevertheless be clearly demarcated by the cultural condition of the popular music that preceded it and by the one that followed it. Prior to its occurrence, musical nationalism was characterized by a quest for essentialist uniqueness through art, folk, and traditional popular music, by an ideology of musical purism. Upon its fulfillment, musical nationalism came to be characterized by the legitimate, sometimes overwhelming and dominant presence of pop-rock music, which means not only the saturation of the sonic environment with electric, electronic, and amplified sonic textures, but also an attitude of constant openness towards, and intensive integration in, the global art world of pop-rock music.

The Musical Event

An additional justification for conceptualizing the transformation of musical nationalism brought about by pop-rock as an event comes from the work of DeNora (2003). Evolving from ethnographic work carried in different settings (2000), and especially the notion of "music as a technology of the self," DeNora developed a model of a "musical event" that demonstrates how engagement with music affects individual life courses and micro situations of everyday life. Methodologically, a musical event is "an indicative scheme for how we might begin to situate music as it is mobilized in action and as it is associated with social effects" (DeNora 2003: 49). The musical event is

> a specific act of engagement with music. The core of the concept can be found in the five components, [it] consists of an actor or actors, composers, listeners, performers, music analysts, and others, who engage with or "do things with" music within specific environments and under local conditions . . . What is key here is how the music is, or comes to be, meaningful to the actors who engage with it. (DeNora 2003: 49)

At the micro, interactionist level discussed by DeNora, a musical event is an act of engagement with music that in some ways alters the life of the individuals involved. The point in portraying the engagement with music as an event comes to emphasize the transformational power of such an engagement. DeNora stresses throughout her empirical cases and theoretical analysis how the engagement with music constitutes individuals as social agents. She emphasizes, in fact, how music itself functions as a cultural agent through the function of *affordance*:

95

[Music is] . . . a resource for – rather than a medium about – world building. Within this dynamic conception of music's social character, focus shifts from what music depicts . . . to what it makes possible. And to speak of "what music makes possible" is to speak of what music "affords" . . . depending upon how it is conceptualized, the concept of "affordance" highlights music's potential as an organizing medium, as something that helps to structure such things as styles of consciousness, ideas, or modes of embodiment. (DeNora 2003: 46–7)

Generalizing the concept to a macro level of larger social units such as nations or significant collective sectors within them, a musical event can be envisaged in terms of how the engagement of collective actors with certain forms of music alters these actors' sense of cultural uniqueness. A musical event would be a sequence of occurrences in which music affords a cultural change, a re-structuring of collective consciousness and ideas. The encounter of large sectors within national societies, and especially musicians, critics, and other music professionals, with the pop-rock aesthetic had exactly this effect.

The historical musical event of pop-rock is, then, the event that altered the way musical nationalism – and, by extension, cultural identity at large – is practiced and experienced by individuals and by collective entities in late modernity. Following the duration of this event, the perception and performance of ethno-national cultural uniqueness has been transformed from one emphasizing essentialism and purism, to one organized around fluidity, relativity, and admitted openness to "otherness." Musical nationalism has mutated from being organized, primarily, around acoustic sonorities to a realm in which amplified, electric, and electronic sounds are the standard mode for making music. By calibrating local, national, and indigenous musical cultures to its sonic textures, aesthetic idioms, and stylistic map, pop-rock music afforded collective entities within national societies, or indeed nations at large, the reconfiguration of their sense of uniqueness. It afforded, among other things, the execution of a change in cultural orientation from being directed toward cultural separatism to one that embodies aesthetic cosmopolitanism.

The Historical Musical Event of Pop-Rock

The introduction of the pop-rock aesthetic into ethno-national musical cultures comprised, then, an "event" not in a strict sense of one occurrence or a happening confined to one place in a short period of time, but rather as a transformational process, a long-term event, that had the effect of a structural transformation in musical culture.

Agency

For the musical event of pop-rock to take place, however, active agency had to be practiced. The event had to be "produced" by social agents whose interests propelled them to engagement with music that constituted the event. These agents might be classified into four basic categories: musicians, critics and media professionals, music industry personnel, and fans. The cultural work of the first three types, those active in the field of cultural production, are discussed below. The cultural work of fans is discussed in the next chapter. All these agents, as the actors in the historical musical event of pop-rock, were in fact those who "made aesthetic cosmopolitanism from within" the national context (Beck and Sznaider 2006). They are the ones who materialized in their actions and practice the interplay between the global field of pop-rock and the fields of national culture, the two-way transference of aesthetic schemes between pop-rock and ethnic or national forms of popular music.

Musicians

Generations of musicians within ethno-national settings, since the 1960s and onwards, once they were faced with, and actually fascinated by the creative possibilities offered by the Anglo-American dominant forms of the art of pop-rock – including the artistic and other ideologies surrounding those creative possibilities – have been self-mobilized into membership and actorhood in the global field of pop-rock. While the adoption of pop-rock might be interpreted, along the cultural imperialism thesis, as a move forced on musicians by the industry, it is rather its willful embracement that has proved crucial. Indeed, if there is a moment, an occurrence, or an act that might be called "cultural imperialism" in this regard, it consists of the imposition and then acceptance of a belief in the cultural significance and artistic value of the creative means and canonic works of pop-rock. As an act of conversion from traditional forms of making music to the creative practices of pop-rock, it signaled the active joining of the field. Thus, a study of creative practices among musicians in 13 countries in all continents during the 1980s found that, in terms of being sources for innovation and stylistic self-definition, pop-rock genres and sub-genres ("rock and its derivatives") are by far the most influential (Campbell Robinson et al. 1991: 210–11).

Furthermore, when examining the musical instruments mostly used by the musicians in the study, the researchers have concluded that "popular music the world over then appears to be dominated by what are now established as the traditional instruments of rock" (Campbell Robinson et al. 1991: 215).

In other words, once they came to perceive themselves as participants in the global field, pop-rock musicians, in all parts of the world, adopted the imperative to keep track and be updated with things that happen at the forefront of dominant, mostly Anglo-American pop-rock (and sometimes other locations as well). Stylistic explorations valorized as innovative, and musicians hailed as prime exponents of such innovations by the dominant (Anglo-American) production of meaning positions in the field, were bound to influence and inspire pop-rock musicians all over the world. Such musicians have willfully let themselves be inspired and influenced, because it served their interest to feel active, updated, and relevant actors in the global field, and to determine their own path of creativity and innovation in it.

These musicians, however, were also actors in the field of national culture, where they were propelled to create works whose form, content, and meaning arguably represent some variants of ethnic singularity or national uniqueness. The field of national culture is the social space in which different identity positions within a given ethno-national setting struggle over what constitutes and defines legitimate national culture (Regev 2000). It is a space of identity positions, each of them "taken" by a specific variant of the national culture, whose practitioners, believers, and representatives struggle to gain recognition, legitimacy, and possible dominance. The issue at stake, around which the field of national culture as an arena of struggle is organized, is the repertory of cultural forms, practices, tastes, sensibilities, elements of knowledge, and canons of art forms and art works – in short, the specific cultural capital and habitus, or the institutionalized cultural repertoire (Lamont 1995) – that defines taken-for-granted, default membership in a national culture. Indeed, one may speak in this regard about *national cultural capital* and *national habitus*, that is, embodied schemes of perception and evaluation, pertaining to specific cultural products, that structure modes of conduct and cultural practices which, in their turn, define membership in a given national community. In the fields of art – both high and popular – art forms and art works hailed as indigenous and native tend to be consecrated as "national art," while members of national communities are expected to master the embodied schemes of perception, the intuitive and spontaneous competence required for decoding them in certain ways. Cultural forms associated with supposedly imported aesthetic elements or with ethnic and other minorities are often engaged in struggles for national legitimacy, struggles for these cultural products to be included in the national cultural capital.

Pop-rock musicians have found themselves most typically struggling for their works to be included in national cultural capital. As members of ethno-national communities, and as artists whose immediate public comes also from those same communities, they have been impelled to make music that can be used by their relevant publics to sustain a certain sense of local national uniqueness, or ethnic singularity. As agents in national fields of popular music, either in dominant or dominated positions, they were familiar with indigenous styles and genres, with the history of local music, with artistic hierarchies in the field. They had the creative dispositions associated with some, if not all of those styles and genres. In short, they were in possession of the field-specific habitus.

Pop-rock musicians, then, have found themselves in the intersection of two fields, a position that has determined the creative trajectories that were opened to them. The creative trajectories that are available to artists at any given moment, the "space of possibles" as Bourdieu calls them, are dependent on the history of their field and on the power relations between genres and styles at that particular moment. Toynbee's (2000) elaboration of this point applies to the work of musicians in the field of popular music, leading him to develop the model of "the radius of creativity." The radius of creativity in pop-rock music is derived from the space of stylistic possibilities encountered by musicians in a given moment and sociohistorical setting. Given this space, there is always a certain likelihood that some stylistic possibilities will be preferred over others. This likelihood is determined by several factors. These include, firstly, the musician's own dispositions, namely his or her training, education and capabilities, as well as knowledge of pop-rock stylistic history and repertoire; secondly, his or her position in the field in terms of personal connections, social background, and stylistic inclination; and thirdly, the readily available creative means, such as access to instruments, recording studios, and rehearsal spaces. The radius of creativity means, in other words, that musicians are structurally channeled into a given cluster of stylistic directions and creative options.

The space of creative possibilities opened to pop-rock musicians in national settings came to consist of both the pop-rock tradition and the ethno-national heritage of which they are successors. It thus directed them to a radius of creativity that afforded a two-way transposition of musical practices, of aesthetic schemes, between pop-rock and indigenous music traditions. At its core, the historical musical event of pop-rock has been about transposing schemes from the global field to the national field and vice versa. Transposition has consisted of taking stylistic patterns of pop-rock and using them within national contexts, and applying ethnic and national traditional patterns into the realm of pop-rock. Transposition resulted, most notably, in making national variants of whatever pop-rock style happened to be in vogue at a given moment. Thus, many countries witnessed locally made rock'n'roll in the early 1960s; music inspired by British rock later in that decade; progressive rock, folk rock, and punk in the 1970s; new wave in the 1980s, and hip-hop or electronic dance in the 1990s. The most salient ethno-national elements in these repertoires consisted of singing in native languages and referring in the lyrics to subjects and issues that emanate from local, national social reality. However, in order to justify this music and gain legitimacy as expression of ethnic or national uniqueness, transposition of creative practices took place also in the other direction. This was done by incorporating stylistic elements and creative techniques associated with local, ethno-national traditions of folk and popular music into pop-rock. Major practices here included the use of native musical instruments (sometimes modified to become electric), incorporation of indigenous vocal techniques in singing, inclusion of traditional rhythmic or melodic patterns, and recording electrified pop-rock cover versions of traditional music. Most of these practices are well captured in the following reference to the success of the song "Miin," by Yŏptchŏndŭl, a band formed in 1974 by Shin Joong Hyun, sometimes referred to as "the godfather of [South] Korean rock":

> "Miin" had a monumental cultural impact. Ordinary people, especially young schoolchildren on the streets, were humming along with the folksy melody and rhyme loosely based on *changt'aryŏng*, the traditional beggar's song for food. Shin blended this with an apparent homage to Jimi Hendrix, borrowing a motif from "Voodoo Chile" to create the famous opening guitar riff in "Miin." In addition, Shin gave it a touch of vibrato akin to *nonghyŏn*, a technique widely used with traditional Korean stringed instruments. As a result, the lead guitar in "Miin" sounds like the *kayagŭm* (a twelve-stringed zither), generating a hybrid of Western rock and traditional Korean music. Even one of the most conservative mainstream newspapers praised Shin's feat: "Shin Joong Hyun's 'Miin' is said to create the Yŏpchŏn style by adding the western rock beat to our *karak* (traditional Korean melody) . . . It is

perceived as a desirable trend against the blind following of western pop music." (Kim and Shin 2010: 220)

In a more general vein, and as already noted in chapter 2, the patterns of transposition were most typically exemplified by ethnic or folk pop-rock singer-songwriters and bands, whose inspiration came from the paths set most prominently by Bob Dylan, but whose notion of "folk" came from their own heritage. Another important influence has been reggae musician Bob Marley, not necessarily by inspiring musicians to follow this particular style, but rather by pointing to the creative path where indigenous music is merged with pop-rock sensibilities and instrumentation (Toynbee 2007). The result has been electric ethno-rock styles, often received with much enthusiasm by domestic critics and audiences for its perceived seamless mixture of indigenous tradition and state-of-the-art modernity. This point is captured by Turino (2000), when he writes about the rise of indigenous-based electric guitar bands in Zimbabwe in the 1970s and 1980s, during the war for independence. These electric guitar bands emerged in the 1960s with music influenced by *rock'n'roll*, Congolese *rumba* (a.k.a. *soukous*) and South African *mbaqanga*. During the 1970s, however, the bands increasingly turned to indigenous styles for influence and inspiration:

> As performed by artists such as Thomas Mapfumo, Zexie Manatsa, Oliver M'tukudzi, and many others, this music became closely linked to nationalism among some sectors of the Zimbabwean population and in international perception during the late 1970s and 1980s. Political nationalism, however, was only one of several elements that came together to influence the practice, style, and meaning of indigenous-based guitar bands. Musicians' professional aspirations and cosmopolitan discourses about artistic creativity and originality were equally important. (Turino 2000: 262)

As already stated, the term "hybridization" is often used to refer to the creative practices employed by pop-rock musicians in many countries when they merge and fuse elements of traditional music with pop-rock. The term certainly illustrates these creative practices. Yet it should be re-stressed that hybridization is not an arbitrary or whimsical imaginative practice of some individuals, but rather an artistic practice structured by the social position of pop-rock music in the intersection of two fields of cultural production.

Critics and media professionals

Musicians were not the only cultural producers that have found themselves in this intersection of the fields of pop-rock and national culture. Critics, commentators, radio DJ's, and music editors – in short, producers of meaning, as Bourdieu refers to these professions – have been in an important position in this regard as well. Their practices of transposition took the form of establishing pop-rock magazines, editing and presenting radio programs, writing reviews and columns in the press, and more. Through these practices they transposed into the local field the knowledge of pop-rock, its criteria of evaluation, its mythology of canon and history and, in short, the artistic ideology of pop-rock. Their work of agency has been, ultimately, to produce the ideological and aesthetic vocabulary, as well as the artistic jus-tification through which pop-rock music could become culturally respectable, and home-made pop-rock could gain recognition as a legitimate expression of ethno-national uniqueness. Starting in many countries as gossip magazines centered on blatant promotion of chart toppers, pop-rock criticism evolved into professional and opinionated forms of writing in independent quality magazines and in the music sections of daily or weekly newspapers. The core of this professional evolution consisted of implementation and adaptation of pop-rock's aesthetic ideology and evaluation criteria, based on the ideology of autonomous art, and successfully imposing them on the local field as a prominent, if not dominant mode for assessing the cultural value of popular music. Thus, for example, self-authorship became a crucial parameter for the appreciation of popular music performers. In the course of the event, a clear artistic hierarchy has been established in many national fields of popular music between singer-songwriters (or bands as fully creative units) and singer-performers, where the latter have been typically relegated to a lower position.

In West European or Latin American countries the emergence of pop-rock journalism was essentially an integral part of a general process of media professionalization and diversification, so that the artistic ideological function was somehow concealed. In a place like 1970s and 1980s Soviet Russia, the ideological function of such jour-nalism was more pronounced. Therefore, while not a typical example of such production of meaning mechanism, a publication like *Roksi* stands as clear manifestation, a sort of blueprint of the cultural agendas of pop-rock journalism almost everywhere. First published in October 1977, "It continued, under three different editorial com-mittees, until 1990, during which time fifteen issues were produced at somewhat irregular intervals" (McMichael 2005: 669).

Roksi's first three issues share a similar format, opening with an edito-rial article, moving through reviews and other articles, and closing with

102

a section called "Spleten", in which the latest gossip of the local rock community is reported. Issues 1 and 2 feature a hit parade of groups and musicians, 'LENGORTOP' (a contraction of Leningradskii gorod-skoi top) ... Reviews of concerts taking place in Leningrad feature prominently, including those by Grebenshchikov's Akvarium, Mashina Vremeni, and Soiuz Liubitelei Muzyki Rok, a Leningrad group formed in 1972 with Vladimir Kozlov as its lead singer. The journal conveyed news of Western musicians' activities, and made space for satirical articles or somewhat mordant fiction about life as a musician or fan. Above all, it appeared to be dominated by what can be described as theoretical articles – that is, articles discussing the meaning and place of rock music in the Soviet Union. Such pieces treated the problems inher-ent in producing rock music that were meaningful both to performers and listeners, and anticipated later attempts to explain the cultural meaning of rock music in its Russo-Soviet context. Debates about language, "Russianness" and the distinction between professional and amateur music-making all feature in the magazine's first three issues. (McMichael 2005: 671)

By the 1980s and 1990s, as local pop-rock matured into its self-confidence phase (see below), the professionalism of pop-rock critics introduced to many countries mechanisms of canonization such as "all time" and end-of-year "best albums" rankings (Antonić and Štrbac 1998), artistic prizes and awards, as well as filmed documen-taries and encyclopedic projects that narrated the history of national pop-rock.

Industry

Although obviously guided and motivated by profit interests, and by the culture of instrumentality and rationality that characterizes all modern organization, the global cultural industries of popular music have ultimately acted, from the perspective of cultural soci-ology, as disseminators of the pop-rock aesthetic. The role of the international music industries as agents of mostly Anglo-American profit interests cannot be neglected, nor can their role in maintain-ing inequalities in rights and working condition of musicians and other music professionals (see Getino 1995; Negus 1996; Wallis and Malm 1984; Yúdice 1999). Nevertheless, the cultural dimen-sion that has ultimately underlined their managerial and creative practices should not be underestimated either. Once the production values that came into being with the pop-rock aesthetic, as well as the organizational structures and managerial practices associated with the manufacturing and marketing of pop-rock music, became the standard professional culture of the music industries (Negus 1992), they have been isomorphicaly replicated in the local music industries of countries around the world. As DiMaggio and Powell (1983) have demonstrated, "highly structured organizational fields provide a context in which individual efforts to deal rationally with uncertainty and constraint often lead, in the aggregate, to homogeneity in structure, culture, and output" (DiMaggio and Powell 1983: 147). They identify coercive, mimetic, and normative isomorphism as the three mechanisms that lead to similarities in the functioning of organizations that work in a given realm, and in their products. In the case of the set of organizations commonly known as "the international music industries," mimetic and normative isomorphism meant, from the 1970s and onward, standardization of production patterns along the pop-rock aesthetic. This meant, in a country like Zimbabwe for example, that the very emergence of a music industry, the rise of popular music as a professional career, came into being only when pop-rock started to have some presence and impact (Turino 2000). In countries where a music industry already existed, its organizations, both as local independent firms or as subsidiaries of transnational corporations, increasingly adapted and adjusted their ways of operation to fit the aesthetic conventions of pop-rock music, because these were perceived by them as the model of sheer professionalism. This was done either by mimicking leading music corporations, in the wake of the emerging belief that it is the efficient way to manage the production of music; or by implementing professional conventions in order to comply with norms set by the leading international firms with which local industries increasingly collaborated in various ways. Thus in Turkey, for example, "[s]ince the mid-1990s, the music industry has grown bigger in size and, resembling global counterparts, marketing has gained importance in terms of the extent of branding activities" (Yazıcıoğlu 2010: 241). Furthermore, the music industry in Turkey has become

> similar to that in the West with creators (copyright owners, musicians/
> artists, and producers/engineers), industrialists (publishers, record com-
> panies, and concert/festival producers/promoters), distributors (media,
> retail, concerts, and festivals), and consumers (record buyers, live
> audiences, media, etc.). Rock bands first start with indies and then are
> transferred to the bigger local record companies. (Yazıcıoğlu 2010: 242)

In other words, the default, taken-for-granted perception of industrial organization and task division in music production became practically synonymous with pop-rock production. This is relevant even to the studio work involved in the creation of sound. As Meintjes

104

discovered, while documenting the difficulties of fully implementing ideal working conditions in the studio in early 1990s South Africa, and contextualizing them in the legacy of apartheid, "for sound engineers who are involved in shaping South African music styles, values about local traditions are co-constructed with ideas about production in high-end studios in the metropoles of the North" (Meintjes 2005: 26). In a similar vein, the ritual periodization of Austropop as a new phase in Austrian popular music is seen as inseparable from changes in the industry, including music production:

> The advent of austropop represents a decisive point in the history of Austrian popular music, and the start of a creative incorporation and acquisition into domestic traditions of the formerly "foreign" rock-based music produced and distributed by the internationally operating recording and entertainment conglomerates. It marks the meteoric rise in the careers of not only musicians . . . But also the beginning of careers by sound engineers/producers . . . of managers . . . as well as a network of support in the broadcasting and print media. (Larkey 1993: 150)

* * *

National, domestic, local or indigenous pop-rock music emerged, then, as an embodiment of aesthetic cosmopolitanism through engagement with music practiced by musicians and critics caught in the intersection between the global field of pop-rock music and the field of national culture, and the isomorphic mechanisms in the music industry. The long-term event of pop-rockization lasted, globally, from sometime in the late 1950s or early 1960s until the 1990s, when it reached its fulfillment. Its progression is portrayed below in some detail as consisting of four phases or periods: an *early historical phase*, a period of *consecrated beginnings*, a phase of *consolidation and rise to dominance*, and a phase of *diversification and glorification*. These four phases partially parallel the four stages suggested by Campbell Robinson et al. (1991) in regard to global changes in the popular music industry, yet significantly differ by focusing on the stylistic lineage of pop-rock and on the implications of musical change for the wider national culture. The quasi ideal-type model of the event discussed below is largely based on the cases of pop-rock in Argentina and Israel, which provide most of the examples for the discussion. Although primarily depicting the course of the event in these two countries, the model serves here for pointing to the internal structure of the event, its cultural logic and evolution. The four stages model also fits, to a large extent, the process that has taken place in other Latin American countries, in Western Europe and in Japan. Countries in other parts of the world have witnessed slightly different variants of the event. China, for example, saw the early emergence of pop-rock only in the 1980s. Nevertheless, the accelerated pace of the event in such countries still followed the logic implied by this model, so that by the late 1990s pop-rockization and aesthetic cosmopolitanism in popular music have been consolidated in large parts of the world.

Early "Pre-History"

This early phase consists of musicians and albums conventionally regarded as the first to introduce rock music into local national culture. However, although their initial contribution to the emergence of national pop-rock is acknowledged by critics and historical narratives, they are portrayed, in most cases, as lacking in artistic quality and authenticity. The musicians in this phase preceded the mythologized, consecrated moment of the "birth" of ethno-national pop-rock, the moment when its proper "history" began, according to ritual periodization practices. The term "pre-history" seems therefore to be suitable here. Argentina and Israel provide two typical cases of "pre-historical" pop-rock, publicly characterized when it first appeared as imitative or inauthentic, and therefore denied consecration. However, while in Argentina the performers associated with this early stage enjoyed commercial success and the status of media teen idols (Kreimer 1970), in Israel the pioneering of pop-rock had the character of a suburban subculture, hardly noticed by the media or record industry (Heilbronner 2011). Performers Sandro and Palito Ortega are the most salient names in Argentina during this phase. Sandro was a local Elvis Presley impersonator. He recorded Spanish cover versions of early rock'n'roll hits, and adopted the corresponding appearance (hair style, body language on stage, etc.). Palito Ortega, on the other hand, was the main figure in the group of performers known as *el club del clan*, after the television show which regularly featured them. The models here were early 1960s North American musicians such as Paul Anka or Neil Sedaka. Known together as 'la nueva ola' (new wave) or 'musica beat,' Sandro and *el club del clan* participants were an intrusion in the popular music of Argentina, dominated by folklore, tango, and other Latin American forms of popular music.

In the case of Israel, the early musicians are usually grouped together under the name *lehaqot ha-qetzev* (the beat groups). The label refers to a number of bands that sang in bad English covers of Anglo-American hits (originally by Elvis Presley, Cliff Richard, The

106

Beatles, The Rolling Stones, The Animals, The Kinks, The Who, etc.). With names such as Ha-Shmenim ve-ha-Razim (The Fat Guys and the Slim Guys), Ha-Kokhavim ha-Kehulim (The Blue Stars), The Goldfingers, Ha-Arayiot (The Lions), Uzi ve-ha-Signonot (Uzi and the Styles) and The Churchills, the bands regularly interchanged members and performed in small clubs in the greater Tel Aviv area, most notably in the town of Ramla. The thin cultural industry of Israel in the mid-1960s hardly noticed the phenomenon, even when toward the end of the 1960s several of these bands recorded some original music. Lehaqot ha-qetzev, if noticed at all by power-holding positions in the field of national culture, were dismissed as totally irrelevant, and at best treated as a threat to the sought after purity of national culture.

Interestingly, a salient source of influence on this early pop-rock in both Israel and Argentina was the Italian pop-rock associated with the San Remo festival, with performers such as Little Tony, Bobby Solo, Rita Pavone, Gianni Morandi, and others. By the early 1960s, following earlier Italian adaptations of *rock'n'roll* (Minganti 1993), the style was starting to have an impact on this major festival of Italian song:

> The San Remo music festival, despite its reputation for melody, co-opted the new current quite swiftly. The more melodic rock singers, such as Tony Dallara – whose 'Come prima' (inspired by various Platters' songs, including 'Only You', and the 'sobbing' delivery style of the group's singer Tony Williams) was seen as the first 'shouted' song – Jenny Luna and Joe Sentieri were followed by Celentano, Mina and Gaber, who offered a more beat-oriented sound. The rocker *urlatori* ["shouter"] first appeared at the San Remo festival in 1961, when Celentano and Little Tony offered competing – but in fact very similar – versions of "24,000 baci" (24,000 kisses) which won second place. (Gundle 2006: 376)

Indeed, Adriano Celentano was the pivotal figure here. Although generally considered the "Italian Elvis," his performances were not as imitative as similar figures in other countries:

> Italian rock – even the Italian rock that had relatively few aesthetic aspirations and was more openly market-directed – was not merely an imitation of foreign models, but developed out of a integration of those foreign models with motifs and requirements that were deeply rooted in the Italian national political and religious culture, aspects that a figure like Celentano – a son of emigrants who was constantly working to balance impulses toward modernization with more conservative

107

and traditionalistic inclinations – seemed to emphasize. (Santoro 2006: 278)

Yet another notable case of a "pre-historical" phase is Russia. Under the Soviet regime, early rock musicians struggled in the 1960s and 1970s with the scarcity or confiscation of electric instruments by the police, with censorship of lyrics, and with pressure from state authorities to play either instrumental folk music or ideologically constructive lyrics (Steinholt 2005). According to Russian rock critic Troitsky (1987), most of the bands during this early phase were highly imitative of Anglo-American pop-rock, until "finally, there appeared a band that sang something original – Time Machine [Mashina Vremeni]. If there's any group on whom we may bestow the honorary title of Russian Beatles in terms of their influence on rock music here, it's probably Time Machine" (Troitsky 1987: 27).

Consecrated Beginning

As already discussed in chapter 2, pop-rock culture in many countries tends to cherish a quasi-mythical moment of the "birth" of its own national rock. This moment is typically a short period, characterized by the appearance of a set of albums and musical activities regarded by critics as the founding or constitutive moment of local pop-rock history. Lasting in the cases of Argentina and Israel, roughly, from the late 1960s throughout much of the 1970s, this consecrated beginning consists of the early work of musicians that, according to conventional narrative, were the first to make local rock music "worthy of its name," in two senses: music that matched – according to local critics – artistic standards set by leading Anglo-American artists of the period; and music that could properly be called locally "authentic" – because of the language it used, the content of its lyrics, a typical sonic texture, the social sources from which it emanated and, most notably, the self-authorship of the musicians. Thus the consecrated beginning of pop-rock in Argentina and Israel is characterized by the appearance of enthusiastically received local versions, yet self-authored music inspired by The Beatles and Bob Dylan, *folk rock, psychedelic,* or *progressive rock,* and to some extent *hard/heavy rock.* Following this period, leading musicians of this phase enjoyed a lasting and influential career well into the twenty-first century. The albums recorded in this phase by these musicians are the consecrated classics of local rock, its essential canon. It is with these albums that

108

in both countries the music was given the proper names of *Israeli rock* and *rock nacional*.

An important feature of this formative moment, as with similar moments in other fields of art, has been its collaborative nature. In each country, the "birth" of ethno-national pop-rock is credited to a small network of musicians that between them formed bands, duos or short-lived projects, participated in each other's solo efforts, contributed production work and authorship of compositions or lyrics to each other's albums, and joined forces on stage in festivals and special concerts. Regev and Seroussi (2004) refer to this network in Israel as the "elite" of Israeli rock. The term can be applied to the parallel network in Argentina as well. Musicians and critics there repeatedly declare the release and success of the single "La balsa" (The raft) by Los Gatos in 1967 as the beginning of *rock nacional*. Litto Nebia, front person of this band, is one member of the "elite" network whose additional prominent names include Luis Alberto Spinetta, Charly García, Nito Mestre, David Lebón, and Leon Gieco. Additional members come from bands fronted by these musicians (Almendra, Pescado Rabioso, Sui Generis, Serú Girán, Pappo's Blues). Other bands often referred to as founders of *rock nacional* are Manal, Vox Dei, and Arco Iris. The first album by Spinetta's band, *Almendra*, is often credited as the constitutive work of *rock nacional* (the album was voted twice, in critics and musicians polls conducted by the daily newspapers *Clarín* in 1985 and *Página/12* in 1992, as the best album in the history of Argentinean rock):

> Everything seemed to be there in place: the sonic world of the 60s, with its diverse replicates, diverse styles, synthesized in thirty minutes. In this sense, it might be said that the influence of the Beatles on *Almendra* was less about direct musical affiliation than about the idea of the integral disc or album, like *Sgt. Pepper's Lonely Hearts Club Band*. (Pujol 2002: 269)

In Israel the elite network consisted of singer Arik Einstein and musicians like Shalom Hanoch, Shmulik Kraus, and Shem-Tov Levy who collaborated with him intensively during this formative stage. The elite also included members of the band Kaveret (Danni Sanderson, Yoni Rechter, Gidi Gov, Alon Olearchik, Yitzhak Klepter) as well as Ariel Zilber, Matti Caspi, and others. Foremost among the albums made by members of this network are *Sof Onat ha-Tapuzim* (End of the Orange Season, 1976), the only album by Tamuz, a band led by Shalom Hanoch and Ariel Zilber, and *Shablool* (1970), by Arik Einstein and Shalom Hanoch.

In a period when Israeli music sounded like a merger of a poor man's San Remo festival and the Eurovision, *Shablool* landed like a thunder on a clear day. A real boom. The most important and best album recorded until this day in the new Israeli music . . . Rock'n'roll in Hebrew. Here, at this point exactly, Israeli rock was born. (Yaakov Gilaad, *Hadashot*, December 5, 1986)

It should be stressed that these valorizations are retrospective. At the actual time of their release, the seminal albums of national rock enjoyed, at best, modest success in the market and received fairly small attention from some curious reviewers. In the 1970s, pop-rock had just started its struggle for legitimacy and recognition within national culture. As Diaz (2005) points out for Argentina, in what amounted to a typical mode of constituting a position or sub-field (within the field of national culture), pop-rock's producers of meaning portrayed it as an invigoration of national culture, as the local implementation of new and exciting developments in world art and culture. In addition, national pop-rock culture was coupled to actual oppositional politics, an aspect that later facilitated its legitimacy. Thus in Argentina rock came to be associated implicitly (and on some memorable occasions explicitly; see Vila 1987) with opposition to dictatorship and the military regime of 1976–83, while in Israel a certain association emerged between rock and opposition to the occupation of the Palestinians.

It should be noted that the association, or even outright identification, of rock with leftist oppositional politics had in certain other countries severe consequences for musicians. Thailand was one such country:

Another rock genre emerged in the 1970s, *Pleng phua chiwit* (songs for life), during a period of great political uncertainty . . . Clashes between the authorities and students' and workers' groups in 1973 and 1976 encouraged students to take up protest rock and after a brutal military coup in 1976 many students took refuge in jungles and mountain retreats. *Pleng phua chiwit* became something of a symbol of the peaceful fight against dictatorial power. It was headed by Caravan, a band formed from two socially conscious bands, Tor Sen and Sunjorn and the Bangladesh band. Using a musical soundtrack culled from Western folk rock, West Coast rock and the protest music of Bob Dylan . . . Caravan added stirring lyrics by intellectuals like Jit Poumisak, and broadcast some of their music from jungle radio stations (Clewley 2005: 217)

South Korea also witnessed a repression of pop-rock, exactly at the point in time when future consecrated musicians like Shin Joong

Hyun or Kim Hong-t'ak were formulating their sonic language within the style known in South Korea as "the group sound."

> The Korean group sound era began with music festivals and contests ... One of the most prominent festivals was the annual Playboy Cup Vocal Group Contest. The grand prize of the inaugural contest in 1969 went to Kim Hong-t'ak's He Six, the band he formed after splitting with the Key Boys ... As a group sound ... He Six was playing psychedelic rock with an audacity and intensity that rivaled Shin Joong Hyun's. He Six occasionally added a flute or an oboe to the psychedelic jam sessions, making an experimental sound comparable to the contemporary British band Jethro Tull. If Shin Joong Hyun's sound evokes Jimi Hendrix, Kim Hong-t'ak's nimble and sophisticated guitar work resembles Carlos Santana's ... The same year the Playboy Cup folded, an outdoor concert festival took place in a riverside resort area near Seoul. During a three-day period the Ch'ŏngp'yŏng Festival drew crowds of thousands, whose communal experiences were similar to Woodstock and the Summer of Love in the United States. The global youth counterculture had arrived in Korea: long hair, bell-bottoms, recreational drug use, and antiauthority attitudes. Rok, along with the fledgling modern folk movement, provided a soundtrack for this new cultural drama. The liberal proponents called it the youth culture (*ch'ŏngnyŏn munhwa*), whereas the conservative opponents had much more sinister names for it. (Kim and Shin 2010: 214–15)

Through most of the 1970s, under Park's regime, pop-rock culture was deemed "decadent" and could not flourish. Still, in later years, the music made during the "group sounds" came to be consecrated and inspirational for Korean pop-rock (Shin 2011).

As much as the alignment of pop-rock with oppositional culture was genuine and sprang out of sincere commitment of musicians and fans, it also proved to serve the interest of pop-rock practitioners to gain legitimacy. Oppositional politics, however, were not the only strategy for gaining legitimacy in authoritarian regimes. In Russia, for example, the mythologized birth of rock is closely associated with the bands that played in and recorded around the Leningrad Rock Club in the early 1980s (Cushman 1995; Steinholt 2005) – Aquarium, Kino, Alisa, and Zoopark amongst others. Although the Club was initiated by musicians, its establishment and functioning was made possible through official bureaucratic procedures that implicitly meant a certain compliance with the regime and the authorities. The Club was premised on an ideology of artistic exploration and creativity and the theme of political resentment played a minimal role, if any.

Indeed, the accomplishment of national pop-rock during this phase was to establish itself as a legitimate, although still minority position in fields of national culture, next to existing positions of traditional popular and folk music. The valorizations quoted above for Argentina and Israel, and similar ones in other countries, were written when pop-rock had already gained prominence and even dominance. They mythologize this phase as a moment of rupture, canonize the pioneering status and avant-garde aura of the albums, and express the sense of achievement shared by pop-rock musicians and critics in a later period, when pop-rock was already a dominant force.

A somewhat different variant of a mythologized beginning of pop-rock is the Spanish case. *La Movida* (the move), a period of intensive cultural activity in Madrid during the early 1980s, is widely regarded as the cradle of pop-rock in that country (Fouce 2006; Lechado 2005). Taking shape during the transition to democracy after 40 years of dictatorial regime, *La Movida* signifies the leap of Spanish arts and popular culture into the stylistic vocabulary of postmodernism (film director Pedro Almodóvar, for example, was a vital person in the network of artists that made *La Movida* happen). Bands and musicians such as Kaka de Luxe, Alaska y los Pegamoides, Radio Futura, Nacha Pop, Loquillo, and El Último de la Fila, inspired and influenced primarily by punk, post-punk, and new wave, were at the core of *La Movida*, and their music swept the radio and the music market. Their output is sometimes referred to as "the golden age of Spanish pop." However, unlike the more typical cases of mythologized beginnings, the music of *La Movida* did not react solely to the light music, associated with traditional Spanish popular song and dance (like the *copla*), to melodic pop (as represented in the 1970s by the enormous success of Julio Iglesias) or to the mimicking of Anglo-American pop-rock by earlier bands. *La Movida* expressed also, implicitly, a negation of the artistic seriousness of three pop-rock phenomena that preceded it in the 1970s. These were the politically committed singer-songwriters, best represented by the likes of Paco Ibáñez or Victor Manuel; the scene of *rock catalán* (Catalonian rock), whose most notable voice was probably Pau Riba; and the flamenco-infused network of *rock andaluz* (Andalusian rock), that ranged from the more straightforward flamenco pop of Pata Negra to the progressive rock of Triana or Alameda. That is, while contrasting the sheer commerciality of the pop that dominated the charts, the music created by the bands and musicians of *La Movida* did not opt for the typical pattern of pop-rock authenticity, but rather took its inspiration from

the attitude of detached irony, associated with the pop-art of Andy
Warhol (who visited Madrid in 1983, in the midst of *La Movida*
and, according to local rumor, walked through the halls of the Prado
museum – home to classic paintings by El Greco and Goya – in just
15 minutes). In other words, although it was not the first instance of
Spanish pop-rock to be credited with artistic authenticity, *La Movida*
stands as the consecrated beginning of pop-rock in this country
because it expressed, in the words of Borja Casani (founder and first
editor of *La Luna de Madrid*, the magazine that gave voice to the
ideas and the protagonists of *La Movida* during the 1980s), the spirit
of cultural change that marked the transition to democracy: "fascina-
tion with the new, the appearance of a new type of intellectual, more
frivolous and less classic, and the creation of a small culture, without
great works nor great masters" (quoted in Fouce 2006: 28).

Consolidation and Rise to Dominance

This is the phase during which pop-rock music rose to national dominance. The 1980s witnessed the pop-rockization of almost the entire
field of popular music in many countries. The historical context for
this phase in Argentina was the demise of the military regime and the
return to democracy. In Israel this phase coincided with the transition to liberal economic policy ushered in by the right-wing Likud
party. Alabarces (1993) refers in this regard to an "explosion" in the
amount and public impact of rock produced in Argentina in the early
1980s, while Regev and Seroussi (2004) write about "the coming
of rock" during this period in Israel. In other words, in this phase,
pop-rock music was firmly consolidated as a leading force in national
fields of music and culture along two complementary channels.
Genres and styles, and the pop-rock aesthetic in general, were being
increasingly indigenized, while some local and traditional genres were
going through a process of pop-rockization.

The rise of pop-rock to national dominance was accomplished
in this phase through interplay between music making and music
journalism, that is, between the growing acceptance of the pop-rock
aesthetic as the major creative platform in popular music production,
and the establishment of magazines, newspaper sections and supplements, as well as radio channels, for which the evaluative criteria
of pop-rock became the default practice of professional popular
music journalism. The expanding use of electric instruments and
sophisticated studio production, as well as the increased following
of Anglo-American stylistic trends, were thus served by a journalistic

113

apparatus that worked to both produce the meaning of this new music and proclaim its artistic value.

In Argentina, magazines like *Pelo* and *Expreso Imaginario* had already started to appear during the 1970s. They were joined by *Cantarock* in the 1980s, a decade in which the widely circulating daily newspaper *Clarin* started its weekly rock supplement under the name *No*. It was soon rivaled by the supplement *Si* of the daily *Pagian/12*. Also notable in these early years is the magazine *Humor*, which featured a pop-rock section written by Gloria Guerrero. These publications were the venues where individuals like Alfredo Rosso, Miguel Grinberg, Pipo Lernoud, Enrique Symns, Claudio Kleiman, and others established their authoritative position as leading critics and commentators of pop-rock in Argentina. Along with the printed press arrived radio stations whose playlists, commentaries, specialized programs, and other formats of broadcasting propelled Argentinean pop-rock to dominance. Foremost among these was the Rock & Pop channel in Buenos Aires which, starting in 1985, devoted many of its music programs to promoting national pop-rock, but also introduced the type of informal, critical, free speaking, and occasionally humorous styles of presenting pop-rock.

Similar developments occurred in Israeli media around the same period. As early as 1973, a local "pirate" radio station, "The Voice of Peace," modeled after offshore stations in the North Sea (i.e., Radio London, Radio Caroline, and Radio Veronica), began broadcasting non-stop pop-rock music from a ship "somewhere in the Mediterranean," as its slogan went. Towards the end of the decade, the Israel Broadcast Authority launched Reshet Gimmel, an all pop-rock station, while Galei Tzahal, the channel operated by the Israel Defense Forces, expanded to a 24-hour format with pop-rock being its major ingredient. By the 1980s, the two latter had increasingly developed a roster of pop-rock programs that ranged from chart hits to specialized shows concentrating on alternative rock.

Pop-rock magazines, however, have been a rare species in the Israeli media. Several attempts to launch specialized publications, most notably *Volume* in 1983, ended after few issues. *Lahiton* was the only long-lasting music magazine, but it was centered primarily on photos and gossip rather than critical reviewing and commentary. More artistically oriented rock journalism did emerge, however, during the 1980s. The three major daily newspapers (*Yediot Aharonot*, *Maariv*, and *Haaretz*) in the country started to feature regular columns and supplements with album reviews, opinionated essays, interviews with musicians, and other material. The short-lived daily newspaper

Hadashot (1984–93) also contributed significantly to the press coverage of pop-rock, while the weekly newspapers of Tel-Aviv (*Ha-Yir*) and Jerusalem (*Kol Ha-Yir*), known as *mekomonim* and modeled after publications like New York's *The Village Voice*, became leading podia for album and concert reviews and, in general, for nurturing and voicing local pop-rock culture.

In the case of music making, several parallel developments amalgamated to consolidate the stature of pop-rock. Most salient is the general adoption of electrification, amplification, and sophisticated studio production – the pop-rock aesthetic – as the standard creative practice in the field of popular music. That is, given that pop-rock musicians have been those who molded and codified the modes for using electric instruments, amplification, and studio production techniques as expressive and creative tools, adoption of these practices, even by musicians whose stylistic classification did not qualify as pop-rock in a strict sense, signaled an acceptance of pop-rock as the realm of innovation for large parts of the field of popular music. It reflected an acknowledgment that pop-rock is the domain in which new sonic patterns and expressive options in electric instruments and studio technology are explored and formulated to later be adopted by other positions in the field. In various countries, and certainly in Argentina and Israel, pop-rock musicians and instrumentalists who had already gained proficiency and reputation during the two early phases, became by the 1980s the national hoard of experts from which studio and supporting musicians as well as producers were recruited for making "state-of-the-art" popular music.

This point is best exemplified by the transformation of traditional melodic pop into so-called "soft rock" or "adult oriented rock." Here, the niche of sentimental ballads has been taken by singer-songwriters such as Alejandro Lerner (in Argentina) or Rami Kleinstein (in Israel), whose inspiration comes from the likes of Elton John, for example. Most saliently, this niche came to be associated with female singers, sometimes characterized as glamorous pop divas, whose grandiose sonic idiom is set within pop-rock parameters of instrumentation and production (synthesizers, electric guitars, etc.). The careers and recordings of female singers such as Rita (in Israel) or Sandra Mihanovich (in Argentina), for example, have blurred the supposedly sharp divisions that existed until the 1980s between the sonic textures of pop-rock and those of traditional, orchestrated, and jazzy popular song. More than any other style, this phenomenon reflects the pop-rockization of popular music and, indeed, the expansion of "rock" to become "pop-rock."

115

A more specific phenomenon that took place within this general trend consists of collaborations and mergers of pop-rock with folk genres. In a move that broadened some tendencies that already existed in earlier works, pop-rock musicians started to record, in rock arrangements, songs from the local folk and traditional popular canon, to create original music in the same vein, and to team up with prominent musicians from those genres. The two-way stylistic exchange that emerged blurred at some points the differences between pop-rock and folk music. Notable examples in Argentina include Mercedes Sosa, a national icon of folklore, who shared the stage in 1982 with Charly García, Leon Gieco, and other *rock nacional* founders, and then moved on to record songs by these and other pop-rock authors such as Fito Páez and Alejandro Lerner. Gieco is indeed an outstanding figure here. A folk rock *auteur*, his oeuvre made him "one of the fundamental protagonists of the history of Argentinean popular music, by situating him in an intermediate point between rock and folklore" (Aguirre et al. 2005: 145). Equipped with a mobile studio, Gieco embarked in 1981 on a three-year trip across Argentina, during which he recorded with local musicians from all the country's provinces self-authored songs as well as traditional ones. The project, carried out together with Gustavo Santaolalla (leader of the progressive folk rock band Arco Iris, and later a prominent producer of Latin American pop-rock), yielded the triple album *De Ushuaia a La Quiaca*, that became a landmark fusion of folklore and pop-rock. Finally, Juan Carlos Baglietto, in his first solo album (1982), which became the first *rock nacional* album to receive "gold" certification from the local industry, performed pop-rock music using a vocal form of delivery, as well as arrangements that owed much to the traditional atmosphere of tango.

In Israel, the first thing to mention is the success of leading rock artists in establishing themselves as inheritors of, rather than rebels against the invented folk tradition of *shirey eretz yisrael*. This was achieved primarily through the series of albums *Good Old Eretz Yisrael*, in which Arik Einstein recorded classic songs from this folk repertoire in soft rock arrangements. The composers and arrangers who collaborated with him on the project, Shem-Tov Levy and Yoni Rechter, emerged in these albums, as well as in other projects, as the rock-inspired heirs of canonic *eretz yisrael* composers such as Sasha Argov, Mordechai Zeira or David Zehavi. From a different angle, the growing presence and legitimacy of *musica mizrahit* (oriental pop music), although sometimes ideologically antagonistic to rock, nevertheless introduced an ethnic form of pop-rock (best expressed in

116

the work of singers Zohar Argov and Haim Moshe). In a similar vein, Yehuda Poliker left his hard rock band Benzin to become one of the country's most successful and beloved musicians with his formula of Greek and other Mediterranean-inspired pop-rock music. Ehud Banai also emerged with a successful career and a sonic idiom that fuses rock with Middle Eastern and Asian influences.

Finally, this phase in the on-going historical event witnessed a new generation of pop-rock musicians whose career took off following collaborations with the founders and under their auspices (Yehudit Ravitz in Israel, Fito Páez in Argentina), or who were influenced by new frontiers of stylistic innovation – most notably punk, post-punk, and new wave (the bands Soda Stereo, Attaque 77 and Virus in Argentina, and Mashina in Israel). Given the already legitimized position of the founders, the entry of these newcomers into the framework of what counts as "national" was smoother and faster, and met with positive reviews about keeping local culture in pace with general artistic innovations. This type of acceptance was facilitated by the discourse, developed in music magazines, newspaper supplements, radio and television shows that flourished at this point, in which the founders of national rock were mythologized and which presented the expansion of pop-rock as a natural, conflict-free linear evolution. While this discourse, as Alabarces notes, neutralizes the oppositional character rock initially had in Argentina, and it therefore "de-ideol-ogizes the ideological, and de-politicizes the political" (1993: 88), the discourse nevertheless depicts the position reached by pop-rock during the 1980 – that of dominance and centrality in the national fields of popular music.

Diversification, Internationalization, Glorification

The final phase of the musical historical event of pop-rock, during the 1990s and into the next century, consisted of stylistic diversifica-tion in accordance with trends in global pop-rock, but also through development of indigenous patterns, decoupled from such trends. In addition, local musicians made forays into the international field with occasional success, thus bringing pride into the national field about its artistic quality and the ability to match Anglo-American dominance. Most importantly, perhaps, and in what amounts to ritualistic self-appraisals, this phase also witnessed the appearance of written or televised histories of national pop-rock and the introduc-tion of prizes and awards by the industry, the media, and the state to honor and glorify the work of pop-rock musicians. In sum, it is the phase in which pop-rock became not only fully accepted, but rather gained national self-confidence to the point of celebrating its own achievements and writing its own history in a glorifying manner.

Diversification along global trends was manifested in the 1990s by electronica and hip-hop, the former represented by the thriving of electronic club cultures in Tel Aviv and Buenos Aires, but also by electro-pop in the case of Argentina (bands like Entre Rios and Miranda!), and by the scene of *goa-trance* in Israel (best represented by duos like Astral Projection and Infected Mushroom). National forms of hip-hop were also successfully introduced in these two countries, usually mixed with strong funk and reggae tones, as in the case of Argentinean bands like Illya Kuryaki & Los Valderramas or Sindicato Argentino del Hip Hop, and Israeli bands like Shabak Samech or Hadag Nahash (Dorchin 2012).

More significant during this phase were the indigenous stylistic developments that indicated a sense of self-assurance on the part of national pop-rock musicians and critics about their ability to generate stylistic innovations, decoupled from Anglo-American trends – a development that to some extent rendered US and UK pop-rock less relevant for national pop-rock cultures (Frith 2004). Unlike earlier hybrids of ethnic or folk rock, which were mostly about connecting rock with tradition and heritage, the stylistic innovations of the 1990s were seen by local critics as domestic stylistic explorations that parallel those taking place in the metropolitan centers of pop-rock. In Argentina, this point became most explicit with the appearance of the trend known as *rock chabón*, whose prominent exponents were bands such as Los Piojos or La Renga (Semán and Vila 2002; Semán et al. 2004). Some of the critique that has been raised among older rockers against its artistic quality and form of nationalism (Marchi 2005) exposed *rock chabón* as a rupture in the perceived smoothness and linearity of *rock nacional*'s evolution (see also Benedetti 2008). Somehow connected to *rock chabón* was the growing presence of Latin American rhythmic influences in rock, most notably the *cumbia*, but also *candombe*, *cuarteto*, and others, best expressed in the sounds and success of the band Bersuit Vergarabat (Citro 2008).

In Israel, the phenomenon to mention is the fusion between the previously conflicting musical cultures of *musica mizrahit* and rock. This fusion was pioneered in the 1990s by bands such as Sfatayim, Knesiat ha-Sechel (The Mind Church) and, most prominently, Tea-Packs, that surfaced from the southern town of Sderot with an ethnic sound owing as much to existing Israeli and dominant Anglo-American pop-rock as to *musica mizrahit*. The "sound of Sderot" thus defied

118

existing categories and was hailed by critics as a quintessential, indigenous Israeli idiom of pop-rock (Saada-Ophir 2006). Another significant step was the collaboration of the pop-rock band Ethnix with singer Eyal Golan, which propelled the latter's career to national stardom. Later on, in the 2000s, the fusion of genres was further consolidated by performers such as Sarit Hadad, Lior Narkis, Kobi Peretz, and others, whose style of "mizrahi light" made them the new mainstream of Israeli pop (Kaplan 2011).

Another aspect of this phase consisted of successful forays of local musicians into the global field and generic sub-fields. With these, national pop-rock critics and musicians celebrated a sense of achievement. Such successes served as proof of the artistic quality reached by national pop-rock musicians, their ability to match or even surpass standards of dominant Anglo-American pop-rock. Israel's pop-rock overseas presence was heralded in the 1980s with "Im Nin'alu," a Jewish Yemenite traditional song performed by Ofra Haza and remixed by Izhar Ashdot to become an international electro-dance hit; and by Minimal Compact, a band that enjoyed success in some European alternative rock scenes. In the 1990s the already mentioned exponents of the electronic style of *goa-trance*, Astral Projection and Infected Mushroom, became world leading names of this genre's scene. In addition, intensive touring of the band Rockfour in the US, as well as the collaboration of Aviv Geffen, a prominent name in Israeli rock since the early 1990s, with Steven Wilson (leader of UK progressive rock band Porcupine Tree) under the name Blackfield, earned a reputation for Israeli alternative pop-rock in this genre's scenes in the US and Europe.

Internationalization in the case of Argentina meant primarily expansion into and a high profile in the framework of Spanish-speaking pop-rock of Latin America, Spain and the US, also known as *rock en español*. During the 1990s, Argentinean bands such as Soda Stereo, Los Fabulosos Cadillacs and Los Enanitos Verdes as well as rock *auteur* Fito Páez became leading names of this scene across the continent, enjoying both market and critical success; the already mentioned transatlantic successful career of Andrés Calamaro made him a prominent pop-rock artist in Spain as much as in his native Argentina. Additional contributions to the sense of international achievement came, for example, from the high profile of Gustavo Santaolalla (originally the leader of the 1970s band Arco Iris) as musical producer of leading names of Latin pop-rock and other genres, and from the warm critical reception in the US and UK rock publications of albums by singer-songwriter Juana Molina. The historical musical event of pop-rock culminated, however, around the turn of the century in these two, and in many other, countries with the broadcasting of television series (*Sof Onat ha-Tapuzim* in Israel, 1998, and *Quizas Porque: Historia del Rock Nacional*, 2009, in Argentina) and the publication of books about the history of national pop-rock (Bitar 1993), by the appearance of album guides (Aguirre et al. 2005), encyclopedic websites (rock.com.ar for Argentina,www.mooma.com for Israel), as well as various critics' polls to elect "the best albums." In addition, local honors patterned after the US Grammies or the UK Brit awards have been constituted in both countries, as annual events of appraisal to current musicians but also for honoring veteran musicians with special "lifetime achievement" awards (the Gardel prize in Argentina, the ACUM and TAMUZ awards in Israel). With these discursive endeavours, media events, and ceremonies, a mythologized narrative of pop-rock history has been institutionalized and a canon of its most acclaimed musicians and works has been erected. These annual rituals, as well as the media and discursive projects, glorified the sense of long history, wealth of repertoire, variety of styles and artistic achievement of national pop-rock. They also marked the strong hold pop-rock music has gained at this point in the national cultural field.

* * *

Symbolically, the ultimate example of the pop-rock musical historical event is probably the one that took place in the former Eastern bloc countries, where the event carried – more than in any other country or region – political meanings. As has been well analyzed and documented in a collection of essays on pop-rock in East Germany, Poland, Czechoslovakia, Hungary, Yugoslavia, Bulgaria, Ukraine, Belarus, and the Soviet Union in general, pop-rock gave voice, from the 1960s onward, to those feelings and ideas that eventually culminated in 1989 with the sweeping transformation of regimes in all these countries (Ramet 1994b):

> Thus rock musicians figured – in the Soviet and East European countries of the 1980s – a bit like prophets. That is to say, they did not invent or create the ideas of revolution or the feelings of discontent and disaffection. But they were sensitive to the appearance and growth of these ideas and gave them articulation, and in this way they helped to reinforce the revolutionary tide. (Ramet 1994a: 2)

Nevertheless, it should be repeated, in conclusion, that the consolidation of pop-rock as a viable, prominent, dominant, and, in any case, legitimate component of musical nationalism did not necessarily follow in every country the clearly demarcated phases outlined above. Thus in Brazil, for example, the "early history" phase of nonlegitimate pop-rock in a sense did not precede but rather coincided with the more legitimate introduction of pop-rock in the 1960s.

> Rock's entry into popular music in Brazil, symbolized by the electric guitar, was marked by the appearance of two distinct modes of musical production: the Jovem Guarda of Roberto Carlos, a vanguard of mass popular music, and Tropicalismo, considered more sophisticated option within a restricted type of musical production (MPB). Jovem Guarda and Tropicalismo both related to the Beatles: Jovem Guarda, accentuating adolescent sentimentalism, and Tropicalismo, through songs with a certain degree of artistic aspiration. (Ulhôa 2004: 204)

Yet the high esteem held for *tropicalismo*, a musical movement whose major musicians' connection to pop-rock was occasional and passing, hindered in a sense the crystallization of a consecrated beginning in the 1970s. Such a moment arrived only in the next decade, thus coalescing in fact the second and the third phases into one:

> By the end of the 1980s *rock brasileiro, rock Brasil, rock nacional*, or even *Brock* – the capital letters emphasize nationality – as it has been variously called, had achieved a certain level of success. (Ulhôa 2004: 204)

As a whole, however, the historical musical event of pop-rock followed the same cultural logic almost everywhere, taking pop-rock from being despised by elitists and purists when it first entered into national cultures, to championing overwhelming presence and cultural legitimacy upon its fulfillment. The transformation is symbolized in some countries by the very rehabilitation of its early non-legitimate idols, making them icons of cultural modernization. This is the case for Johnny Hallyday, France's prime pop-rock performer:

> When he became France's first rock idol in 1961, pop was feared by the cultural and political establishment everywhere as a dangerous influence on youth, and, in Gaullist France particularly, as a vehicle of US cultural imperialism. (Loosely 2005: 200)

By the 1990s, however,

> [t]he image of the singer as thieving magpie, switching from one popular-cultural movement to the next and embarrassing the nation in the process, is often recast . . . Johnny today is constructed as more a *chanteur* than a rock star . . . What this underscoring of a *chanson* lineage

at the expense of his rock credentials is designed to achieve is Johnny's aesthetic and cultural authentication. His rock'n'roll origins are not denied . . . but they are discreetly sidelined . . . In the process, Hallyday is re-nationalised, converted from Trojan horse of America to public space given over to a kind of Frenchness. (Looseley 2005: 196, 198)

The transformation of musical nationalism, then, as it took place throughout the historical musical event of pop-rock, revolved essentially around the production of meaning, about establishing a firm belief in artistic value and cultural significance of domestic pop-rock music. The event was carried out primarily by critics, journalists, media professionals, and, most obviously, by musicians and music industry people. It was, in other words, an event that took place in the field of cultural production. Concurrently, and in the wake of the occurrences of the event, Anglo-American and domestic pop-rock genres and styles took hold in the tastes and life-worlds of ardent fans and casual listeners. Pop-rock genres became the foci of socio-cultural entities, variously known as subcultures or scenes, and in the musical preferences of various groupings and individuals in many countries. The nature of this cultural and experiential place of pop-rock at the level of reception and consumption is the subject of the next chapter.

— 5 —

AESTHETIC CULTURES

The cluster of styles known to the uninitiated by the labels *heavy metal*, or simply *metal*, has been a globally thriving form of pop-rock since at least the 1980s (Wallach et al. 2011). Locations of metal consumption and production have been researched and documented, among other places, in Turkey (Hecker 2005, 2010), Israel (Kahn-Harris 2007), Brazil (Avelar 2003), Basque country (Weston 2011), Malaysia and Indonesia (Lockard 1998), Japan (Kawano and Hosokawa 2011) and the Nordic countries (Hagen 2011). Emma Baulch describes the emergence of devoted fandom and activity around the sub-style of *thrash metal* in Denpasar, Bali (Indonesia) as having its roots in a late 1980s radio program called "1921," in reference to its twice-weekly slot (from 19:00 to 21:00, every Saturday and Sunday), and broadcast on a local community radio station, Radio Yudha. The program gradually became dedicated to *thrash metal*, and later *death metal*. Broadcasting music by Anglo-American bands such as Megadeth, Kreator, Slayer, and Metallica, a *thrash metal* fandom was taking shape in Denpasar:

> [I]ncreasing numbers of enthusiasts responded to the new show by visiting the studio at the time of the broadcasts. In this way, 1921 did not merely link otherwise disparate listeners in the manner of a cyber chat room, e-mail discussion list or subscriber-based community radio, but operated as a call to prayer, sucking disparate enthusiasts from family compounds scattered all over Denpasar, and bringing them together in a space in which fixity was achieved through tape swapping, information exchange, the production of self-designed black tee shirts and the kind of uniquely Balinese drinking rituals that serve to knit male solidarity. (Baulch 2003: 196–7)

Baulch goes on to assert that the Balinese thrash metal scene was not "steeped in blue collar ethos" (Weinstein 2000: 115), as the Western heavy metal fans are typically portrayed (see also Bryson 1996). Rather, the Balinese metal enthusiasts were "distinctly bourgeois, and for the majority of them, the future seemed relatively bright. Most of them were university students whose parents had helped them to buy guitars and approved of their music-related 'hobby'" (Baulch 2003: 199). Thrash metal fandom in Indonesia (as elsewhere), however, was not confined to the small group of enthusiastic and active fans in Bali. Concerts by the internationally successful Brazilian metal band Sepultura in 1992, and by the US band Metallica in 1993, were held in a large stadium in Jakarta, drawing audiences of thousands. The concerts "attracted both middle class and elite fans able to afford ticket prices, as well as lower class metal and punk funs who, unable to purchase tickets, eventually resorted to frustrated rioting" (Bodden 2005: 7). The mass enthusiasm generated by the Indonesian concerts of Sepultura and Metallica, however, came to be seen by the Balinese fans as "instances of inauthenticity" (Baulch 2003: 199). They consequently shifted their preferences to other, more extreme sub-styles of metal that go by labels such as *death metal* and *grindcore*. Baulch also points out that, in the case of the Balinese metal devotees and musicians, no attempt has been made to indigenize the music by way of hybridization. Responding to the commercialization of traditional Balinese culture amid the massive tourist industry on the island, the metal fans adhered to music by Anglo-American bands, to cover versions by their local bands, and to English lyrics in their original songs. As marginal as this group's activity was, adhering to an imagined notion of a global "elsewhere," as Baulch calls it, was their way to assert a sense of authentic identity that does not succumb to the stereotyped image of authentic Balinese culture. Either as occasional listeners and concert goers or as ardent participants in a ritualized symbolic exchange of knowledge and objects, *metal* fans in Indonesia have displayed and practiced, in their engagement with this genre, active membership in the global aesthetic realm of metal music. Engagement with these styles of pop-rock music, as practitioners of the rituals surrounding thrash and death metal and as occasional concert goers or record buyers, afforded young people in early 1990s Indonesia the possibility to shape their local identity as participants in what they perceived as a creative aesthetic frontier of late modernity. Ardent or casual, metal fandom served them as a strategy for entering modernity and participating in it, to paraphrase Garcia Canclini (1995).

Metal fandom in Indonesia well illustrates the complex and some-times seemingly paradoxical ways in which pop-rock music functions in the life-worlds of its fans, and how it is articulated in terms of socio-cultural identities. For the small group of Balinese devotees, extreme metal music served as a cultural tool for erecting boundaries, for differentiating themselves, their lifestyle, from larger society. For the massive audiences that congregated in Jakarta to watch and listen to Sepultura and Metallica, extreme metal music was most probably one element in their otherwise wider and eclectic taste in both local and global pop-rock music. With these two modes of consumption, metal music fandom in Indonesia resonated with similar trajectories of pop-rock styles such as punk, hip-hop, or electronic dance music. It is a dynamic in which small groups of devotees develop a sense of identity based on their enthusiasm for certain musicians and bands that most typically create works in the sphere of innovative, avant-garde, or experimental sonic textures. Eventually, however, some of these musicians tend to expand their attractiveness to wider audi-ences, where their music becomes an ingredient of eclectic tastes of various groups. They move from avant-gardism to commercialism, either within the generic sub-field, or indeed into the central sub-field of pop-rock. At the same time, never-ceasing experimentation and creative exploration supplies new sub-styles for the still existing or newer small groupings that emerge and seek to differentiate them-selves from wider society through a set of rituals focused around music consumption.

Research has responded to this dynamic functioning of pop-rock as an object of taste and consumption by studying its reception, its cultural uses among fans and audiences, from two major perspec-tives. One is ethnographic by nature, concentrating mostly on the role of music in the everyday lives of fans, especially as it pertains to construction and definition of socio-cultural identities in terms of carefully designed aesthetic styles. The other perspective consists of survey-based sociological research that focuses primarily on the linkage between taste preferences and sociological variables, includ-ing socio-economic status, occupation, and education level. Two major terms are associated with the first approach, namely *subculture* and *scene*, while the other approach has flourished since the 1990s around the concept of *omnivorous* cultural consumption. That is – and returning briefly to the metal fans in Indonesia – while the group of devotees in Bali almost perfectly fitted the notion of subculture (as indeed Baulch refers to them), for the middle-class masses that came to the Sepultura and Metallica concerts in Jakarta, metal music has been most probably one element in their omnivorous taste preferences for nationally specific and global styles of popular music. As much as these two approaches have produced a rich body of knowledge on pop-rock reception and consumption, their parallel and separate existence calls for a certain integration, for a more general and comprehensive theoretical framework for understanding the cultural functioning of pop-rock styles in the life-worlds and the taste patterns of fans around the world. Moreover, most of the research under these two approaches has concentrated on consumption practices in the metropolitan West or, in some cases, specific countries. Studies of pop-rock subcultures and taste patterns as world phenomena are scarce.

Following a short discussion of the two approaches, then, a theoretical framework for understanding pop-rock fandom and taste preferences will be outlined below. Taking a lead from concepts developed in the sociology of science and knowledge, the notion of *aesthetic cultures* is proposed for describing the nature of pop-rock fandom. The chapter then proceeds to examine the functioning of pop-rock aesthetic cultures, especially in light of the advent of Internet platforms, which have greatly intensified the working of such aesthetic cultures in fans' life-worlds, and rendered them *global microstructures*. The chapter concludes with a detailed examination of the aesthetic culture of *indie/alternative* pop-rock as an exemplary case.

Subcultural Scenes to Aesthetic Cultures

For a long period, from its very origins in the 1970s, a substantial part of pop-rock scholarship was engaged in empirical studies and theoretical formulations in order to come to terms with one of the most obvious and trivial observations about pop-rock fandom and cultural consumption, namely that fans and musicians of pop-rock music in general, and of specific styles and genres in particular, share certain feelings of connection, participation, sometimes even a sort of camaraderie, that stem from their common interest and shared taste in a particular genre of pop-rock. These sentiments are translated into collective patterns of worshipping and visual styles of appearance that jointly construct an aesthetic lifestyle, in some cases augmented with a socio-political ideology. In other words, pop-rock fandom has been generally and widely regarded as a socio-cultural entity that amounts to more then just a category of individuals with similar taste and consumption patterns. Notable examples of such phenomena include the mods (centered on 1960s English pop-rock), the hippies (centered on psychedelic and folk rock), and the aesthetic styles associated with punk, reggae, metal, hip-hop, and electronic dance. The term "subculture," originally associated in sociology with the study of youth delinquency, was applied in the 1970s to these types of socio-cultural identities of adolescents and young adults. Marked by a neo-Gramscian approach, subcultural studies interpreted these collective phenomena as rituals of resistance against hegemonic culture, ultimately destined to be incorporated into that same hegemonic culture through different mechanisms that neutralize their critical stance (Hall and Jefferson 1976; Hebdige 1979; Willis 1978). Subcultural theory came under critique when youth cultures were found to be hierarchical (Thornton 1995) and looser aggregations then originally perceived. New terms that were suggested for characterizing the phenomenon, most notably *scenes* and *neo-tribes* (Bennett 2000, 2004a; Straw 1991), led to a polemic about the proper nomenclature (Bennett 2006a; Hesmondhalgh 2005), which focused around the issue of youth consumption. It has been argued that over time, as the first generations of pop-rock fans have grown older, the correlation between music consumption and youth has greatly decreased. The notion of scene has consequently gained much currency (Bennett and Peterson 2004), as a term depicting networks consisting of fans and musicians that are looser and not necessarily young, nor geographically focused. Scenes of pop-rock music can be virtual and composed of older fans or pre-teen girls (Bennett 2004b, 2006b; Vroomen 2004; Baker 2004).

A quite different line of research about popular music consumption is the one centered on the concept of omnivorous consumption. Developed by Peterson in the early 1990s (Peterson and Kern 1996; Peterson and Simkus 1992), the concept proved to be a fertile ground for numerous studies and debates about the nature of cultural consumption in late modernity. The core finding and major proposition of omnivore studies has been that the performance of status distinction by upper-middle classes in late modernity has shifted from practices of exclusivity concentrated around high culture arts and products, to practices of eclectic consumption that include popular culture as well (Peterson 1997). Arguably a critique of Bourdieu's findings about distinction and cultural capital, the concept of omnivorousness was later interpreted as being, in fact, an extension of Bourdieu's work (Coulangeon 2003; Lizardo and Skiles 2008). In the case of music, it has been shown repeatedly and across countries that upper-middle-class omnivores tend to include in their tastes, next to classical music and jazz, some genres of pop-rock music, thus demonstrating status superiority through conspicuous openness to diversity (Ollivier 2008).

One shortcoming of omnivore studies, at least from the perspective of popular music scholarship, and especially pop-rock research, is that they miss the nature of omnivorousness prevalent among pop-rock listeners. That is, by surveying the consumption of popular music genres next to classical music or jazz, existing research tends to overlook those omnivores whose taste does not exceed the stylistic range of pop-rock, yet it covers a diverse repertoire, from metal and hip-hop, through electronic dance and mainstream pop to alternative pop-rock. The opposite of univores within popular music publics are not necessarily those whose taste covers pop-rock and classical music, but most often those whose taste preferences exist within the stylistic contours of pop-rock – yet nevertheless possess taste preferences for numerous pop-rock genres. These are the pop-rock omnivores.

However, even if the notion of a pop-rock omnivore is acknowledged and considered, it still stands as a mode of consumption quite removed from the mode of membership in a scene, let alone in a subculture, of a pop-rock genre. In terms of theoretical interpretation, the two modes stand in scholarly writing as if there is no relation between them, under two separate traditions of research. Three facets of pop-rock consumption, however, indicate that the notions of omnivorous consumption and subculture or scene have to be bridged and the relations between them made clear. Firstly, almost all genres of pop-rock that function as the nucleus of a subculture or a scene are also, at the same time, components in the eclectic repertoire of pop-rock omnivores. Second, when a subculture dissolves, the pop-rock genre associated with it still survives as a component in the tastes of old and new fans, next to their taste in additional genres. Finally, during their life cycle as music lovers, individuals may move from being devoted participants in a subculture or a scene to being less involved, yet still interested consumers of a given genre, who at the same time broaden their tastes to include additional styles.

It is, then, their co-existence, as well as the movement of taste patterns between the two modes, that call for bridging the notions of subculture or scene with pop-rock omnivorousness. As proposed early on by Fabbri (1982), and realized empirically by Lena and Peterson (2008) and Lena (2012), one possible way of doing this is by using the notion of genre itself as a socio-cultural framework, and especially the trajectories that genres take between different possible incarnations. However, the analysis of genre trajectories implies that genres cannot exist concurrently in multiple incarnations – at any given moment a genre's incarnation is either avant-garde, scene-based or industry-based. But genres do tend to exist, concurrently, in more than one mode. As socio-cultural entities, and as discussed in chapter 3, genres should be seen as sub-fields that can be simultaneously avant-gardist or scenic and industrial – that is, commercial. In addition, given the strong connotation of the term genre as referring to purely musical conventions, it seems that even as a socio-cultural unit, the term should be seen as pertaining primarily to the sphere of production and much less to consumption. The following section therefore proposes an understanding of pop-rock fandom as a continuum of practices, an axis that stretches from active fans, whose entire social identity revolves around engagement with one genre, to listeners with passing, occasional interest in one or more pop-rock styles. Pop-rock fandom is portrayed below as membership in *aesthetic cultures*, varying from ardent to occasional participation.

Aesthetic Cultures

Taking a lead from work in the sociology of science, and especially the notion of epistemic culture, the stylistic universe of pop-rock music and its functioning in the lives of fans and audiences can be portrayed as a set of *aesthetic cultures*, while pop-rock at large can be seen as an aesthetic meta-culture. The idea of an epistemic culture "refers to those sets of practices, arrangements and mechanisms bound together by necessity, affinity and historical coincidence which, in a given area of professional expertise, make up how we know what we know. Epistemic cultures are cultures of creating and warranting knowledge" (Knorr Cetina 2007: 363). Paraphrasing this formulation, an aesthetic culture may be envisaged as a cluster of practices, arrangements, and mechanisms bound together by affinity and historical coincidence which, in a given area of artistic and professional expertise, make up how we experience, evaluate, and sense the world of objects that conventionally belong to a given form of art, and what we know about it. Aesthetic cultures are cultures of creating and warranting criteria of evaluation, modes of worshipping, cognitive and emotional dispositions pertaining to a given world of artistic objects. The notion of aesthetic culture has some parallels with the concepts of field and habitus. However, while Bourdieu's concept of field refers primarily to the space of production practices, the emphasis here is on the space of knowledge and dispositions as it exists primarily among fans and consumers. Indeed, the notion of aesthetic culture is quite similar to the concept of habitus. It is suggested here as an enhancement, allowing a focus on sets of aesthetic sensibilities not only as they exist in individuals' bodies and practices, but as realms of knowledge that exist publicly in the media and other channels. Also, as will be discussed below, the notion of aesthetic culture allows discussing partial membership and participation, thus avoiding the dichotomous nature associated with habitus, where one is supposed to either have it or not.

When understood in this way, various genres of pop-rock may be seen as aesthetic cultures, while pop-rock at large, its range of styles and sub-styles may be understood as the aesthetic meta-culture of pop-rock. Thus we may speak about the aesthetic cultures of metal, of hip-hop, of alternative/indie rock, of electronic dance music, to name the most obvious, but also the aesthetic culture of mainstream pop, for example. The aesthetic cultures of pop-rock should not be seen as rigidly bounded realms of cultural sensibilities, dispositions, and practices, but rather as fluid, constantly changing and reshaped realms. Many of them overlap each other, and their boundaries are anything but clearly defined when it comes to classifying musical works and musicians. Moreover, the aesthetic meta-culture of pop-rock itself is not clearly bounded from other aesthetic cultures of music. Overlaps and blurred boundaries may be found between it and other aesthetic cultures of popular music, of jazz, of art music, and more. On the other hand, fervent practitioners of certain pop-rock aesthetic cultures obviously tend to ritualize boundaries, in order to clearly separate one aesthetic culture of pop-rock from another.

Membership and participation in any given aesthetic culture of pop-rock can be envisaged as a series of expanding circles. The innermost circle consists of experts and ardent fans of the aesthetic culture. They have detailed knowledge and highly refined taste. These are the aficionados, the knowledgeable individuals, the active amateurs Hennion (2001, 2004) refers to, for whom engagement with music amounts to much more than fleeting moments of listening, those who often possess large music collections. They are also the ones who tend to ritualize boundaries between one aesthetic culture and another, and construct group identities around their engagement with music – in other words, they are the makers of subcultures and scenes. The outermost circles, on the other hand, consist of individuals who are occasional fans, with superficial knowledge of one or another work or musician. Participation in a given aesthetic culture is for them just a partial practice, one taste preference among others. These individuals might equally well be partially engaged in the outer circles of several aesthetic cultures of pop-rock. Some of them might be characterized as omnivorous pop-rock consumers, individuals whose taste covers several pop-rock genres. Disseminated from their Anglo-American origins since the 1950s, with an aura of rebellion, fun and hedonism, experimentalism and exploration of uncharted sonic and aesthetic grounds, aesthetic cultures of pop-rock have continually attracted adolescents and young adults in almost any part of the world. Seeking to become full participants in pop-rock aesthetic cultures, they have established local variants of scenes and subcultures. Alternatively, or as they became older, pop-rock genres were integrated into their taste spectrum in an eclectic manner.

Joining aesthetic cultures of pop-rock and participating in them, however, involves acquaintance with relevant knowledge. It thus depends on the availability of, and accessibility to, such knowledge. In order to participate in a given aesthetic culture of pop-rock, individuals have to become aware not only of its very existence, but gain a certain mastery of the specific knowledge that pertains to this aesthetic culture. When acquired, the knowledge that evokes and affords active participation in such culture has to be available and accessible. In the early days of pop-rock, up until the 1980s at the least, acquiring the relevant knowledge of and about its aesthetic cultures was in many countries complicated, difficult, sometimes even a risky task. The advent of the Internet has afforded since the 1990s greater, tighter, more efficient, and more immediate participation in the aesthetic cultures of pop-rock. Practicing and performing aesthetic cosmopolitanism, in the case of pop-rock aesthetic cultures, was immensely upgraded with the Internet. Being initially a loose chain of relatively isolated instances, global aesthetic cultures of pop-rock have become, with the aid of Internet platforms, tight and culturally effective networks. An understanding of this process entails some elaboration about the notion of pop-rock knowledge.

Forms of Pop-Rock Knowledge

The ultimate meaning of being a participant or a member in an aesthetic culture of pop-rock is about having as much knowledge as possible regarding its music. Pop-rock knowledge, however, consists of two basic types. One type of knowledge is informative, or rather, a database type of knowledge, which is mostly about names of musicians, albums, songs, genres, genealogies of styles and periods, etc. It most often consists also of acquaintance with the institutionalized evaluative hierarchies of pop-rock in general, or of a specific aesthetic culture. That is, knowledge about which bands and musicians are the sanctified master artists, and which musical works are the masterpieces of pop-rock and of its specific styles. The other type of knowledge consists of acquaintance with the music itself, with its actual sounds. In terms of accessibility, there is an important qualitative difference between the two types of knowledge. The first type of knowledge is informational and discursive by nature. One can obtain it by reading or through conversation. The other is experiential. The only way to gain it is by listening to the music itself, usually more than once, until acquiring a sort of cognitive and affective ownership of it that allows one to say that he or she knows, likes, and enjoys a musical work or a genre. Indeed, this second type of knowledge is ideally embodied and fully realized in collecting, in ownership of albums or other phonograms, or in any other practice that allows unconditional listening to favorite music whenever one wants. To give a simple example, a member in the aesthetic culture of metal anywhere in the world may know about the existence of a band called Led Zeppelin in the 1970s, know the names of band members and that the band has recorded eight studio albums, including their titles and order of release. One may also know that some Led Zeppelin albums are unanimously considered in pop-rock history as definitive masterpieces of early metal, and in fact of pop-rock in general. And then there is acquaintance with the actual sounds of the music recorded by Led Zeppelin, and owning them culturally, in the sense of being able to recognize songs when they are played, follow melodies and song progressions as already recognized sound sequences, hum them, have them inside one's body and mind.

Until the 1990s, membership and participation in the aesthetic cultures of pop-rock were structurally characterized – in many, if not most countries – by a gap, a disparity, between discursive knowledge and experiential knowledge. That is, while discursive knowledge was in many cases easier to obtain, gaining experiential knowledge, and materializing it in collecting, was a much harder task. Be it through magazines and newspapers, radio talk or conversation among fans, discursive knowledge has been relatively available and accessible. Acquiring experiential knowledge of the music itself, and especially materializing this knowledge into collecting, was more problematic. For most aspiring participants, acquiring this type of knowledge was at best partial. The availability of records and their prices, particularly in countries and regions culturally, economically, and politically removed from the West, made it difficult to build a large private collection of works. Pop-rock programs on radio and television were an important source of acquaintance, but these – when available – were by their nature fleeting and ephemeral. The database knowledge of the average pop-rock music fan, and even of experts, was most often better and wider then their acquaintance or familiarity with the actual sounds of the music they sometimes knew so much about. Ownership of albums containing that music was even less likely. Aspiring participants in aesthetic cultures of pop-rock in many countries were often in a position where they heard talk about bands, musicians, and works, they might have heard some fleeting excerpts from the music itself, but were in great difficulties to get hold of full albums. In this regard, the aesthetic cultures of pop-rock were lacking in cultural effectivity. That is, many participants could not fully accomplish or practice the core experience of membership, which consists of being acquainted with the actual sounds of large portions of the pop-rock repertoire from all periods and styles.

Full-fledged participation in aesthetic cultures of pop-rock, in countries for which such cultures were initially an import, was gradually established with the arrival of upgraded and more sophisticated modes of dissemination such as cable and satellite television, cassette recorders, CD burners, computer audio-file players and, most significantly, Internet connections and facilities. The possibilities for producing and exchanging informative knowledge as well as actual music on Internet platforms, the improved circulation and activation of both types of knowledge in the life-worlds of fans, have afforded an optimized participation in the aesthetic cultures of pop-rock, rendering them *global microstructures* (Knorr Cetina 2005) of sorts. Before looking into the immense upgrading of the cultural effectivity the Internet has afforded the aesthetic cultures of pop-rock, a brief discussion of some practices of acquiring knowledge and localizing it from earlier periods is in order. In what follows, early attempts to join aesthetic cultures of pop-rock in different countries are presented and discussed, in order to emphasize the eagerness, even fervor, that characterized those early efforts of adolescents and young adults in the 1970s and 1980s.

Early Participation

As partial as its presence was in many countries, the affective power of pop-rock on actual or aspiring participants in its aesthetic cultures was as strong as in its metropolitan centers. An ardent fan of punk in Medillín, Colombia, for example, tells how he and friends became acquainted in the 1980s with the knowledge of and about this aesthetic culture:

> Punk gave us an opportunity of freedom, of confronting our social reality head-on. Some of us began to do research, looking into some foreign books and magazines that talked about punk ... we also translated some Sex Pistols lyrics from a cassette that a friend in Bogotá had lent us. (Freddy Rodas, "El Chino", quoted in Muñoz and Marín 2006: 138, and credited as "one of the first initiated into punk in Medillín")

Joining an aesthetic culture like punk meant, for most participants, adopting its typical rituals and worshipping practices, becoming experts about the names of musicians, bands, and works that make up these cultures and, most importantly, getting to know the music itself. It all became, together, the fertile ground from which locally created music in the same vein could emerge. In the case of punk, membership went most often hand in hand with ideologies and attitudes of rebellion against larger society, political and educational institutions, and other aspects of social life.

However, joining and participating in pop-rock aesthetic cultures was not everywhere and always involved with straightforward rebellion. There were cases where it took the form of accommodating the aesthetic culture of pop-rock music into existing local ideologies and cultural institutions of a given country. One notable case is the Soviet Union, that is, Russia, in the 1970s and 1980s. An illuminating analysis of this practice is presented by Yurchak (2003), when discussing the ideological work of Andrei (born 1954), an active member in the Komsomol (the youth division of the Communist Party in the Soviet Union):

> When Andrei studied in school in the early 1970s, he, like millions of his contemporaries, became a fan of Anglo-American rock music. He and his school-mates fantasized about having their own band, occasionally jammed at home, and named their impromptu band in English – The Boys from a Morgue. At the university, between 1973 and 1976, Andrei met more music fans, and started participating in an active exchange of tapes. Officially, the music of most Western rock bands did not exist in the Soviet universe – one could not purchase the records of Alice Cooper, Led Zeppelin, Pink Floyd, or Deep Purple in stores, hear them on the radio or see them in concert. Moreover, this type of music was regularly denounced in official publications as an example of bourgeois culture. Yet in the daily life of Andrei's generation this music was in vibrant existence. Small numbers of Western records were brought into the Soviet Union from abroad by Soviet sailors, copied over and over on reel-to-reel recorders, and in this reduplicated form spread at

an exponential rate among members of the younger generation around the country. (Yurchak 2003: 499)

As part of his work at the university during the 1970s and into the 1980s, Andrei organized youth dances, where he routinely played recorded copies of this "non-existent" Western music. He also gave short lectures about different Western pop-rock bands, and organized concerts of so-called "amateur" Russian bands that started to emerge in that period. These events, says Yurchak, had to be approved by a local Communist Party Secretary. Andrei usually secured such approval by presenting the dances and concerts in his reports as "ideologically sound forms of Komsomol youth life" (Yurchak 2003: 500). Yurchak goes on to explain that young people like Andrei genuinely believed that the aesthetic value of pop-rock music, although officially condemned as bourgeois music, was commensurable with Soviet culture. This was possible because "Soviet youth," says Yurchak "did not necessarily interpret Western rock music and culture the way it was interpreted by Western audiences in Western contexts" (Yurchak 2003: 502). This point is further strengthened by the story of Nikolai, a teenager (born 1959) from the Siberian cities of Yakutsk and Novosibirsk. In letters to a teenager friend from Leningrad, written in the late 1970s, he strongly expressed his commitment to and belief in the ideals and ethics of Communism, but at the same time advocated the aesthetic value of Western rock music. Nikolai writes to his friend "that he had just heard recordings of the British bands Queen and King Crimson, and that the latter band especially 'impressed me quite a bit' and 'I'd like to find out more about them'" (Yurchak 2003: 502). When the friend from Leningrad complained about his high-school teacher of aesthetics, Nikolai responded by saying:

> [T]ell your teacher of aesthetic that one cannot view the world around from a prehistoric position . . . Because from a higher ground one can clearly see that rock music and its relatives are worthy successors of classical music, and that the Beatles *is an unprecedented phenomenon of our life whose impact on the human mind* is, perhaps, comparable with space flights and nuclear physics . . . One cannot educate us not knowing how we live, over what we suffer and what and why we love. Tell her that I love Bach, Vivaldi, Tchaikovsky, Rakhmaninov, Shchedrin. And yet, with no reservation, I can put next to them Paul McCartney. (Yurchak 2003: 503; emphasis in original)

In other words, says Yurchak, "Nikolai actively reinterpreted Soviet ideology, rendering it compatible with the Communist ideals as he understood and admired them . . . by explicitly linking Western rock to the officially celebrated achievements of Soviet socialism (e.g., space exploration, nuclear physics) and of 'good' non-bourgeois international culture (e.g., classical music)" (Yurchak 2003: 503).

By initiating local variants of pop-rock scenes and subcultures like punk or metal, or by enthusiastically embracing pop-rock works into their taste preferences for sheer aesthetic purposes, young adults in different parts of the world have been actively seeking to acquire both discursive and experiential knowledge of pop-rock. The gap between discursive and experiential knowledge, between knowing about the music and becoming closely familiar with the music itself, has significantly narrowed down, to the point of not really existing, with the advent of Internet facilities. Local scenes of metal, punk, or reggae in different countries, as well as straightforward taste preferences for progressive rock or mainstream pop, have evolved from being loosely connected units into tight, inter-connected, well informed and therefore effective translocal aesthetic cultures of pop-rock. Interaction characterized by one-directional flow of knowledge, with local national scenes and fans usually perceiving themselves as lagging behind and peripheral or, at any rate, clearly separated from the metropolitan centers of pop-rock in the UK and the US, has turned into a sense of "real-time" participation.

Global Microstructure

Jumping two or three decades ahead, it is most obvious that with the platforms made available by the Internet, the aesthetic meta-culture of pop-rock has grown to become one of the most fully realized incarnations of aesthetic cosmopolitanism. With these platforms, aesthetic cosmopolitanism became a routine, ordinary, and trivial cultural condition for countless pop-rock fans around the world. Internet platforms have greatly advanced the scope and amount of discursive information available to the uninitiated. Acquiring information and data about all periods, styles, musicians, and works of pop-rock became a matter of few computer-mouse clicks – especially for those in some command of the English language. The most significant advancement brought about by Internet platforms, however, was the improvement in availability of and access to experiential knowledge, to the actual sounds of music (as well as to visual forms like filmed concerts and videos). These platforms afforded immediate engagement with new music as it is released, made historical recordings from all periods and styles of pop-rock available for listening and collecting, and – often, in the case of locally based websites, written in native languages – presented local and global, metropolitan and peripheral knowledge in coexistence. By affording all this, Internet platforms have optimized the presence and role of pop-rock in the life-worlds of fans and consumers, rendering their participation in pop-rock aesthetic cultures smoother and more effective than ever before. One way to sociologically make sense of this enhanced shift in the functioning of pop-rock aesthetic cultures is to adapt the notion of global microstructures. Stemming from work on financial markets (Knorr Cetina and Bruegger 2002) and terrorist groups (Knorr Cetina 2005), the concept refers to socio-cultural "structures of connectivity and integration that are global in scope and microsociological in character" (Knorr Cetina 2005: 215). That is, forms of social organization whose various units and participants are geographically distant from each other, yet communicate between them in modes that resemble face-to-face interaction, while lacking typical aspects of formal organization. The analysis of global microstructures, furthermore, stresses the role of Internet practices in tightening the effectiveness of such structures. In other words, the impact of the Internet is understood as facilitating the transformation of already existing forms of socio-cultural organizations into a more efficient and tight mode of functioning – and not as the ushering of previously non-existent groups or organizations.

Indeed, pop-rock aesthetic cultures, as socio-cultural units geographically dispersed around the globe in the form of scenes and subcultures, or as instances of taste preference, have long existed and functioned along microsociological modes of interaction between fans. Yet Internet platforms, as they have been increasingly present and available, have greatly upgraded and tightened for fans across the world their sense of equal participation in aesthetic cultures of pop-rock. Affording fans unhindered intensive engagement with almost endless amounts of local and global music, participation in aesthetic cultures of pop-rock have become a full-fledged materialization of aesthetic cosmopolitanism. As global microstructures, then, pop-rock aesthetic cultures have transformed into realms of socio-cultural activity that engulf face-to-face encounters, consumption of traditional media in the form of magazines, radio, television, and CDs, and Internet platforms, in which most of these modes converge in various ways (see Jenkins 2006 on this point). In order to better grasp the enhanced existence of pop-rock aesthetic cultures as global microstructures, the infrastructure of Internet platforms that affords this should be reviewed in some detail.

Internet Platforms

There are numerous modes of music flow over the Internet. Documenting or keeping track of them may prove a complicated task, as some of these modes constantly change and transform, while others disappear because new ones render them obsolete. In addition, their ever-enhanced sophistication makes it hard to classify them according to functions and services. Roughly, however, they can be divided into those platforms dedicated for listening to vast repertoires of music; and those that serve as platforms for transferring audio files. In other words, they can be divided into platforms of streaming and platforms for downloading music. Some of the services offered by such platforms are regarded by international copyright laws as illegal, while others, especially those owned by corporations, are confined by these laws to limited regions. Yet pop-rock fans all over the world seem to be industrious and inventive, so that eventually, in one way or another, Internet platforms that afford engagement with music tend to be widely available. The focus in the following review is therefore on the impact of such practices on the aesthetic cultures of pop-rock, and not on their legal, technological, or corporate aspects. Another important element contained in most of these platforms is the option to chat and discuss the music. Be it in the form of casual comments or lengthy evaluative explanations, through exchange of opinions or forwarding of additional information about songs and musicians, almost all platforms consist of personal forms of interaction that give these platforms a microsociological character.

Streaming

Extending traditional formats of music broadcasting, Internet radio stations are one widespread form of pop-rock streaming. Unrestricted in their range, music radio channels on the Internet either duplicate their conventional airwave transmission, or exist exclusively as web stations. In either case, pop-rock channels are typically devoted to specific styles. Fans can tune in to them and get acquainted with recent or older works in given genres or stylistic categories of music. Some channels bind their streaming into podcasts, so that repeated loop listening to long playlists is possible. The disadvantage of such radio stations is the arbitrariness of the selections and lack of listener control over what one gets to hear. Certain advances in this regard are provided by websites that offer guidance in constructing personal playlists. These are listening lists built by experts, either in the form of critics' choice, or by adjusting playlists to users' preferences. Some notable websites have devised special software that allows listeners to delineate their musical preferences (by stating names of bands and musicians, for example), and the software responds by offering music along similar stylistic lines. In this type of websites, fans have more control over the playlists, and they can steer their preferences to the point of constructing personal playlists and keeping them under their own account on the website, for repeated listening. Such websites also serve as guided courses into styles and genres, learning about works previously unknown to the listener. Another take on streaming that seems to be gaining much impact on listening habits among pop-rock fans is provided by services that allow listening to full albums. Stocking thousands of albums in their servers, and making them available for a monthly fee, such services are offering, in effect, an alternative to collecting and personal ownership of albums.

Finally, the realm of music streaming has been overwhelmingly dominated since the mid 2000s by the video streaming website, YouTube. Although far from being exclusively a music website, the music video section has proved to be an almost endless well for music, past and new. Allowing users from all parts of the world to upload and watch music videos, or songs with some sort of visual images attached to them, the music channels on this website became a leading world source to get acquainted with music of all genres, all countries, and all periods. In addition to all the above, embedding of videos and insertion of links have made social network sites yet another major platform for disseminating and sharing music. Halfway between streaming and transference are audio-file (mp3) blogs. These are per-sonal websites, in which individual fans – sometimes a group of them – upload audio files of their favorite music, for other users to listen to or to download, to comment upon and chat about. While many of these blogs are devoted to new releases, others tend to upload older materials. The vast number of audio-file blogs has resulted in the emergence of websites that function as guides to such blogs, web locations that concentrate and provide links to numerous audio-file blogs, including statistics of the most listened to songs. As much as all the streaming platforms make large portions of pop-rock repertoires available for multiple listening, they do not satisfy fans who are keen on collecting music and having it ready for their own engagement anytime and anywhere.

File transference

At their optimal utilization, platforms for transference of audio files between computers situated anywhere in the world, facilitate the construction of large personal music collections. Internet music stores that sell music on-line provide one obvious source for acquisition of music in the form of audio files, and thus rapid acquaintance with new and large repertoires of music. Stores usually allow listening to music samples only, but, on the other hand, they offer the possibility of immediate collecting. New songs and albums can be purchased as they are released, while old music that has not been available for a long time becomes so, thus fans in remote or peripheral regions no longer depend on local retailers. Purchasing from Internet stores entails, however, financial transactions that not everyone can afford, nor are such transactions feasible everywhere. In addition, copyright agreements between countries and companies hinder access to major stores in many countries.

In terms of building personal collections, file sharing, the transference of audio files between personal computers (peer-to-peer, or P2P up/downloading) is probably the ultimate platform the Internet offers as these lines are being written. File sharing makes it possible for large numbers of fans to become collectors of music in a mode previously limited to much fewer individuals. This type of software thus has the greatest contribution to narrowing the gap between discursive and experiential knowledge, and transforming fans into owners of a wide variety of pop-rock works and styles.

Micro relations

A major feature of most, if not all pop-rock streaming and transference platforms is the microsociological nature of expression and interaction that complements the music. Fans and bloggers constantly comment, discuss and chat about the music in an informal manner, assuming their readers as equal peers. Surfing through many of the radio stations, streaming platforms, and especially blogs, one encounters pieces of texts that range from short appraisals (or harsh critique) to lengthy analysis, all written in a conversational manner, resembling almost intimate acquaintance with the potential, anonymous readers, and expressing a sense of parity, of being part of a community. Needless to say, the responses come from surfers situated in various parts of the world. Thus, on the website of a Romanian radio station (radio3net.ro/10001) that allows listening to the "1001 albums one must know," one could read responses from listeners situated not only in Romania, but also in Chile, Brazil, Portugal, and Russia (accessed in July and August 2010), congratulating the station for allowing them to listen to "great music."

The sense of community, of parity, is best expressed around the exchange of music on file sharing platforms. Two interaction elements, which exist on other platforms as well, are most clearly manifested in file sharing platforms. These are *anonymity* and *reciprocity*. The point about anonymity is that, when downloading music, the downloader does not know who the person is at the other end of the connection, whose audio-file she or he receives, nor is it possible to know that person's location on the globe. Individuals exist as usernames that most often have nothing to do with their real names. Still, downloading is based on the assumption that on the other end of the file sharing connection there is a real person, whose taste preference in music parallels that held by the downloader. Based on the technical possibility to browse files in remote computers, reciprocity in file sharing stands as a sign of mutual confidence and trust between fans and therefore also as an ethical imperative and norm. This is expressed in the instant messages that sometimes accompany file sharing. Thus when an individual downloads from others without sharing files, he or she may be banned by other participants and in addition receive castigations and even insults.

These, for example, are a question and then a warning, received through the instant messaging function of one file sharing platform on September 2007: "Why do you share so little music?" and "If you want to download, you better answer." A different variant of this type of communication is manifested in the following request, sent as instant message in June 2007: "Man, would you mind pulling your upload limit up a bit? I mean, that's what p2p is all about, right?" On the other hand, a certain intimacy is manifested when messages are sent regarding queues and exchange, like the following message received by one downloader in December 2006: "I would very much like to get all 3 discs of *Back to Mono* from you. Please let me know if you'd like to be put first in line for anything of mine"; or when people apologize for having to shut down their computer in the middle of downloading, as expressed in this short message (originally in Spanish) on a Saturday in February 2007: "I'm sorry, but I have to go. On Monday you can go on downloading." And finally, a message of courtesy sent to the whole downloading community in July 2007: "A message to all downloading users: folks, get what you can from me now. I'm going to be traveling for 2 weeks, so you won't see me. Enjoy." Between them, anonymity and reciprocity account for a peculiar form of relationship, one that strips individuals of any personal characteristic and distills them into a sort of abstract entity of music collectors that communicate with each other through file sharing software.

141

Moving from this general outline of the infrastructure that allows the tightening of aesthetic cultures of pop-rock, and their mutation into global microstructures, the following section goes into some detail by looking at one particular aesthetic culture of pop-rock, organized not just around a particulat genre, but around expertise in pop-rock knowledge, namely, the aesthetic culture of the pop-rock intellectuals, the pop-rock *intelligentsia*, which to a large extent overlaps the aesthetic culture of alternative or indie pop-rock.

The Pop-Rock *Intelligentsia*

The aesthetic culture of pop-rock discussed in this section – and especially its core inner circle – is in fact the *intelligentsia* of pop-rock, its *literati* and *cognoscenti*. It is the aesthetic culture whose participants tend to perceive pop-rock music in artistic and intellectual terms, individuals who take it upon themselves to be the carriers, transmitters, and reproducers of pop-rock knowledge along lines parallel to those of art historians or *cinephiles*. Given that the knowledge about pop-rock history and pop-rock stylistic genealogy scarcely exists in the curriculum at any level of the education system – certainly so in non-Anglo-American countries – the pop-rock intelligentsia fulfills the role of educators and reproducers of pop-rock heritage. The pop-rock intelligentsia largely overlaps with, but is not fully identical to, the aesthetic culture of *alternative* or *indie pop-rock*. A discussion of the scene, or rather the notion of indie/alternative rock therefore precedes a review of this aesthetic culture in several countries and a detailed elaboration on the practices of the pop-rock intelligentsia in Israel.

Indie/Alternative Pop-Rock

As already outlined in chapter 3, throughout pop-rock history, since the 1960s, one of the sub-fields of pop-rock consisted of musicians and bands whose works were hailed by critics and fans as the inventive explorations of pop-rock, as the expansions of its aesthetic idioms, as extensions of its expressive possibilities and, most importantly, as the musicians whose work is motivated by pure creative impulses. Although covering a wide range of pop-rock styles and periods through the years, this body of works, many of which became part of the essential artistic canon of pop-rock music, has been referred to routinely since the 1990s by critics, historians, and

142

scholars as *alternative pop-rock*. Applying this tag retrospectively, one characterization refers to it as a

> broad label . . . which has been used since late 1960s for popular music seen as less commercial and mainstream, and more authentic and "uncompromising". At the historical heart of alternative music was its rejection of the commercial music industry, and the emphasis it placed on rock music as art or expression rather than as a product for sale for economic profit. This makes the "function" or meaning of alternative rock the classic purpose of "art." (Shuker 1998: 6)

This meaning of the term *alternative pop-rock* is somewhat broader than its vernacular and sometimes scholarly use since the 1990s, when it came to depict one specific aesthetic culture, including musicians and fans (Bannister 2006; Fonarow 2006; Kruse 2003). In the UK, alternative rock has also been referred to as "indie" music, an abbreviation of the alleged independence of this music's production firms from the control of large music corporations. In fact, however, as recurrent studies about organizational concentration and stylistic diversity have shown (Peterson and Berger 1975; Dowd 2004), and as Hesmondhalgh argues specifically about the "indie" scene in the UK (1999), the relations between small music companies associated with innovative music and large music corporations has always been more complicated than the dichotomous image implied by the term "indie." More than depicting an organizational reality of the music industry, the term in fact "was becoming widely used to describe a new phase in the cultural politics of alternative pop-rock in Britain," while the music itself "turned to 'jangly' guitars, an emphasis on clever and/or sensitive lyrics inherited from the singer/songwriter tradition in rock and pop, and minimal focus on rhythm track" (Hesmondhalgh 1999: 38).

Alternative pop-rock (or "indie") is used here, then, as a cultural label, referring to the whole range of styles, musicians and works, including already canonized and fully consecrated musicians and works, that occupy the institutionalized artistic, explorative, and innovative positions, or in short, the creatively autonomous poles in the field. By the 1990s, and into the twenty-first century, the range of alternative pop-rock broadened to include sub-categories like *intelligent dance music* (a.k.a. IDM), *alternative singer-songwriters*, or *alternative rap*. As a catchphrase then, alternative pop-rock stands here as signifier for the music perceived within the aesthetic meta-culture of pop-rock as its past and present creative frontiers, music that tops the artistic hierarchy in the field. Moreover, as an

143

aesthetic culture, alternative pop-rock consists since the 1980s of fans and musicians who are knowledgeable about this tradition, highly literate in its stylistic genealogy, committed to preserve and reproduce this knowledge, and constantly in search of new music that in their view continues the exploratory spirit of pop-rock. As Bannister (2006) notes, there has been a strong correlation between the emergence of the alternative scene in the 1980s and the rise of archivalism, archeology of knowledge and connoisseurship in pop-rock history. This was reflected, for example, in the success of Nick Hornby's novel *High Fidelity* (1996), and in the words of David Buckley, who in his biography of REM (one of the most success-ful and influential American alternative bands) stated that around 1980, with the wealth of genres and styles already existing in pop-rock history, and in order to determine its radius of creativity "a great rock group . . . needed a pop *historian*" (quoted in Bannister 2006: 78–9). Put differently, participants in the aesthetic culture of alternative pop-rock are to large extent knowledgable pop-rock omnivores.

In countries for which pop-rock was an import, practically all styles and aesthetic cultures of pop-rock music were initially an "alterna-tive" to dominant popular music. However, upon the consolidation and full legitimation of domestic forms of pop-rock in the 1980s, and with the growing diversification of national pop-rock in the 1990s, the aesthetic culture of alternative pop-rock began to turn up in various countries. Following the models set in the US and UK fields, these local manifestations of alternative pop-rock have proclaimed themselves guardians of pop-rock knowledge and bastions of artistic innovation. Excavating into their own history and into globalized Anglo-American pop-rock, fans and musicians in countries with an already established pop-rock tradition have started to shape local variants of the aesthetic culture of alternative pop-rock. Becoming experts and cognoscenti of pop-rock history and knowledge in a way that combines local and Anglo-American music on a level par, while practicing this expertise with an artistic aura of avant-garde, has rendered alternative pop-rock fans and musicians prime exponents of aesthetic cosmopolitanism.

One country in which alternative/indie aesthetic culture thrived during the 1990s is Italy. Rising from the social centers that emerged in Italy during the 1980s as loci for radical cultural activities, alter-native pop-rock was an integral part of a broader movement of intellectual and critical forms of expression:

One of the most important alternative circulation channels of the record industry is made up of the circuit of "centri sociali" ("social centres") and places that are inadequately organized from the commercial and production point of view, but are particularly active in promoting music at a local level, thanks also to forms of political involvement on the part of music groups and the audiences themselves ... In general, centri sociali have played an important role in bringing to a wider audience music that is aesthetically different by means of channels of communication other than those controlled by national culture ... From the end of the 1990s, then, independent music began to achieve small but significant successes in the Italian music market. Some groups from the independent music world, such as CCCP, Almamegretta, 99 Posse, Marlene Kuntz and Massimo Volume, attracted considerable attention – in truth, in terms more of criticism than market success – to the extent of being described by the national music press as the rise of 'new Italian rock' ... In short, the new decade has seen the independent producers transforming themselves into a sector that is for the most part characterized by political engagement, local cultural ferment and, more generally, the skill of the connoisseur. (Magaudda 2009: 299–300)

Less imbued with socio-political messages, alternative pop-rock in South Korea was more about musical style and cultural association vis-à-vis Anglo-American pop-rock. It was mostly a reaction of intellectually oriented fans and musicians toward the hyper commercialism of K-pop. Thus in the 1990s,

the terminology, ideology and attitude of all things "indie" began to develop in Korea ... Contemporary forms of Anglophone pop-rock styles were the main sources of inspiration for these emerging Korean indie bands, and this music starkly contrasted with mainstream Korean pop, which strongly referenced American R&B and Japanese idol (*aidoru*) music. The scene began to grow when the bands found support from local critics and enthusiasts, and infrastructure and a critical mass began to form in the Hongdae area [of Seoul]. One of the pivotal events in the early indie scene was held in 1995 ... titled *A Tribute Concert for Kurt Cobain*, the event was held as a mark of respect to the Nirvana singer-songwriter who had died the previous year, and it attracted young people who were fans of the grunge sound ... Once a steady number of indie bands emerged in the scene, musical events dedicated to indie were intermittently held; they were welcomed as a component of the new generation's culture. Indie bands may have been agents of cultural and creative change. (Shin 2011: 153)

A third example where alternative pop-rock prospers as a network of knowledgeable fans and musicians is Sweden, in which, as elsewhere, there is a thriving independent music scene . . . [it has] hubs in Gothenburg, Malmö, Umeå, and Stockholm. Swedish indie bands play around Sweden and make brief forays to neighboring countries, but few launch international tours . . . Swedish independent music gets little radio airplay, even in Sweden, and its fans depend on the Internet to locate new music and to connect with one another. Though there may be particular bands getting buzz at any given moment, Swedish indie fandom as a whole is more concerned with monitoring and promoting multiple bands on multiple labels . . . they build community through a network of sites, building their own and taking advantage of those already on offer to strengthen their engagement with Swedish indie music and their social ties with one another. (Baym 2007)

Alternative Pop-Rock on the Web

Indeed, with webzines (that is, web magazines), blogs, social networks, radio podcasts, and other platforms, the Internet became a major site for consolidating alternative pop-rock as a global microstructure and for performing aesthetic cosmopolitanism. Two websites have gained prominence by the second part of the 2000s as influential junctions for the worldwide dissemination of knowledge of and about alternative pop-rock. One is *Pitchfork* (pitchfork.com), a webzine of reviews and commentary, including links to or embedded pieces of music. The other is the *Hype Machine* (hypem.com/#), a website that serves as an aggregator of music blogs; that is, a location on the web where one can find lists of, and links to, many different audio blogs that either stream or offer to download music.

One particular Internet project that exemplifies the extent to which the aesthetic culture of alternative pop-rock is in fact a global microstructure is MAP, Music Alliance Pact. Started in 2008 by a music blogger from Scotland who identifies himself as the Pop Cop, the project brings together music blogs from some 36 countries (one from each country). Each blog uploads on the 15th day of each month one piece of music by a musician or a band from its own country, a piece that the blogger likes or at least finds interesting and innovative. Adding a short description of the artist and the music, each of the blogs then publishes on its own website the full podcast of all the 36 tracks. Interested fans are thus exposed on the 15th of each month to a playlist of 36 new tracks of alternative pop-rock, each from a different country, to be listened to or downloaded. In addition to being a mechanism of distribution and a sort of meeting place for participants in this aesthetic culture, MAP is a showcase of pop-rock knowledge, of acquaintance with and expertise in the vocabulary of adjectives for talking about music, the names of styles, the careers of musicians. The following are a selection of quotes from music characterizations by MAP bloggers. It should be noted that while most blogs replicate the English texts about the songs, Zonaindie and Musikorner, the Argentinean and Spanish participants in MAP (respectively), translate them into Spanish (MAP playlists were accessed through The Guardian Music Blog, guardian.uk/music/musicblog, and through Zonaindie, zonaindie.com.ar, during October 2011):

Fakuta is one of the best bets in the current Chilean musical scene. Behind that moniker, architect Pamela Sepúlveda builds introspective synth-pop songs filled with detailed soundscapes and warm textures. (Super 45, Chile, September 2011)

From the west coast of Finland, The New Tigers are a guitar-driven pop band that might remind you of Yo La Tengo, Sonic Youth or Galaxie 500. (Glue, Finland September 2011)

The Baggios could be described as the Brazilian version of The White Stripes. It's the fusion of blues/garage rock from the Detroit duo transposed to the arid feel of Brazil's hot north-west and its 70s rock. (Meio Desligado, Brazil, August 2011)

Ode Buat Kota, which means "an ode to the city," is taken from Bangkutaman's latest concept album about hard life in Jakarta – the pollution, traffic, crime, house loans, etc. Their music is influenced by The Stone Roses, The Byrds and The Mamas & The Papas. (Deathrockstar, Indonesia, November 2010)

JJay's ear-melting vocals coasting smoothly over dreamy soundscapes peppered with catchy, thudding beats and soaring synths have earned him a serious fanbase … he returned to Shanghai and met B6 with whom he shared a passion for Depeche Mode, Kraftwerk and Royksopp. (Woozy, China, November 2010)

Aggressive and arrogant, otherworldly and expressive, Mimicry fuses electroclash with psychedelic techno, ethnic beats and garage rock. (Popop, Estonia, April 2011)

The history of Iguana Lovers goes as far back as 1991 when they released Universo, their first album, which had a limited run in cassette format. Along with big acts such as Babasónicos and El Otro Yo, they managed to create a whole new movement within Argentine rock music, with a post-punk sound influenced by British bands like Happy Mondays, The Stone Roses and New Order. (Zonaindie, Argentina, February 2011)

Counting on their readers' acquaintance with the names of the bands they mention, on familiarity with the sub-style labels they keep referring to in order to describe the music, and on the vocabulary used to depict sonic textures, these bloggers manifest the universe of knowledge around which the aesthetic culture of alternative pop-rock is organized. MAP is obviously only one project on each blog's website. All the blogs participating in the project offer additional music and links to other websites, either in their own country or elsewhere, with links to Pitchfork and the Hype Machine featured in almost all of them.

As much as the aesthetic culture of alternative pop-rock thrives as a global microstructure through Internet platforms, much of the local activity is augmented, however, with traditional media like radio broadcasting, magazines, and music sections in newspapers, as well as by fan interactions in clubs and other venues. These, together with Internet sites in native languages, give local alternative pop-rock fans in a given country a sense of national particularity, yet by being local instances of a global microstructure, they function as performances of aesthetic cosmopolitan. The case of Israel may serve as one example.

Extended Case: Israeli Cognoscenti

Israeli fans and musicians can obviously follow and be updated about alternative pop-rock knowledge through transnational channels of information. Writing and presenting in Hebrew, as well as the ability to share knowledge about Israeli alternative pop-rock, constitutes the added value of local practices that draws members of the aesthetic culture into reading and listening, chatting and discussing in local venues. As cultural sites that bring together metropolitan and local musical sounds and discursive knowledge, in Hebrew, the work and practices of Israeli pop-rock critics and journalists (press and Internet), radio editors and presenters, club owners, record store vendors, bloggers and chatters, function as performances of aesthetic cosmopolitanism not only in the content of the knowledge they perpetuate, but also in their formats and patterns of presentation. These performances of pop-rock knowledge, in which local alternative pop-rock is presented and discussed in ways that assert its parity with and participation in the same global aesthetic culture can be characterized as *rites of aesthetic cosmopolitanism*. These rites can be divided, roughly, into those that involve the actual sounds of music in one way or another, and those which are purely discursive. The following review focuses on how these performances routinely merge alternative pop-rock from Israel and other countries into one stream of knowledge and information, sonic or discursive.

Music: Radio shows and stations

These are sites where fans and audiences are afforded the possibility to get acquainted with the actual sounds of new or already canonized works of alternative pop-rock music. Typically presented by expert and knowledgeable radio DJs, this channel also supplies information like names of musicians participating on the recording that is being played, as well as biographic details about them, including where they played in the past and with whom. The music is thus contextualized into a knowledge framework about networks and histories of pop-rock bands and musicians, leading returning listeners into certain familiarity not just with the sounds, but with the genealogical evolvement of styles and genres, and of collaborations between musicians. Radio stations that stand out in the Israeli media space as exponents of alternative pop-rock expertise are 88fm, which is part of the Israel Broadcasting Authority (IBA) system, Kol ha-Kampus, the campus voice, a college radio station operated in Tel Aviv by communication students of the College of Management, and Radio Har-ha-Tzofim (Mount Scopus radio), another student channel, operated by students at the Hebrew University of Jerusalem. Some of the regional radio stations in other parts of the country also feature special programs devoted to this type of music.

Historically, and constituting a certain cultural paradox (Soffer 2012), radio shows playing mostly alternative pop-rock were largely associated, since the 1970s, with Galei Tzahal, the army radio station. In the 2000s, its leading program in this niche was "ha-Katzé" (the edge), broadcast several evenings a week on Galgalatz, the music channel affiliated to Galei Tzahal. This program was exemplary of the way alternative rock radio shows function. Edited and presented by two radio editors who were also active musicians, one in hip-hop and the other in electronica, it presented over two hours of tracks by bands and musicians considered as innovative, exceptional, and uncompromising. The show featured music from the US, UK and occasionally other countries, and from Israel as well. Glimpsing at the playlist of one random show, broadcast on October 26, 2008, it included, among many others, tracks by established alternative rockers from the US such as TV On The Radio and Mark Lanegan, by the (then) upcoming US band Deerhunter, as well as by Israeli punk band Useless ID and singer-songwriter Ruth Dolores Weiss. Like similar radio programs and channels in other countries, "ha-Katzé"

149

presented annually, in December, a series of programs in which the editors and listeners selected the albums which, in their judgment, have been the best artistic achievements of the past year. In 2009, the annual summary was amplified by becoming a decade summary, presenting "the best" albums of alternative pop-rock released from 1999 up to 2009. With albums by UK and US bands such as Radiohead, LCD Soundsystem, Interpol, the Strokes, or Arcade Fire (a Canadian band) topping the list, the editors and listeners of "ha-Katzé" produced an end-of-decade summary not dissimilar to lists produced by Anglo-American leading websites and magazines. Manifesting thereby up-to-date taste and state-of-the-art awareness with US and UK alternative pop-rock, they also placed at the relatively respected position of No. 32 the album *menoim shketim* (quiet engines) by the Israeli band Algere. Thus, while self-positioning themselves as participants in the translocal scene of alternative pop-rock, it was also made clear that local music itself plays a role in that scene.

Music: Venues, clubs, concerts

Places for "live" music are obviously an important element in the cultural performance of cosmopolitanism in pop-rock music. Various music venues, especially small clubs, by constructing their image as home to alternative pop-rock music, become locations in which fans gather to collectively worship the objects of their taste, namely, local or foreign bands and musicians. In addition to offering a place for collective gathering and joint exposure to the sounds of the music, the clubs contribute to the sense of refined taste through their typical design, which is quite similar to that of alternative rock music clubs in other countries.

Usually located in basements or in industrial parts of the city, rock clubs tend to be dimly lit and in general designed in an aesthetic of shabbiness. Catering to a relatively small audience, some of these clubs tend to disappear after operating for just a year or two. However, at any given moment since the 1990s or so, Tel Aviv has had 10 to 15 small clubs or pubs that acted as home to local alternative rock bands. The more successful ones, like Barby, Zappa, and Levontin 7, are the ones that occasionally hosted alternative rock bands and musicians from other countries. A partial list of US/UK and other non-Israeli alternative pop-rock bands and musicians that played these venues in the 2000s includes new and upcoming, as well long-active names such as Dinosaur Jr., Echo and the Bunnymen, Low, Kurt Wagner, M83, dEUS, Gong, Devendra Benhart, Okkervil River, Bill Callahan and Yo La Tengo. Many of these concerts

150

featured, as warm-up performances, Israeli bands or musicians. In addition, the posters and brochures which publicize the concerts by foreign musicians conventionally list them as items in the monthly or weekly roster, next to shows by local musicians and bands.

In addition to the clubs, the experience of being a community has been fostered in the 2000s through initiatives to hold festivals of Israeli alternative music in the countryside. The first of them was the Hutzmize ("out of it") Festival that took place in the mountains of Galilee, and was held for its third and final year in September 2009. As it declared on its website:

> The Hutzmize Festival is the first festival of its kind that paves the way to connect lovers of Israeli indie music with nature. With its help, and in its wake, it became possible to hold similar events like the In-D-Negev Festival. In the world, the connection between indie music and nature is immediate and clear, whereas in this country the alternative scene fences itself mostly in Tel Aviv pubs. The purpose of the Festival is to place the underground scene in a different setting, open and lit in the nature, away from the smoke-full basements of the city, and allow the public that lives in the north to take part in the celebration. (magamaga.com/hutzmize2/about.html, accessed October 2010)

Listing prominent names of Israeli alternative pop-rock musicians that will perform, such as Asaf Amdurski, Amir Lev, Gilad Kahana, Eatliz, Electra, and many others, the website went on to announce the participation of the electro-noise duo Les Trucs, from Berlin. Citing a source that defines the duo as "one of the most original and exciting underground bands in Europe today," the Festival website characterizes their music as "Nintendocore – electronica that merges the 8-bit of bands such as Crystal Castles and the IDM [i.e. *intelligent dance music*] of Aphex Twin." Taken together, in this festival as in other venues, the settings and presentations of concerts by bands from the US, UK, and other countries, interweave them into the routine flow of concerts by Israeli musicians, thus creating an image of continuity, connection, and parity between Israeli and metropolitan alternative pop-rock.

Critics' discourse: Newspapers, magazines, Internet
Writing about music is a major channel for expressing and demonstrating knowledge that takes place, traditionally, in music magazines. In Israel, as already noted, music magazines are a rare species of journalism. Pop-rock reportage and criticism thrives mostly in daily newspapers, entertainment guides, and weekly city newspapers

151

(known in Hebrew as *mekomonim*, i.e. "locals"). In the 2000s, the Internet also became an important stage. More than just supplying information and evaluations on albums and concerts, music columns function as platforms for demonstrating expertise and diffusing knowledge on stylistic genealogies of pop-rock, musical biographies of musicians and reproduction of canons. Adapting into Hebrew a jargon that originates in British and American music magazines, Israeli music critics foster a discourse of familiarity with pop-rock knowledge and meanings. This, for example, is a quote from a review of a song by the Arctic Monkeys, written in *NRG*, the website associated to the daily newspaper *Ma'ariv*:

> It's not a coincidence that it reminds us of songs from the golden age of punk . . . this is not a hollow gesture in the style of Weezer, but rather two ends of the same umbilical chord. These teenagers from Yorkshire with their funny accent are the first real answer of the myspace generation to the Undertones, the Buzzcocks and the Jam. Everything we got so far in the years 2000 was a preparation for the real thing . . . The Strokes awakened rock'n'roll from its grave, the Libertines put back drugs and sex in it, and Franz Ferdinand the artistic façon. With the Arctic Monkeys, rock'n'roll finally returns to its roots, as an exciting language of beautiful young people who celebrate the fact that this is what they are. (Achi Raz, *NRG*, January 31, 2006)

Thus, in a short passage, and as if just in passing, a brief history and an appraisal of some high points in alternative rock are recapitulated for the believers and introduced for the benefit of newcomers into the pop-rock knowledge community.

A notable facet of advertent aesthetic cosmopolitanism in the case of pop-rock is the delight that emerges among critics when Israeli musicians gain some translocal artistic recognition. This is exemplified in the case of Asaf Avidan and the Mojos, a much applauded Israeli band (who sing in English). Opening a report with the words "global honor," the music section of the leading Israeli website *Ynet* (associated to the Israeli daily newspaper, *Yedioth Ahronot*) told its readers in December 2008 that:

> A single by Israeli singer Asaf Avidan and his band, The Mojos, entitled "The Reckoning," will be distributed with the next issue of music magazine *Rolling Stone* in Europe . . . This is not the first time that the important magazine expresses its appreciation of Avidan: Last year the Mexican edition of *Rolling Stone* praised the young artists' music and branded him "a new messiah." (Or Barnea, *Ynet*, December 24, 2008)

Some eight months later, after a concert tour in Europe, the band was signed to an international contract by the German branch of the Sony-Columbia music corporation. The reports about this event in Israeli music repeatedly quoted the words of the senior vice president who signed the band:

> You don't know what to expect when you listen to Asaf Avidan and The Mojos for the first time, but you soon learn to expect the unexpectable ... This is the sort of music that draws its influence from the smoking joints of the 70's ... if Jeff Buckley was still alive he surely would have joined them on stage (quoted in the music section of another leading website, *Walla*, on August 12, 2009).

The critics are clearly proud, if not enthusiastic, to report and express the ultimate achievement of local alternative rock – to prove itself as standing in the same line of artistic innovation with canonical names from the metropolitan centers of alternative pop-rock.

Fans discourse: Blogs, forums, chats

Internet forums, either as part of established websites, or in the form of personal blogs, offer another channel that allows existing and aspiring members of the pop-rock knowledge community to express opinions and knowledge, or to ask advice and information. Most of the leading alternative pop-rock radio stations keep, next to their Internet broadcasts, adjunct forums that allow fans to express their comments on the music played, and to seek advice and additional details. Thus, for example, on December 11, 2009, the following exchange took place in the listeners' forum of 88fm:

> Listener: "There is a song that was played on the program on Dec. 9, around 11:40, I could not get its name properly, but it's something like 'has an end'."
> Editor: "Hi there, the song is 'There's no end', by Holly Golightly and the Greenhornes. Have a nice week."
> Listener: "Thanks."

The sites in which advertent cosmopolitanism is performed most intensively, however, are the personal blogs written by devoted fans, by ardent cognoscenti. One advantage of these platforms is that they afford mixing of discursive and experiential knowledge. That is, bloggers often not only evaluate and express opinion, but also upload music, either as a streaming channel or as actual files. Fans can thus read evaluations and details about music, while at the same time listening to it. The webpage of Ha-Katzé radio show had links to

153

15 alternative pop-rock blogs, all written in Hebrew and extensively engaged in re-crowning and re-consecrating past names from the canon, while at the same time mediating knowledge, in word, sound, and image, about the most recent, "hyped" names in alternative pop-rock. Declaring Pitchfork as a major source of inspiration, one prominent website in this regard was ha-Sharat ha-'eever (the blind server/janitor; www.hasharat.co.il) whose managers declared that

> [it] is dedicated to music reviews and recommendations contributed by music loving surfers . . . it has two major goals: one – constructing an arsenal of wide and diverse musical knowledge, for the use of Hebrew speaking music fans. The second – provide a platform for good music from the more remote corners of the margins, in order to expand the horizons and the love of the esoteric as an ideology . . . The musical world of the janitor consists of music made from sometime in the 1950s until the foreseeable future, music that is somehow connected to rock, pop, their roots and all the off-shoots of contemporary music, including those that wandered to totally different planets, like hip-hop and black music, electronica, industrial music, instrumental fusion, etc.

Since it went up on the Internet in 2001 and until it stopped its updates some ten years later, this website published hundreds of album and concert reviews, as well as fervent forum discussions, about classic and recent musical works from the arsenal of local and foreign alternative pop-rock. Thousands of contributors have used the website over the years to express opinions and demonstrate knowledge, as well as for uploading pictures and links to sites of downloadable or streaming music. Stored in the sections and pages of the website, it all added up to a rich repertoire of knowledge on pop-rock, all presented in Hebrew. Thus, for example, a contributor that identified himself as yir-miklat (city of sanctuary, after a song by Israeli ethnic rocker Ehud Banai), published between 2004 and 2008 some 15 posts, among them reviews of albums by the German electro-pop band Lali Puna, the English band Echo and the Bunnymen, as well as reviews of works by Israeli musicians such as Quami, Asaf Amdurski, and the band Eatliz. All reviews were followed by responses and discussions from up to 30 other members of the website. Containing hundreds of similar cases, ha-Sharat ha-'eever best exemplified the cultural performances of pop-rock cognoscenti on the Internet.

Music stores

Record stores were a declining institution in the 2000s, but some specialist stores still existed as shrines where knowledge-seeking pop-rock fans congregated to exchange information, gain knowledge, and acquire new music. Some of these were second-hand stores, where old CDs and vinyls were sold at cheap prices. One common characteristic of such stores was the expertise of the vendors, who were specialists in pop-rock knowledge. In addition to records, music stores of this type usually displayed posters, brochures, and other informative handouts about music events in clubs, pubs, and other locations. The prominent institution of this kind still operating in Tel Aviv as these lines are being written, with branches in Jerusalem and other cities, is Ha-Ozen ha-Shlishit (the third ear). Evolving from a small second-hand record store, it became a cultural complex that, in addition to its specialized record shop, also has a small performing room (called Ozen-Bar) where new bands and musicians often get their first opportunity to perform. The "ozen," as it is often referred to by its regular customers, also publishes once in a while a small magazine. Its December 2009 issue was dedicated to (yet another) decade summary, written by its expert vendors. One of them wrote the introductory article, which focused on the still existing advantage of record stores and their vendors over the Internet. It is an example not only of a defense of this declining institution, but also as a sort of ideological manifestation of alternative pop-rock cognoscenti:

All over the world creatures like me work in record stores – usually a store that specializes in a wide range of music that includes the different, the interesting, the other, the rare, the old and the new . . . my store, ha-ozen ha-shlishit, is exactly this kind of store . . . The emergence of [websites such as] All-Music-Guide, Pitchfork, forums, blogs and the like, turns anyone, by a push of keyboard, into an expert . . . And here, at this junction, I, as a records vendor, realize that my role in the world did not end yet. The thing a record vendor possesses, something that internet experts do not possess, is the big picture, the perspective, the distance of years and in particular the specific taste that he has developed. The knowledge on the web is . . . built from patches, from many different people, it is also fragmentary and superficial . . . Me and my experienced colleagues all over the world have already done, and still do the hard work, and that is why people who want a recommendation, who want to talk about new and old records, who want to learn from the thousands of music hours that have passed through your ears, arrive to the store. (Tzahi Rolnik, *Ha-Ozen ha-shlishit magazine*, December 2009)

Indeed, "ha-ozen" is routinely visited by a steady influx of customers, not to say pilgrims, who seek the advice and recommendation of vendors about local and foreign music, and who fill up the intensive roster of the music rooms in order to attend gigs by local alternative pop-rock musicians. This is one place where the quasi-virtual community of alternative pop-rock cognoscenti, that exists as readers of newspapers, as web surfers, or as radio listeners, is materialized into an actual, face-to-face interacting community.

* * *

Returning, in conclusion to this chapter, to the case of *metal*, and remaining with the Israeli context, it should be noted that the translocal and global nature of some aesthetic cultures of pop-rock infuse their discourse with semi-romantic notions about pop-rock music forming a bridge between hostile nations, religions, and other groups. This point is exemplified by the case of the Israeli band Orphaned Land. "Defining their music as Oriental *doom death* or simply Middle Eastern *metal*, they are merging *metal* sounds with traditional tunes and instruments (e.g., *oud, saz, buzuki*)" so that "the music and concept of the band is appealing to metalheads throughout the Middle East" (Hecker 2010: 336–7). Discovering the music of Orphaned Land over the Internet, the band gained significant popularity during the 2000s among metal fans in Arab and other Muslim countries. Furthermore, festivals held within the metal scene in Turkey – a Muslim country that maintains relations with Arab nations and Israel – proved to be venues in which fans from Arab and Muslim countries like Iran, Jordan, Lebanon, Syria, Iraq, and Egypt (countries whose residents cannot travel freely to Israel) could attend concerts by Orphaned Land. The accentuated Arab tinge to Orphaned Land's music, augmented by anti-war and peace messages in song lyrics and in declarations made by its members, have raised adoring statements from fans in Arab countries (placed on the band's website) as well as the assertion that

> [a]ll these words of warmth and friendship exchanged between people who are supposed to hate each other as a result of a long history of political and religious conflict in the region illustrate a new dimension of social relations within the realms of global metal. In that sense, the lines separating different religious, national, and ethnic spaces from each other are being transgressed and contested. (Hecker 2010: 338)

The functioning of pop-rock aesthetic cultures, *metal* or any other, as agents of political reconciliation still remains to be seen. But the example above, as well as many others, demonstrate the impact of pop-rock aesthetic cultures in creating greater cultural connectivity and expanding shared aesthetic ground between groupings in friendly or hostile nations. As they evolved in the new century into global microstructures, this translocal cultural effectivity of aesthetic cultures of pop-rock is the culmination, at the consumption level, of the long-term event of pop-rock.

Aesthetic cultures of pop-rock music have been present in countries all over the world since the 1960s, if not earlier. From a simple demographic perspective, this means that by the early twenty-first century, large numbers of young and adult individuals, some of them over 60 or 70 years of age, carry experiential and discursive pop-rock knowledge in their personal cultural arsenal. Be it as active members in the inner circles of *punk, metal, hip-hop, electronic dance, alternative,* or *progressive rock,* or as occasional listeners to *mainstream pop, soul, psychedelic rock, folk,* and *ethnic rock,* generations of fans throughout the second half of the twentieth century have made pop-rock music into a significant cultural element of their everyday life-worlds. And, as has been demonstrated, taste and involvement in pop-rock aesthetic cultures does not necessarily dimiminish with age (Bennet 2006a; Bennett and Taylor 2012; Hodkinson 2011).

Therefore, as much as each aesthetic culture of pop-rock in itself serves as an interesting case for understanding the cultural work of pop-rock music in the life-world of fans, another highly relevant point from a historical perspective of cultural sociology is the cumulative effect of the aesthetic cultures of pop-rock over the years. That is, for participants in the aesthetic cultures of pop-rock, either as occasional consumers or as ardent followers, pop-rock styles and genres obviously function as major cultural building blocks of their identity and sense of being in the world. They eagerly listen to the music; they are familiar with its sounds. But beyond the active engagement of such individuals with pop-rock music, there is also a more general phenomenological aspect to the prominent presence of pop-rock music in the cultural public sphere of many countries since the 1960s. The accumulated presence of pop-rock aesthetic cultures over the years has rendered the sounds of pop-rock styles and genres ubiquitous and omnipresent in late modernity, especially in urban settings, all over the world. They are crucial elements in the cultural design of urban environments and audio-visual products like films, television series, and advertisements, building on individuals' knowledge of and acquaintance with them. In a sense, this aspect is the ultimate consequence of aesthetic cosmopolitanism as manifested by pop-rock. The last chapter examines this point in some detail.

— 6 —

SONIC VOCABULARIES, SPACES, AND BODIES

Niila unbuttoned his shirt and produced the lukewarm single. I sol-
emnly placed it on the record player and lowered the pick-up arm.
Turned up the volume. There was a faint scratching noise.
    Then CRASH! A thunderclap. A powder keg exploded and blew
up the room. All oxygen was sucked out, we were hurled against the
walls, squashed into the wallpaper, and the whole house spun around
at breakneck speed. We were like stamps on an envelope, all our blood
rushed into our hearts, formed a gut-red clump – then suddenly everything changed direction, torrents raged into fingers and toes, red spurts
of blood to every extremity of our bodies till we gaped cod-eyed.
    An eternity later the spinning stopped. Air was sucked back in
through the keyhole and we splatted down on the floor in tiny damp
heaps.
    Rock'n'roll music.
    Beatles.
    It was too good to be true.
    We couldn't speak for ages. We just lay there bleeding, drained,
happy in the echoing silence. Then I stood up and played it one more
time.
    Same thing again. Incredible. This couldn't possibly be a human
creation.
    One more time.
    (Mikael Niemi 2003: 72)

This literary evocation of teenagers' first encounter with The Beatles
(specifically, with the band's version of "rock'n'roll music," authored
and originally recorded by Chuck Berry), in early 1960s northern
Sweden, vividly captures the effect pop-rock music had on its listeners' bodies. The occurrence is depicted as a physical experience
of revelation, as a corporeal response to the sounds, to what they

158

signify. The sounds of the recording, emanating from the record player, triggered the boys in the novel to experience their bodies in a new way. What they felt, one might argue, was an embodiment of cultural change.

Some four decades later, while strolling the streets of Beijing in the summer of 2010, and sampling the music played in the city's shopping centers, fashion stores, restaurants, cafés, and taxis, the list of songs that sets the city's public musical soundscape includes items by Anglo-American pop-rock performers, as well as songs by Chinese (including Hong Kong and Taiwan) pop-rock artists. While not necessarily recognizing the songs, the sounds that fill up the urban environment are nevertheless very familiar. These are the sounds of electronic dance, soft electric-guitar ballads and occasional hip-hop. Some of the songs that most typically kept turning up in the playlists of these public places turned out to be hits by the duo Shui Mu Nian Hua (known in English as The Age of Water & Wood), whose mixture of Chinese folk elements and slightly distorted electric guitars best expressed the banal aesthetic cosmopolitanism of Beijing's public cultural sphere. That is, a smooth, taken-for-granted fusion of native, indigenous sounds with sonorities associated with universal modernity. A sense of locality, of Chineseness, is efficiently integrated with the global sounds of pop-rock to create one culturally coherent soundscape. Beijing obviously resembles in this regard many other cities, like, for example, Indonesian urban landscapes, where

> [E]lectronically amplified pop music is omnipresent. Several Western artists are well known, but there is also a lively Indonesian pop scene which comes in two varieties. One is called "rock Indonesia" and the other *dangdut* (an erotic mixture of Indonesian, Indian, and Western sounds and instruments). Loud pop music is common in the not-too-posh shopping malls . . . Music is also played on many public transport vehicles. (Colombijn 2007: 262)

In other words, activities like sitting in cafés, shopping for food or clothes, dining in restaurants, riding public transportation, or simply taking a walk in a modern city, almost anywhere in the world, seem to be accompanied in early twenty-first century by the constant presence of soaring electric guitars, electronic beats, and guttural vocals emitted from loudspeakers. Either in the form of ballads or as danceable rhythms, the amplified sonorities of local and international pop-rock styles and genres dominate the musical soundscapes. Electric, electronic, amplified musical sounds became ubiquitous, a taken for granted component of the modern urban environment. Pop-rock music is by the early twenty-first century one of the most common building blocs of modern musical soundscapes.

The contrast between the teenagers in early 1960s, when pop-rock music first struck the bodies of listeners around the world and evoked strong reactions, and the already accustomed urban masses of the 2010s, for whom the electric, electronic, and amplified sounds of pop-rock are as trivial as advertising boards or modern skyscrapers, speaks for itself. The difference between the reactions to the physical presence of pop-rock sounds at these two points in time reflects the deep cultural change for which these very sounds served as major agents. It is a cultural change that exemplifies McClary's dictum that "music is a powerful social and political practice precisely because in drawing on metaphors of physicality, it can cause listeners to experience their bodies in new ways" (McClary 1991: 25), as well as DeNora's assertion that music has the potential to "structure things as styles of consciousness, ideas, or mode of embodiment" (DeNora 2003: 47). This potential, one should add, is sometimes fulfilled through encounters with musical textures that have never been heard before. Once encountered and absorbed into a music culture or personal taste, such textures have the potential to usher in new modes of individual and collective experiences, alter the physical reality of public spaces, and in general affect cultural performance at the individual and collective levels. And this is indeed one of the major cultural consequences of pop-rockization. Pop-rock genres and styles – by introducing new sonorities, sound patterns, and textures generated by electric and electronic instruments and by amplification, and through their enormous range of dissemination – acted as agents of cultural change at the material, physical levels of human bodies and urban spaces. Pop-rock heralded the emergence and consolidation of global *electro-amplified soundscapes* and *aesthetic cosmopolitan bodies*. The constitution of such soundscapes and bodies was a direct outcome of growing habitual familiarity, shared by individuals around the world, with the typical sonorities of pop-rock, its characteristic sonic and musical units of signification. These, as a repertoire of auditory communicative elements, as a vocabulary of sounds and stylistic elements, became building blocks for modes of bodily experience and patterns of spatial consciousness that were new in the 1960s and became ubiquitous and omnipresent several decades later. This chapter looks, then, at the physicality of pop-rock music as sound, at its materialization in bodies and spaces. It is based on the premise that one of pop-rock music's essential contributions to modern cultural reality is found in its typical sonorities, in the fact that, as an art form organized around recording, its stylistic history has been in fact an exploration of sonic vocabularies.

> Now that it was possible to manipulate the sound properties of both instruments and voice and reproduce them precisely, the focus of musical performance gradually shifted from the written parameters, pitch, dynamics and formal development, from the melodic and harmonic aspects, to the reproducible details of expression of sound. Thus, sound became the central aesthetic category of rock music. (Wicke 1990: 13)

Although not really embracing or following it, this chapter is partially inspired by certain methodological prescriptions suggested by Latour's explication of actor-network theory (Latour 2005), and especially his insistence on looking at objects, at "things," as actors and participants in the social. As he puts it, "anything that does modify a state of affairs by making a difference is an actor" (Latour 2005: 71), and thus "in addition to 'determining' and serving as a 'backdrop for human action', things might authorize, allow, afford, encourage, permit, suggest, influence, block, render possible, forbid, and so on" (Latour 2005: 72). Consequently, "no science of the social can even begin if the question of who and what participates in the action is not first of all thoroughly explored, even though it might mean letting elements in which, for lack of a better term, we would call non-humans" (Latour 2005: 72). In relation to objects and things, then, sociology has "to produce scripts of what they are making others – humans or non-humans – do" (Latour 2005: 79). This chapter seeks to offer a script of how the sounds of pop-rock music, its sonic vocabularies as "things," have altered listeners' styles of consciousness and caused individuals to experience their bodies in new ways. This requires a preliminary step of discussing the nature and sonic characteristics of pop-rock music as "things."

Sonic Vocabularies

Verbal characterization of sounds is known to be a difficult, if not an impossible task (Barthes 1991). A much quoted comment attributed alternatively to pop-rock *auteur* Elvis Costello and to actor Martin Mull, argues that "writing about music is like dancing about architecture." In other words, it is practically impossible to really convey the qualities of music in written or spoken words. Still, in order to

161

explicate the cultural change inflicted by the sonorities of pop-rock, the sonic textures that give this meta-aesthetic culture its singularity vis-à-vis other musical cultures, it is essential to discuss in some minimal way their attributes. The sonorities that became highly familiar to the modern human ear through pop-rock music can be classified into a physical dimension that includes the sonic textures and effects devised by studio technology as well as the timbral signatures of the most emblematic musical instruments, i.e., electric guitars and electronic keyboards; and a rhetorical dimension, namely the meanings and symbolism of specific musical phrases (Zak III 2001). Using terms associated with musical semiotics, yet in a rather crude and lay mode, quite removed from the precision of that discipline, these two categories will be referred to below, respectively, as tones and timbres, and as museme stacks or strings.

Tones and Timbres

Tones and timbres are, so to speak, the raw materials of musical texts. These are the physical materials whose combinatorial configurations characterize the singularity of a given rendition of a musical work or, in the case of most pop-rock music, define the specificity of each song and recorded track. Musical tones and timbres are conventionally generated by the human voice and musical instruments. The singularity and uniqueness of the human voice, especially in the case of singers, has been notably discussed by Barthes (1977). The "grain of the voice," as he calls it, is the trait that renders each singer's voice identifiable and unique. In the same vein, musical instruments also have their unique tonal and timbral characteristics. Like human voices, musical instruments usually have a set of typical sonic signatures that render them recognizable. Being an art of recording, however, in pop-rock the sonic characteristics of musical instruments are never heard in their supposedly direct and original form. "The range of sound colors encountered on records is vast and ever increasing. Among these one might list the sounds of musical instruments of all sorts, sound effects, synthesized sounds, and simulated ambient images, any of which can be shaped with various electronic processors" (Zak III 2001: 63). In pop-rock, Zak III contends, tones and timbres are not simply the product of musical performance. Rather, the sounds are given form by using a broad and ever evolving repertoire of technologies of modification and manipulation of sound, most of which occur in the recording studio.

162

Recordists manipulate these characteristics as they create their sonic tapestry. They do not simply *record* sounds; . . . they tailor the sound image in some way using the tools and techniques at their disposal . . . one of the most pervasive practices in rock recording is the search for some distinctive sonic quality . . . As they go about getting sounds, often in adventurous ways, rock recordists' search for distinctive colors may lead them far from acoustical reality and deeper into a sound world born of the imagination. (Zak III 2001: 65–6)

In other words, one of pop-rock music's major impacts has been, time and again, the introduction of new tones and timbres, new sonorities. The sounds of electric guitars, the instrument's palette of tones and timbres, stand here as an emblematic example. Any attempt to describe the specificity of the sonic textures of the electric guitar is bound to end up as a list of adjectives that never truly transmit the essence of those sounds.

Gracyk (1996) offers an alternative way of doing this by discussing the technology of the electric guitar and the difference between the sounds generated by it and those of acoustic instruments. As he explains, "electric guitars send their signal to the amplifier from a set of magnets called pickups . . . Any motion of the metal strings alters the electric current flowing through the pickups; registering this motion rather than the sound of the strings, the pickups generate the actual frequencies sent for amplification, including harmonic overtones that are not otherwise present" (Gracyk 1996: 112). And thus, "because sound is produced by any signal emanating from the current in the pickups, an electric guitarist can audibly sustain the same note at the same pitch many times longer than on any acoustic." And "because different wiring and pickup designs yield 'purer' signals than others, the frequencies sent to the amplifier are not a precise replication of the movement of the strings" (Gracyk 1996: 120). Consequently, the sound of the electric guitar gains a mechanical specificity unlike that of any other instrument. In the case of this instrument, physical dimensions of sound, like amplitude, frequency, duration, and form of waves, whose perceptual correlatives are volume, pitch, length, and timbre (or tone color), respectively, acquire unique and distinctive qualities that do not exist in acoustic instruments.

In addition to the volume and tone controls on the guitar and on the amplifier, electric guitars come with a broad series of accompanying devices, referred to by professionals as "stompboxes" or effects pedals. These are used in order to modify the electrical output, manipulate the sonic palette of their instrument, diversify, and expand it. The tones and timbres associated with the use of these devices, the "sound effects," are conventionally referred to by adjectives and verbs such as tremolo, wah-wah, overdrive, vibrato, chorus, delay, flanger, and, most notably, distortion and fuzz. The sound of the electric guitar almost seems to "speak" when used in conjunction with special effects equipment, and is therefore "able to express much more than the melodic pattern which it is actually playing" (Wicke 1990: 13).

The tones and timbres of the electric guitar are probably the definitive sonic metonyms for pop-rock music. However, sounds generated by synthesizers, samplers, and other electronic sound generators have also been a prominent component of pop-rock sonic vocabularies. With the advent of electronically generated tones and timbres, first analogically and later digitally, the sonic palette of pop-rock has exponentially grown to countless options and possibilities. In their search for tones and timbres that will richly paint their work, musicians and producers have explored and formulated digitally controlled sounds, making them a core source of creativity in pop-rock. Fales (2005) argues that the characteristics of electronic sounds can be understood as standing at one extreme of a sonic continuum, whose opposite end is occupied by conventional sounds. "While not pointing to a specific referent," conventional sounds "indicate sources that follow the rules of the acoustic world, and they conform to our canonical sense of how sound works in the world" (Fales 2005: 170). Electronic sounds, at the other end of the continuum, especially those used in pop-rock styles like *techno* and *house*, belong to a category of sounds that is "a kind of catch-all bin."

> This category contains sounds that lack any vestige of contextualization . . . they inhabit a sort of forsaken universe where the very notion of a humanly bounded soundscape is meaningless. Sounds in this category exist in total autonomy from any canon of sounds we might favor. A deluge of these sounds makes us anxious for a foothold, for something familiar to direct our auditory efforts . . . they are so diverse, formless, and unstable that they deprive us of anything to describe, even if we had the vocabulary . . . these sounds are some kind of noise, unpitched and purely timbral. (Fales 2005: 170)

Drawing an analogy to Baudrillard's notion of simulacra (1994), Fales concludes that at their extreme realization, electronic timbres suggest "that perception is caused by nothing in the external world but is rather a hallucination, a product entirely of the listeners' minds" (Fales 2005: 170).

Taken together, then, pop-rock music's impact in its materiality as sound has been the constant injection of new sonorities, sound textures, and tapestries. Regardless of whether they were received enthusiastically and emphatically or with resentment, pop-rock's palette of electric, electronic, and amplified sonorities have joined the repertoire of sounds routinely perceived as ingredients of the musical realm. However, musical tones and timbres do not exist as isolated elements. They arrive in strings and stacks, as sequences and layered structures of sounds that amount to phrases and units of meaning.

Museme Stacks and Strings

Musemes are minimal units of musical meaning. The term is a neologism coined by Seeger (1960) as a sort of musicological analogue to the linguistic term morpheme. However, as Tagg (1987, 2012) demonstrates, the analogy to linguistics is problematical, and in any case an exact definition of musemes that takes into account all the layers and components of a short musical sequence, is hardly achievable. Tagg therefore prefers the notion of musematic structures that "occur as stacks or strings" (1987: 292). Musical meaning, that is, depends on "note *sequences* (the diachronic, 'horizontal' aspect)" as well as the "*simultaneous layering* (the synchronic, 'vertical' aspect) of notes" (Tagg 2012: 232–3; emphasis in original). Inferring from Tagg, museme stacks and strings, as units of musical meaning, are then culturally specific musical structures that different members of the same music aesthetic community can consistently identify, (re) produce, and recognize as having a rather fixed function or meaning. Beyond musicological analysis, when used in a looser way, the terminology of museme stacks and museme strings offers to cultural researchers a convenient and useful tool to talk about musical phrases that conventionally connote – within given cultural communities, at least – relatively fixed meanings like a mood or emotion, a historical period, a national or ethnic entity, and many other notions. It also allows us to point to cross references between musical works, styles, and periods, and thus to talk about connections, influences, and inspirations between them. Indeed, lacking a proper nomenclature, a common way to identify specific museme stacks and strings is to refer back to canonized and well-known musical works where particular musematic structures have been prominently featured. Some of the quotes used in the previous chapter to illustrate the discourse within the aesthetic culture of alternative pop-rock tend to describe a given piece of music by alluding to earlier works.

Throughout its history since the 1950s, and relying on its typical tones and timbres, pop-rock music has generated an ample amount of museme stacks and strings that gained global cultural currency for signifying a broad range of cultural notions. Take, for example, the musematic structure that consists of a slow paced sound of an electric piano, joined by moaning or whining vocal, with a soft "woosh-ing" synthesizer in the background, sometimes resembling a string ensemble (and occasionally augmented with soft-sounding electric guitar or trumpet). It can be heard opening many pop-rock ballads from the 1980s, such as "Hello" by Lionel Richie (1983), "Against All Odds" by Phil Collins (1984), or "Saving All My Love For You" by Whitney Houston (1985). The global success of these and other songs has affixed the variations of these museme stacks and strings as signifiers of romanticism, of yearning and aching for a loved one. It has since become a frequently used musical phrase in countless pop-rock ballads all over the world, like Alejandro Lerner's "Verte sonreir" (Argentina), Laura Pausini's "Strani amori" (Italy), or Filipp Kirkorov's "Cruel love" (Russia).

Other well-established musematic structures are those explored and formulated by electronic musicians such as the British musician Brian Eno, the German band Kraftwerk and French composer and instrumentalist Jean Michel Jarre. Their work propelled various synthesizer-based museme stacks and strings to become signifiers of futuristic realities, outer space exploration, and notions of mechanical worlds. Another well-established museme string associated with electronics is the repetitive playing of a short melodic piece by a high pitched "metallic" sound of a synthesizer, backed by a pulsating monotone electronic rhythm. It can be heard emblematically on a track like "God is a DJ" by Faithless (1998). The museme was explored earlier in that decade by musicians in various sub-styles of electronic dance music, like *techno* and *goa-trance*. Two examples are the track "Hablando" (1991) by the Italian team of musicians known as Ramirez, and "Kabalah" (1996) by the Israeli duo Astral Projection. The museme string came to signify ecstatic dancing typical of rave and club culture of the 1990s and then postmodern forms of partying in general. Throughout the 2000s, standardized variants of this museme string could be heard on countless dance floor hits across the world, such as the international hit "Blue (Da Ba Dee)," by the Italian band Eiffel 65, where variants of this museme string are played in the background of the vocals and in the instrumental refrain.

Some, if not most of the emblematic museme strings and stacks of pop-rock are associated with the sounds of electric guitars. Over the years, electric guitarists have explored the possibilities of sonic expression "hidden" in the instrument, and some of them emerged as the innovators and virtuosos who defined and formulated the vocabularies and musical idioms of the instrument (Waksman 1999; Walser 1993), including certain museme stacks and strings. One notable example, mentioned already in the opening of this book, is the "soaring" electric guitar solo. A defining performance of this museme string can be heard in Led Zeppelin's song, "Stairway to Heaven" (1971). Following its formulation and extensive use in 1970s hard rock, this museme string came to signify emotional transcendence and elevation (Waksman 1999). It has been adapted for this purpose within numerous stylistic contexts, not necessarily hard or heavy rock. Thus, even in a style like Israel's *musica mizrahit*, which in the Israeli context is sometimes positioned in opposition to rock, the museme string has been adopted for expressing emotional elevation. Songs like "Hayity be-gan-eden" by Sarit Hadad (1999) and "Lohemet" by Eyal Golan (2007), the style's most successful female and male performers in the 2000s, well exemplify this practice.

Another example of a typical pop-rock museme string that gained widespread cultural currency is the one sometimes referred to as "chiming" or "jangling" guitar. Its origins are conventionally attributed to the 1960s band The Byrds, and it can be heard in songs like "Eight Miles High" (1966) or in their cover of Bob Dylan's "Mr. Tambourine Man" (1965). A slightly distorted but mostly pleasant-sounding chord progression, the museme string came to signify a melodic, warm dimension of electric guitar use in pop-rock, yet one that nevertheless retains a sense of power and vigor. The chiming and jangling guitar sound was further explored to critical acclaim by a band like Big Star in the 1970s, and then became one of the most identified sound signatures of the band REM throughout their entire career – and in fact of a major current in the aesthetic culture of alternative pop-rock. The use of this museme string, however, has far exceeded its original generic context and is intensively adapted by pop-rock musicians in different countries to convey a feeling of energetic warmth. It is extensively used in the repertoire of the Spanish band Amaral (the song "Te Necesito" may stand as a good example) and featured occasionally in songs by the Chinese band Shui Mu Nian Hua (The Age of Water & Wood) mentioned above.

Pop-rock has generated over the years many and diverse museme stacks and strings that became standard currency in contemporary culture. Most typically, they were originally explored and conceived in given stylistic contexts of pop-rock, like *metal, hip-hop, punk, funk*, *reggae*, or, indeed, any other genre. The repertoire of pop-rock musematic structures has grown and expanded, becoming a rich set of sonic phrases, each with its own more or less affixed connotation in terms of mood and emotion. It would probably be a never ending task to actually collect and classify pop-rock's museme stacks and strings. Yet the cultural point about their accumulation and global distribution is indeed the establishment of a vast repertoire of musical expressions, aural units of meaning, immediately identifiable as carriers of specific meanings.

A telling example of the signification power acquired by pop-rock sonic vocabularies is found in the work of audio resources' companies that function as sonic banks, selling short audio tracks for the film, television, and advertisement soundtrack industries. As much as such enterprises tend to be despised from the perspective of pop-rock's artistic ideology, they nevertheless attest to the cultural impact of pop-rock's musematic repertoire. Thus, one such company publicizes its studio products on the Internet and offers a short museme string of a chiming electric guitar. The track is characterized as "positive, upbeat short track for car commercials, household goods, appliances, DIY [do-it-yourself] stores, corporate use. Great when you need a short, simple, happy track . . . Happy, good, jangly, uplifting, hopeful, carefree, optimistic, vibrant, joyful, light, celebratory, bright, inspiring, successful, simple, bouncy, confident, friendly, fun." Also publicized is a short soaring electric guitar solo, described as "Evocative soulful, emotional and passionately moving solo electric guitar soars above an orchestral background . . . Suitable for film/TV. Soulful romantic drama, emotional loss, nostalgic and tearful scene. Loss, longing and heartbroken. Painful memories . . . Sounds like Pink Floyd. Evocative, longing, sad, retrospective, melancholic, lost, alone, heartsick" (audiosparx.com; accessed 13 November 2011).

Global Electro-Amplified Soundscapes

Music is territorial; its sounds fill up both closed and open spaces. There are "many ways in which popular music is spatial – linked to particular geographical sites, bound up in our everyday perceptions of place, and a part of movements of people, products and cultures across space" (Connell and Gibson 2003: 1; see also Johansson and Bell 2009; Leyshon et al. 1998). One particular and most prominent way is the construction of national space, of cultural locality and domesticity. Territories are domesticated to become cultural

168

environments possessed, owned, by national or ethnic communities. Such domestication shapes a given territory as the "homeland" of a given ethnic group or national community. The visual dimension of such domestication is materialized through architectural styles and other material designs, appearances of people and the linguistic landscapes (Landry and Bourhis 1997). With their typical prosodies, the latter also form part of the sonic dimension of cultural space. This sonic dimension, however, is predominantly defined by music. The musical sounds emanating from cars and buses, the music played by vendors in markets and street corners, or the background music in shopping centers are some of the sources that construct the musical aspect of cultural spaces, or the musical soundscape. Music, in other words, greatly contributes to the specificity of cultural spaces, to the aesthetic uniqueness that sets apart one ethno-national space from another, and therefore to the perceived familiarity, the sense of "being at home" shared by members of ethno-national communities in the territories they inhabit and possess (Stokes 1994). Originally referring to all sounds and to the confined space of the house, Barthes has asserted that "for the human being . . . the appropriation of space is also a matter of sound: domestic space . . . is the space of familiar, recognized noises whose ensemble forms a kind of household symphony" (Barthes 1991: 246). Narrowing down this assertion to the sounds of music, and extending it to public, collective space, it holds also for the appropriation and domestication of space by national, ethnic, and other communities. This is done by filling the space they inhabit with sounds of familiar music, music they consider their "own." This practice was conventionally associated with indigenous folk and popular musical idioms.

The growing presence of Anglo-American pop-rock music in the musical space of many countries in the world since the 1960s has disrupted the soundscape that existed in them. By breaching the existing musical soundscape (Pinch and Bijsterveld 2004) with the new tones and timbres of electric, electronic, and amplified sound, Anglo-American pop-rock music initially created a clear-cut division between the local, folk, or traditional musics that have conventionally composed the uniqueness of ethno-national musical space, and the new foreign music, perceived as cultural invasion. Media policies were sometimes devised to minimize the presence of Anglo-American pop-rock, in order to maintain the "homeland" feeling of uniqueness (Looseley 2003a; Malm and Wallis 1992). However, once local, national, and ethnic styles of pop-rock started to emerge and gain legitimacy, if not dominance, in local fields of popular music, the nature of the uniqueness of ethno-national musical spaces has been significantly transformed. The experience of being culturally "at home" in a person's own country, associated originally in the case of musical space with sonic vocabularies of traditional, indigenous music, has been gradually converted to prominently include sounds of electric and electronic instruments, of music conceived for being amplified and emitted from loudspeaker systems. With repertoires of songs and musematic structures already known to local audiences as their "own" music, national pop-rock has naturalized electric sounds into public spaces. With the legitimacy gained by local pop-rock, electric sounds were no longer perceived as intrusions, but rather as conventional elements of domestic cultural space.

Bologna, Italy, autumn of 2011. Sampling the music played in the city's supermarkets, shopping centers, fashion stores, restaurants, cafés, and taxis, the list of songs that sets the city's public musical soundscape includes items by well-established Italian pop-rock artists like Jovanotti, Biagio Antonacci or Vasco Rossi, by recent Italian pop-rock successes like Marco Mengoni or Emma Marrone, and also by classic and recent Anglo-American pop-rock performers like Elvis Presley, Santana, Boston, Adele, Beyonce, and others. Bologna echoes Tel Aviv, where a similar survey conducted in the summer of 2010 found the city's musical environment to be filled with canonized Anglo-American pop-rock songs by the likes of The Red Hot Chili Peppers, the Pet Shop Boys, Bruce Springsteen, REM, Elton John, as well as by trendy pop acts Chromeo, York, Mutya Buena, and the Black Eyed Peas. Intertwined with them, the space was filled with recent and old Israeli pop-rock songs by Kaveret, Shlomi Shabat, Ehud Banai, Arik Einstein, Sarit Hadad, and others. The situation repeated itself in Bangkok, March 2012. Small restaurants, market vendors and shopping malls provided a mixture of current hits by the likes of Lady Gaga, Britney Spears, Adele, as well as hits by Thai pop-rock names such as Potato, Punch Worakam, Luang Kai, Bie, Jirasak Panphun, and others.

In these three cities, as in many other urban settings around the world, pop-rock in local language, indigenous repertoires of national pop-rock, are smoothly woven together with Anglo-American pop-rock, to create one public musical soundscape composed primarily of electric and electronic sonic vocabularies. The local elements in the sonic environments render it domestic, creating the feeling of Italian-ness, Israeliness or Thai-ness in the examples above. They afford the sense of being at home to members of the national community, to individuals for whom these cities are a cultural home. Yet the presence of Anglo-American pop-rock hits, as well as the electric and electronic nature of local music, makes the space into one that shares much aesthetic common ground with those of other urban settings in the world. Local urban musical environments thus become global electro soundscapes, places where one feels local and global at the very same time. Culturally, they become aesthetic cosmopolitan landscapes.

The permeation of pop-rock's sonic vocabularies and song repertoires into the public cultural sphere, its dominance of cultural landscapes in urban settings worldwide, means that it became a major musical "device of social ordering" (DeNora 2000), especially in consumerist contexts. As already noted, by the 1990s and into the new century, practically all styles of pop-rock sonic vocabulary came to be intensively used in the media, marketing, and advertisement industries for projecting moods and images into film and television dramas and onto consumer goods, either as licensed excerpts from known songs, or as commissioned original music (Taylor 2007). In addition, historical repertoires of pop-rock – either Anglo-American or nationally specific – enjoying the status of "classics," came to be prominently featured in various urban settings as background music – most prominently in shopping centers (Sterne 1997).

From the point of view of pop-rock's artistic ideology – and indeed from the perspective of the ideology of autonomous art at large – as well as from a folk and nationalistic purist standpoint, the intensive presence of pop-rock sonic vocabulary and classic repertoire in the public sphere is sometimes portrayed, in a somewhat derogatory manner, as elevator music, as "muzak." That is, as music totally turned into utilitarian formulas, aimed at constituting docile individuals, and channeling them into consumerist behavior. But a more detached, ethnographic perspective cannot but point to the transformation of the musical environment in late modernity into one overwhelmingly dominated by the repertoire of pop-rock music and by its sonic vocabularies. Even attempts at constructing collective or personal spaces that oppose and counter the dominant one – in urban neighborhoods or through personal gadgets – most often rely on genres and sub-genres of pop-rock music (Bull 2006; Whiteley et al. 2005). Extreme metal, hardcore hip-hop, reggae, experimental electronics, radical alternative rock, or ethnic pop-rock styles in diasporic settings may serve the construction of oppositional cultural spaces, or of personalized music universes. But when compared to the folk, ethnic, and traditional purism of past environments, or to the sonic vocabularies of symphonic orchestras, these oppositional audioscapes clearly belong – just as the musical spaces against which they supposedly react – to the realm of pop-rock music.

Aesthetic Cosmopolitan Bodies

The use of pop-rock music in advertisements and film scores, in shopping malls and in gym halls, in order to manage emotions of spectators and to engineer moods of consumers is based on the assumption that the bodies of modern individuals are already equipped with cultural knowledge of, and competence to decipher, the museme stacks, the tones and timbres of pop-rock music. All these cultural technologies take advantage of the fact that pop-rock's sonic vocabulary is already inscribed in the auditory memory of individuals in late modernity.

> Musical experiences are rooted in the most primitive bodily experience. There are probably no tastes – except perhaps in food – more deeply rooted in the body than musical tastes . . . Music is a "bodily thing." It ravishes, moves, stirs, carries away; it is not so much beyond words as below them, in movement of the limbs and body, rhythms, excitements and slowings, tensions and releases. The most "mystical," the most "spiritual" of the arts is perhaps simply the most corporeal. That's probably what makes it so difficult to speak of music except in adjectives or exclamations. (Bourdieu 1993b: 104–5)

As discussed and analyzed repeatedly, the cultural work of music is realized primarily through its direct, material impact on the human body (DeNora 2000, 2003; Frith 1996; Meyer 1956; Middleton 1990; Shepherd and Wicke 1997). Music makes the body move, vibrate, and tremble, not just in the obvious case of dancing, but rather through its multiple effects on internal organs, the brain, and states of consciousness. Individuals tend to absorb and store in their auditory memory certain types of musical sounds, including melodies and harmonies. These, in turn, define the auditory imagery of individuals, namely, their ability to imagine musical sounds (see Crowder 1993). Through its embodied effects, its invasion of the body, its nature of being "in the body," music plays a central role in all forms of collective rituals and ceremonies, or indeed in many types of social gathering. Music is a prime cultural tool in countless social encounters where certain authorities, institutions, or organizations seek to monitor or discipline the bodies of subjects, or when such monitoring and disciplining is sought by a person's own self for various purposes (see reviews in Martin 2006; Shilling 2005). In order to achieve their

172

goals and to be culturally effective, such uses of music depend, in most cases, on cultural familiarity with music – if not with the actual musical works, then at least with the sonorities of the music being used. In other words, the cultural effects of a given type of music are dependent upon its typical sonorities being already inscribed in the bodies of its listeners (or not, in cases where the aim is to shock or even torture). These individuals have to be members and participants in aesthetic cultures of music, or at least acquainted and familiar with the aesthetic culture to which these sonorities belong. This means familiarity with the tones and timbres of certain musical instruments, feeling comfortable with their sonorities, being able to intuitively and spontaneously enjoy the aural characteristics produced by specific instrumental ensembles in which certain musical instruments are prominently featured.

Unfamiliarity with the aesthetics of a musical culture often takes the form of amazement and puzzlement towards the tones and timbres of its typical musical instruments and their combined sonic palette, towards its typical musematic patterns. Such sounds might be perceived as strange or exotic, or even evoke bodily reactions of rejection and repulsion because they come across as "non-musical," as "noise." This was indeed one initial reaction to electric and electronic musical instruments and to the overall sonic palette of pop-rock when its sonic vocabularies were first introduced. However, as pop-rock became, in the wake of the historical musical event, ubiquitous and dominant in national cultural settings around the world, individual members in them have acquired familiarity and acquaintance with its tones and timbres, as well as habitual, intuitive capability of deciphering its musematic patterns. All over the world, generations of adolescents and young adults from the 1960s and onwards, have either actively participated in the aesthetic cultures of pop-rock or developed taste preferences for one or more genres of pop-rock. By and large, by the turn of the century, numerous adults the world around were already equipped with the corporeal knowledge pertaining to the deciphering of pop-rock music and enjoying it. The bodies of all these individuals have become intuitively receptive to the sonorities of pop-rock.

The crystallization of embodied familiarity with the tones and timbres and the musematic structures of pop-rock entailed, in addition, a cultural pattern of listening, one that is closely linked to pop-rock's qualities as recorded and amplified music, emitted from loudspeakers. Pop-rock ushered the bodily absorption of a form of corporeal receptiveness to music, a mode of listening, a cultural competence that is routinely performed in the everyday life of passive and active listeners in most countries and cultures of the world. Writing about the cultural trajectory of pop-rock in Argentina, and specifying the experience of listening to music designed to be heard on stereo equipment or earphones, Diaz (2005) outlines the essence of this change. He does it by arguing against Baudrillard's assertion that in the mode of listening to recorded music enabled by sophisticated technologies, "one does not 'hear' . . . for the distance that allows one to *hear* music, at a concert or somewhere else, is abolished" (Baudrillard 1991: 30). This might be true for music not designated for such technologies. But pop-rock, says Diaz, unlike earlier forms of music, is created through interaction with technology and it is designed to invade the body, all the body, and not just the ears. Pop-rock evokes in this regard a new pattern of musical perception. It is an experience in which one may hear, for example, some opening electric guitar notes coming from "the left," while subsequent sounds may come from "the right." Then some soft drums appear from "the back," while the bass and the bass drum are felt in the abdomen, as coming from somewhere "below" (Diaz 2005: 202). The rock fan, contends Diaz, is "into" the music; with pop-rock, one does not listen to sounds but is rather taken by them, is immersed in them, filled up with them (writing in Spanish, Diaz uses the jargon of rock fans about being "copado" by the sound). Pop-rock constructs, according to Diaz, a new location of music reception, a new way of being situated in the musical space, in which there are no longer lines between body and musical sound, because music fills the entire environment. In other words, the mode of music perception implied by pop-rock music, the tones and timbres, as well as the musematic structures of pop-rock, have been absorbed into the musical auditory memory and the musical auditory imagery of individuals in countries and cultures where pop-rock became prevalent and dominant. Pop-rock tones and timbres have been digested into the cultural vocabulary stored in agents' bodies across the world. The sonorities of pop-rock became ingredients in the cultural tool-kits of individuals almost anywhere in the world, to be retrieved and used for decoding and for enjoyment of music.

One significant effect of pop-rock's long-term impact on the body has to do with the cultural performance of musical nationalism. As it has been typically constituted by national movements and nation-states in their formative phases, musical nationalism was organized around traditional forms of music that are played on acoustic and often indigenous instruments. Such forms of music served the interest

174

of nationalism in establishing itself as directly continuing ancient traditions and as a reflection of existing folklore. National culture and its embodiment in individuals' sense of identity thus became associated with the sounds and sonic textures of these instruments, and therefore with concomitant modes of corporeality. Much of the musical idioms associated with specific national and ethnic cultures are based on the typical sonorities of certain musical instruments, on ensembles in which they are prominently featured, and on typical musematic patterns emitted by such ensembles. The tones and timbres, as well as typical musematic patterns, associated with instruments such as sitar and tabla, ûd, bouzouki, balalaika, bandoneon and charanga, accordion and zourna, or with ensembles in which these instruments are prominently featured, might immediately evoke notions of Indian, Arab, Greek, Russian, Argentinean, French and Armenian cultural uniqueness, respectively. This evocation may connote identifiable and possibly exotic otherness to listeners who are not themselves members of these national cultures. For individuals who are native members of these cultures, however, the corporeality evoked by the typical sonic textures of these instruments amounts, in fact, to a bodily performance of membership in their national cultures. Upon listening to such music and recognizing in it, spontaneously and intuitively, their collective identity, they are engaged in the cultural performance of musical nationalism. The daily encounters with music, especially with music one knows and likes, amount to "performing rites," as Frith (1996) calls them. In such rites, he contends, music "both articulates and offers the immediate experience of collective identity" (Frith 1996: 273). Intuitive, spontaneous bodily recognition of a given musical piece as one we know or like, one that "belongs" to our collective cultural identity, amounts to a performance of membership in this collective entity. The bodily recognition of a piece of music as being Argentinean or Spanish, Israeli or Japanese, when the individual perceiving knows himself or herself to be a member of the nation in question, amounts to a cultural performance, a re-assertion, of membership in the nation.

The cultural transformation encapsulated in the sonic vocabulary of pop-rock therefore means, at the individual level, an alteration of the corporeality through which memberships in nations or ethnicities are performed. With the growth of sectors within national societies who adopted national pop-rock styles as the music that expresses and symbolizes their collective identity, the bodily experience and performance of national identity has been transformed. The bodily experience associated with folk/traditional acoustic instruments has been augmented, at times replaced, by the bodily experience associated with pop-rock. It became a bodily disposition that affords experiences of cultural homeyness and domesticity through sonic vocabularies that are at one and the same time native and foreign, indigenous and alien. Put differently, when bodies come to identify and experience the sense of a cultural home, as this is mediated through musical sound, with the sonic vocabularies of pop-rock, they become aesthetic cosmopolitan bodies.

Discussing round-the-world travelers' preparations and experiences, and especially their "bodily practices of flexibility, adaptability, tolerance and openness to difference," Molz (2006: 2) suggests the notion of cosmopolitan bodies. While her use of the term refers to traveling and movement and to physical competence, the term can nevertheless be applied to the cultural competences involved in taste, in the corporeal flexibility and adaptability to aesthetic diversity. An aesthetic cosmopolitan body is therefore not just a body capable of recognizing, accepting, and adapting itself to otherness, to aesthetic idioms and circumstances associated with cultural materials other than those familiar to him or her from his or her native culture, but rather a body that articulates its own local identity by incorporating elements from alien cultures. Aesthetic cosmopolitan bodies are bodies whose very corporeality is inscribed with cultural dispositions and sensibilities, schemes of aesthetic perception and evaluative criteria shared by many other bodies across the world. Once the bodies of modern individuals adapt their senses, and knowingly incorporate elements from other cultures into the experiential repertoires through which they articulate cultural locality and homeyness, their bodies become aesthetic cosmopolitan bodies. In the case of food, for example, when tastes, dishes, and practices of eating that originate in one country are integrated into the food culture of other countries, when such an influx becomes a constant, regular feature, and the bodies become accustomed to the mixture of traditional and new, native and alien tastes as practices of contemporary locality, we may talk about aesthetic cosmopolitan bodies – bodies in which aesthetic cosmopolitanism is inscribed.

With the auditory perceptual schemes of individuals all over the world becoming accustomed to the distorted sounds of electric guitars and to the indefinable timbres of electronic music; with the tones and timbres of pop-rock being absorbed into the canonical auditory knowledge of listeners across the world; with the musemes of pop-rock becoming familiar and recognizable as musical elements by listeners in almost any culture, ethnic group, and nation; when all the above become elements in the cultural performance of contemporary musical nationalism, it becomes plausible to assert that pop-rock music has constituted its listeners as aesthetic cosmopolitan bodies, that is, as bodies inscribed with musico-aural knowledge that affords a sense of being local and translocal at one and the same time.

Actants of Intercultural Phenomenological Proximity

The sonic vocabulary of pop-rock – as tones and timbres, as musematic stacks and strings, as genres and styles, as concrete musical works – has modified the state of affairs in the global musical and cultural fields. In Latour's terminology, and in that of actor-network theory in general, the sounds of pop-rock therefore qualify as *actants*, as "things" in the world whose presence have a certain transformative effect on reality. Pop-rock music has generated and provided a repertoire of actants that mediated new ways of experiencing the body, new styles of consciousness and modes of embodiment, new designs of the musical public sphere. When referring to non-human actants, the terminology of actor-network theory typically talks about objects. Gadgets and instruments, but also (in the case of science) molecules and microorganisms are most often mentioned as examples of actants. In addition, modifications of the state of affairs are usually explored in terms of short time spans, in which the effects of occurrences and events associated with given actants can be felt and observed quite instantaneously, mostly at the micro level of individuals and small groups. Musical instruments and musical sounds also have immediate effects, as DeNora demonstrates (2000). In addition, musical sounds are mediated by a broad range of devices, gadgets, and equipment. In this regard, personal music players, for example, might be viewed as actants who modify their users' state of consciousness and conduct. But the musical "objects" that in fact function as actants are the sounds themselves (Gomart and Hennion 1999), the sonic vocabularies of styles and genres, the tones and timbres emitted from musical instruments and loudspeakers. It is therefore through its materiality as sound that music in general, and musical genres in particular, ultimately function as actants. That is, as modifiers of cultural states of affairs, as transformers of cultural conditions. In addition, the collective cultural transformation brought about by musical genres is gradual; it accumulates over a long period of time. It is only after the sonic vocabularies of genres have been fully digested and absorbed into the bodies of many members in sociocultural collective units, only after these musical sounds have been legitimized and institutionalized to the point of being used for practical purposes in the cultural public sphere, that the transformational power such genres in fact have over the cultural state of affairs can be fully assessed. Or, returning to the actor-network terminology, it is only when certain, formerly innovative and disruptive musical idioms become fully integrated into the "normatively standardized bodily packages" (Moser and Law 1999) of individuals, that the actual functioning of musical genres as actants is realized.

Given the constant emergence of styles and genres of pop-rock, where each one expands the palette of tones and timbres and of museme stacks, pop-rock history can be envisaged as the serial appearance of clusters of actants. One significant modification brought about into world culture by these serial clusters of actants, by the long and expanding stylistic lineage of pop-rock genres, is essentially about growing cultural propinquity between national formations. The corporeality evoked by their sounds and the qualities they radiate on cultural spaces, have grown to become a conventional and legitimate ingredient in the experience of national cultural uniqueness in many different countries. Pop-rock sounds have thus brought formerly distant and separate cultural spaces into greater proximity. As Tomlinson (2000) notes, one implication of cultural globalization is the experience of cultural proximity shared by individuals in different ethno-national settings. While he understands this phenomenological proximity as the experience of being constantly aware of the existence and relevance of other cultures, it seems that, following the discussion above of electro soundscapes and aesthetic cosmopolitan bodies, a somewhat different meaning of the term can be discerned, namely, phenomenological proximity as a condition of cultural overlap, in which the experience of cultural uniqueness in one national formation comes to share much common aesthetic ground with the experience of uniqueness in other such formations.

If, as Frith asserts, music "gives us a way of being in the world, a way of making sense of it" (1996: 272), then the particularity of that mode of being in the world which is the experience of membership in a given national formation, as mediated by music, has been transformed by pop-rock. It is no longer a way of being in the world that is, or at least strives to be, totally different from that of national formations other than one's own. Rather, it is a way of being in the world whose particularity intentionally shares much common expressive ground with that of other national formations. That is, as the same expressive materials – electric and electronic tones and timbres, pop-rock musematic structures – are used to produce the experience

SONIC VOCABULARIES, SPACES, AND BODIES

of musico-cultural uniqueness of different national formations, the cultural overlap between these formations is enhanced and intensified. The mutual sense of otherness between different national or ethnic formations is reduced, shrunk to a minimum, while the proportion of shared aesthetic perceptions grows and expands. And this is, perhaps, the core of aesthetic cosmopolitanism – the shriveling and withering of cultural otherness. Not its disappearance, but its mutation into something always familiar, never fully alien or strange. Listening to girl groups from Japan, to hip-hop from Turkey, to flamenco-tinged rock from Spain, and to a female or male rock *auteur* from any country, pop-rock fans anywhere in the world will always encounter in each of the above some electric and electronic sounds, vocal techniques, and musical phrases familiar from their very own national music.

REFERENCES

Abrams, M.H. (1989) Art-as-Such: The Sociology of Modern Aesthetics. In: *Doing Things with Texts*. W.W. Norton, New York, pp. 135–58.

Adorno, T. (1941) On Popular Music. *Studies in Philosophy and Social Science* IX, 17–48.

Aguirre, J., Roveta, M., Correa, M. and Tijman, G.A. (2005) *Diccionario del rock argentino*. Musimundo, Buenos Aires.

Alabarces, P. (1993) *Entre Gatos y Violdores: el rock nacional en la cultura argentina*. Ediciones Colihue, Buenos Aires.

Antonić, D. and Štrbac, D. (1998) *YU 100: Najbolji albumi jugoslovenske rok i pop muzike*. YU Rock Press, Belgrade.

Appadurai, A. (1990) Disjuncture and Difference in the Global Cultural Economy. In: Featherstone, M. (ed.), *Global Culture*. Sage, London, pp. 295–310.

Avelar, I. (2003) Heavy Metal Music in Postdictatorial Brazil: Sepultura and the Coding of Nationality in Sound. *Journal of Latin American Cultural Studies* 12, 330–46.

Baker, S. (2004) Pop in(to) the Bedroom: Popular Music in Pre-Teen Girls' Bedroom Culture. *European Journal of Cultural Studies* 7, 75–93.

Bannister, M. (2006) "Loaded": Indie Guitar Rock, Canonism, White Masculinities. *Popular Music* 25, 77–95.

Baranovitch, N. (2003) *China's New Voices*. University of California Press, Berkeley, CA.

Barthes, R. (1977) *Image, Music, Text*. Hill and Wang, New York

Barthes, R. (1991) *The Responsibility of Forms*. University of California Press, Berkeley, CA.

Baudrillard, J. (1991) *Seduction*. Palgrave Macmillan, New York.

Baudrillard, J. (1994) *Simulacra and Simulation*. University of Michigan Press, Ann Arbor, MI.

Baulch, E. (2002) Creating a Scene: Balinese Punk's Beginnings. *International Journal of Cultural Studies* 5, 153–77.

Baulch, E. (2003) Gesturing Elsewhere: The Identity Politics of the Balinese Death/Thrash Metal Scene. *Popular Music* 22(2), 195–215.

Baulch, E. (2007) *Making Scenes: Reggae, Punk and Death Metal in 1990s Bali*. Duke University Press, Durham, NC.

Baym, N. (2007) The New Shape of Online Community: The Example of Swedish Independent Music Fandom, *First Monday* 12, firstmonday.org/issues/ (online journal).

Beck, U. (2006) *The Cosmopolitan Vision*. Polity, Cambridge.

Beck, U. and Sznaider, N. (2006) Unpacking Cosmopolitanism for the Social Sciences. *British Journal of Sociology* 27, 3–23.

Benedetti, C.M. (2008) El rock de los desangelados. Música, sectores populares y procesos de consumo. *Trans* 12, sibertrans.com/trans/publicaciones (online journal).

Bennett, A. (1999) Hip-Hop am Main: The Localization of Rap Music and Hip-Hop Culture. *Media, Culture & Society* 27, 77–91.

Bennett, A. (2000) *Popular Music and Youth Culture: Music, Identity and Place*. Macmillan, London.

Bennett, A. (2004a) Consolidating the Music Scenes Perspective. *Poetics* 32, 223–34.

Bennett, A. (2004b) New Tales from Canterbury: The Making of a Virtual Scene. In: Bennett, A. and Peterson, R.A. (eds.) *Music Scenes: Local, Translocal and Virtual*. Vanderbilt University Press, Nashville, TN, pp. 205–20.

Bennett, A. (2006a) In Defence of Neo-tribes: A Response to Blackman and Hesmondhalgh. *Journal of Youth Studies* 8, 255–9.

Bennett, A. (2006b) Punk's Not Dead: The Continuing Significance of Punk Rock for an Older Generation of Fans. *Sociology* 40, 219–35.

Bennett, A. and Peterson, R.A. (eds.) (2004) *Music Scenes: Local, Translocal and Virtual*. Vanderbilt University Press, Nashville, TN.

Bennett, A. and Taylor J. (2012) Popular Music and the Aesthetics of Ageing. *Popular Music* 31, 231–43.

Beumers, B. (2005) *Pop Culture Russia! Media, Arts and Lifestyle*. ABC-CLIO, Inc., Santa Barbara, CA.

Billig, M. (1995) *Banal Nationalism*. Sage, London.

Birgy, P. (2003) French Electronic Music: The Invention of a Tradition. In: Dauncey, H. and Cannon, S. (eds.) *Popular Music in France from Chanson to Techno*. Ashgate, Aldershot, pp. 225–42.

Bitar, M.F. (1993) *Historia del Rock en Argentina*. Editorial Distal, Buenos Aires.

Bloch, L.R. and Lemish, D. (2003) The Megaphone Effect: The International Diffusion of Cultural Media via the USA. In: Kalbfleisch, P.J. (ed.) *Communication Yearbook* 27. Lawrence Erlbaum Associates, Mahwah, NJ, pp. 159–90.

Bloom, A. (1987) *The Closing of the American Mind*. Simon & Schuster, New York.

Bodden, M. (2005) Rap in Indonesian Youth Music in the 1990s. *Asian Music* 36, 1–27.

Bourdieu, P. (1984) *Distinction: A Social Critique of the Judgment of Taste*. Routledge, London.

Bourdieu, P. (1992) *The Rules of Art*. Polity, Cambridge.

Bourdieu, P. (1993a) *The Field of Cultural Production*. Polity, Cambridge.

Bourdieu, P. (1993b) Music Lovers: Origin and Evolution of the Species. In: *Sociology in Question*. Sage, London, pp. 103–7.

Brierre, J.D., Deplasse, H., Eudeline C., Perrin, J.É. and Thoury J.W. (eds.) (2000) *L'Encyclopédie du rock française*. Edition Hors Collection, Paris.

Bryson, B. (1996) "Anything but Heavy Metal": Symbolic Exclusion and Musical Dislikes. *American Sociological Review* 61, 884–99.

Bull, M. (2006) *Sounding Out the City: Personal Stereo and the Management of Everyday Life.* Berg, New York.

Calderon, N. (2009) *The Second Day: On Poetry and Rock in Israel after Yona Wallach.* Dvir, Tel Aviv (in Hebrew).

Campbell Robinson, D., Buck, E.B. and Cuthbert, M. (1991) *Music at the Margins.* Sage, London.

Cateforis, T. (ed.) (2006) *The Rock History Reader.* Routledge, London.

Chapple, S. and Garofalo, R. (1977) *Rock'n'roll is Here to Pay: The History and Politics of the Music Industry.* Nelson-Hall, Chicago, IL.

Christgau, R. (2000) *Christgau's Consumer Guide: Albums of the 90's.* St. Martin's Press, New York.

Chua, B.H. (2004) Conceptualizing an East Asian Popular Culture. *Inter-Asia Cultural Studies* 5, 200–21.

Citro, S. (2008) El Rock como un ritual adolescente. Trasgresión y realismo grotesco en los recitales de Bersuit, *Trans* 12, sibertrans.com/trans/public aciones (online journal).

Clarke, P. (1983) "A Magic Science": Rock Music as a Recording Art. *Popular Music* 3, 195–213.

Clewley, J. (2005) Thailand. In: Shepherd, J., Horn, D. and Laing, D. (eds.) *Continuum Encyclopedia of Popular Music of the World, vol. V: Asia and Oceania.* Continuum, London, pp. 214–20.

Colombijn, F. (2007) Toooot! Vroooom!: The Urban Soundscape in Indonesia. *SOJOURN: Journal of Social Issues in Southeast Asia* 22, 255–73.

Condry, I. (2006) *Hip Hop Japan: Rap and the Paths of Cultural Globalization.* Duke University Press, Durham, NC.

Connell, J. and Gibson, C. (2003) *Sound Track: Popular Music, Identity and Place.* Routledge, London.

Cotter, J.M. (1999) Sounds of Hate: White Power Rock and Roll and the Neo-Nazi Skinhead Sub-Culture. *Terrorism and Political Violence* 11, 111–40.

Coulangeon, P. (2003) La Stratification sociale des goûts musicaux: Le modèle de la légitimité culturelle en question. *Revue française de sociologie* 44, 3–33.

Crane, D. (2008) Globalization and Cultural Flows/Networks. In: Bennett, T. and Frow, J. (eds.) *The Sage Handbook of Cultural Analysis.* Sage, London, pp. 359–81.

Crowder, R.G. (1993) Auditory Memory. In: McAdams, S. and Bigand, E. (eds.) *Thinking in Sound: The Cognitive Psychology of Human Audition.* Oxford University Press, Oxford, pp. 113–45.

Cushman, T. (1995) *Notes from the Underground: Rock Music Counterculture in Russia.* SUNY Press, Albany, NY.

Darling-Wolf, F. (2008) Getting over our "Illusion d'Optique": From Globalization to *Mondialisation* (through French Rap). *Communication Theory* 18, 187–209.

DeCurtis, A. and Henke, J. (eds.) (1992) *The Rolling Stone Illustrated History of Rock and Roll.* Straight Arrow Publishers, New York.

de Kloet, J. (2010) *Red Sonic Trajectories: Popular Music and Youth in Urban China.* Amsterdam School for Social Science Research, University of Amsterdam, Amsterdam.

del Val, F., Pérez Colman, M. and Noya, J. (2011) Movida promovida: El canon estético del pop rock Español. Unpublished paper.
DeNora, T. (2000) *Music in Everyday Life*. Cambridge University Press, Cambridge.
DeNora, T. (2003) *After Adorno*. Cambridge University Press, Cambridge.
Diaz, C.F. (2005) *Libro de viajes y extravíos: un recorrido por el rock argentino (1965–1985)*. Narvaja Editor, Unquillo.
DiMaggio, P. (1987) Classification in Art. *American Sociological Review* 52, 440–55.
DiMaggio, P. (1992) Cultural Boundaries and Structural Change: The Extension of the High Culture Model to Theater, Opera and the Dance, 1900–1940. In: Lamont, M. and Fournier, M. (eds.) *Cultivating Differences: Symbolic Boundaries and the Making of Inequality*. The University of Chicago Press, Chicago, IL, pp. 21–57.
DiMaggio, P. and Powell, W. (1983) The Iron Cage Revisited: Institutionalized Isomorphism and Collective Rationality in Organizational Fields. *American Sociological Review* 48, 147–60.
Dorchin, U. (2012) *Real Time: Hip-Hop in Israel/Israeli Hip-Hop*. Resling, Tel Aviv (in Hebrew).
Dowd, T. (2004) Concentration and Diversity Revisited: Production Logics and the U.S. Mainstream Recording Market, 1940–1990. *Social Forces* 82, 1411–55.
Dunn, C. (2001) *Brutality Garden*. University of North Carolina Press, Chapel Hill, NC.
Eagleton, T. (1990) *The Ideology of the Aesthetic*. Basil Blackwell, Oxford.
Epstein, S. (2000) Anarchy in the UK, Solidarity in the ROK: Punk Rock Comes to Korea. *Acta Koreana* 3, 1–34.
Esterrich, C. and Murillo, J.H. (2000) Rock with Punk with Pop with Folklore: Transformations and Renewal in Aterciopelados and Café Tacuba. *Latin American Music Review* 21, 31–44.
Fabbri, F. (1982) What Kind of Music? *Popular Music* 2, 131–44.
Fales, C. (2005) Short-Circuiting Perceptual Systems: Timbre in Ambient and Techno Music. In: Greene, P.D. and Porcello, T. (eds.) *Wired for Sound: Engineering and Technologies in Sonic Cultures*. Wesleyan University Press, Middletown, CT, pp. 156–80.
Featherstone, M. (1991) *Consumer Culture and Postmodernism*. Sage, London.
Feld, S. (2000) A Sweet Lullaby for World Music. *Public Culture* 12, 145–71.
Fonarow, W. (2006) *Empire of Dirt: The Aesthetics and Rituals of British Indie Music*. Wesleyan University Press, Middletown, CT.
Fouce, H. (2006) *El Futuro ya está aquí: Música pop y cambio cultural*. Valecío editores, Madrid.
Fraser, N. (2001) Recognition without Ethics? *Theory, Culture and Society* 18, 21–42.
Frith, S. (1981) *Sound Effects: Youth, Leisure and the Politics of Rock'n'Roll*. Pantheon Books, New York.
Frith, S. (1986) Critical Response. *Critical Studies in Mass Communication* 3, 75–8.
Frith, S. (1987) Towards an Aesthetic of Popular Music. In: Leppert, R. and McCalry, S. (eds.) *Music and Society: The Politics of Composition, Performance and Reception*. Cambridge University Press, Cambridge, pp. 133–50.

Frith, S. (1988) *Music for Pleasure*. Routledge, London.
Frith, S. (1996) *Performing Rites*. Harvard University Press, Cambridge, MA.
Frith, S. (2002) The Discourse of World Music. In: Born, G. and Hesmondhalgh, D. (eds.) *Western Music and its Others*. University of California Press Berkeley, CA, pp. 305–22.
Frith, S. (2004) Does British Music Still Matter? *European Journal of Cultural Studies* 7, 43–58.
Fung, A. and Curtin, M. (2002) The Anomalies of Being Faye (Wong): Gender Politics in Chinese Popular Music. *International Journal of Cultural Studies* 5, 263–90.
Gammond, P. (1993) *The Oxford Companion to Popular Music*. Oxford University Press, Oxford.
Garcia Canclini, N. (1995) *Hybrid Cultures: Strategies for Entering and Leaving Modernity*. University of Minnesota Press, Minneapolis, MN.
Garofalo, R. (2005) *Rockin' Out: Popular Music in the USA*. Pearson Prentice Hall, Upper Saddle River, NJ.
Getino, O. (1995) *Las industrias culturales en la Argentina*. Ediciones Collihue, Buenos Aires.
Gilroy, P. (1993) *The Black Atlantic: Modernity and Double Consciousness*. Verso, London.
Gomart, E. and Hennion, A. (1999) A Sociology of Attachment: Music Amateurs, Drug Users. In: Law, J. and Hassard, J. (eds.) *Actor Network Theory and After*. Sociological Review and Blackwell, Oxford, pp. 220–47.
Gonzalez, J.P. (2012) Vanguardia primitiva en el rock chileno de los años setenta: música, intelectuales y contracultura. *Música Popular em Revista* 1, 75–92.
Gracyk, T. (1996) *Rhythm and Noise: An Aesthetic of Rock*. Duke University Press, Durham, NC.
Greene, P. (2001) Mixed Messages: Unsettled Cosmopolitanisms in Nepali Pop. *Popular Music* 20, 169–87.
Grinberg, M. (1993) *Como vino la mano: Origines del rock Argentino*. Distal, Buenos Aires.
Grossberg, L. (1986) Is There Rock after Punk? *Critical Studies in Mass Communication* 3, 50–74.
Grossberg, L. (1992) *We Gotta Get Out of This Place*. Routledge, London.
Gundle, S. (2006) Adriano Celentano and the Origins of Rock and Roll in Italy. *Journal of Modern Italian Studies* 11, 367–86.
Hagen, R. (2011) Musical Style, Ideology and Mythology in Norwegian Black Metal. In: Wallach, J., Berger, H.M. and Greene, P.D. (eds.) *Metal Rules the Globe: Heavy Metal Music around the World*. Duke University Press, Durham, NC, pp. 180–200.
Hall, S. and Jefferson, T. (eds.) (1976) *Resistance through Rituals: Youth Subcultures in Post War Britain*. Hutchinson, London.
Hammond, A. (2005) *Pop Culture Arab World! Media, Arts and Lifestyle*. ABC-Clio, Santa Barbara, CA.
Hannerz, U. (1990) Cosmopolitans and Locals in World Culture. In: Featherstone, M. (ed.), *Global Culture*. Sage, London, pp. 237–52.
Hannerz, U. (1992) *Cultural Complexity*. Columbia University Press, New York.
Hatch, D. and Millward, S. (1987) *From Blues to Rock: An Analytical History of Pop Music*. Manchester University Press, Manchester.
Hebdige, D. (1979) *Subculture: The Meaning of Style*. Methuen, London.

Hebdige, D. (1990) Fax to the Future. *Marxism Today*, January, 18–23.

Hecker, P. (2005) Taking a Trip to the Middle Eastern Metal Scene. *Nord-Süd Aktuell* 05/01, 57–66.

Hecker, P. (2010) Heavy Metal in the Middle East: New Urban Spaces in a Translocal Underground. In: Bayat A. and Herrera L. (eds.) *Being Young and Muslim: New Cultural Politics in the Global South and North*. Oxford University Press, Oxford, pp. 325–39.

Heilbronner, O. (2011) "Resistance through Rituals": Urban Subcultures of Israeli Youth from the Late 1950s to the 1980s. *Israel Studies* 16, 28–50.

Heller, D. (2007) "Russian Body and Soul": t.A.T.u. Performs at Eurovision 2003. In: Raykoff, I. and Tobin, R.D. (eds.) *A Song for Europe: Popular Music and Politics in the Eurovision Song Contest*. Ashgate, Aldershot, pp. 111–22.

Hennion, A. (2001) Music Lovers: Taste as Performance. *Theory, Culture and Society* 18, 1–22.

Hennion, A. (2004) Pragmatics of Taste. In: Jacobs, M.D. and Hanrahan, N.W. (eds.) *The Blackwell Companion to the Sociology of Culture*. Blackwell, London, pp. 131–44.

Hesmondhalgh, D. (1996) Rethinking Popular Music after Rock and Soul. In: Curran, J., Morley, D. and Walkerdine, V. (eds.) *Cultural Studies and Communications*. Arnold, London, pp. 195–212.

Hesmondhalgh, D. (1999) Indie: The Institutional Politics and Aesthetics of a Popular Music Genre. *Cultural Studies* 13, 34–61.

Hesmondhalgh, D. (2005) Subcultures, Scenes or Tribes? None of the Above. *Journal of Youth Studies* 8, 21–40.

Hesmondhalgh, D. (2007) *The Cultural Industries*. Sage, London.

Hirsch, P. (1972) Processing Fads and Fashions: An Organization-Set Analysis of Cultural Industry Systems. *American Journal of Sociology* 77, 639–59.

Hirshberg, Y. (1995) *Music in the Jewish Community of Palestine*. Oxford University Press, Oxford.

Hodkinson, P. (2011) Ageing in a Spectacular "Youth Culture": Continuity, Change and Community amongst Older Goths. *British Journal of Sociology* 62, 262–82.

Holm-Hudson, K. (ed.) (2002) *Progressive Rock Reconsidered*. Routledge, New York.

Hornby, N. (1995) *High Fidelity* [a novel]. Riverhead Books, New York.

Horowitz, A. (2010) *Mediterranean Israeli Music and the Politics of the Aesthetic*. Wayne State University Press, Detroit, MI.

Iwabuchi, K. (2002) *Recentering Globalization: Popular Culture and Japanese Transnationalism*. Duke University Press, Durham, NC.

Jenkins, H. (2006) *Convergence Culture: Where New and Old Media Collide*. New York University Press, New York.

Johansson, O. and Bell, T.L. (2009) *Sound, Society and the Geography of Popular Music*. Ashgate, Aldershot.

Jones, A.F. (1992) *Like a Knife*. East Asia Program, Cornell University, Ithaca, NY.

Jones, S. (1992) *Rock Formations: Music, Technology and Mass Communication*. Sage, London.

Jordán González, L. and Smith, K.D. (2011) How Did Popular Music Come to Mean Música Popular? *IASPM@Journal* 2, 19–33.

REFERENCES

Kahf, U. (2007) Arabic Hip Hop: Claims of Authenticity and Identity of a New Genre. *Journal of Popular Music Studies* 19, 359–85.
Kahn-Harris, K. (2007) *Extreme Metal: Music and Culture on the Edge.* Berg, Oxford.
Kaplan, D. (2011) Neo-Institutional Analysis of the Rise of Light Mizrachi Music on Israeli Radio, 1995–2010. *Israeli Sociology* 13, 135–59 (in Hebrew).
Kaplan, D. (2012) Institutionalized Erasures: How Global Structures Acquire National Meanings in Israeli Popular Music. *Poetics* 40, 217–36.
Karahasanolu, S. and Skoog, G. (2009) Synthesizing Identity: Gestures of Filiation and Affiliation in Turkish Popular Music. *Asian Music* 40, 52–71.
Käryä, A.V. (2006) A Prescribed Alternative Mainstream: Popular Music and Canon Formation. *Popular Music* 25, 3–19.
Katz, E. and Liebes, T. (1990) *The Export of Meaning: Cross-cultural Readings of "Dallas".* Oxford University Press, New York.
Kawano, K. and Hosokawa, S. (2011) Thunder in the Far East: The Heavy Metal Industry in 1990s Japan. In: Wallach, J., Berger, H.M. and Greene, P.D. (eds.) *Metal Rules the Globe: Heavy Metal Music around the World.* Duke University Press, Durham, NC, pp. 247–70.
Keeler, K. (2009) What's Burmese about Burmese Rap? *American Ethnologist* 36, 2–19.
Kendall, G., Woodward, I. and Skrbis, Z. (2009) *The Sociology of Cosmopolitanism.* Palgrave Macmillan, New York.
Kim, P.H. and Shin, H. (2010) The Birth of "Rok": Cultural Imperialism, Nationalism, and the Glocalization of Rock Music in South Korea, 1964–1975. *Positions* 18, 199–230.
Knorr Cetina, K. (2005) Complex Global Microstructures: The New Terrorist Societies. *Theory, Culture and Society* 22, 213–34.
Knorr Cetina, K. (2007) Culture in Global Knowledge Societies: Knowledge Cultures and Epistemic Cultures. *Interdisciplinary Science Reviews* 32, 361–75.
Knorr Cetina, K. and Bruegger, U. (2002) Global Microstructures: The Virtual Societies of Financial Markets. *American Journal of Sociology* 107, 905–50.
Krätke, S. (2003) Global Media Studies in a Worldwide Urban Network. *European Planning Studies* 11, 605–28.
Kreimer, J.K. (1970) *Agarrate!!! Testimonios de la musica joven en Argentina.* Editorial Galerna, Buenos Aires.
Kruse, H. (2003) *Site and Sound: Understanding Independent Music Scenes.* Peter Lang, New York.
Laing, D. (1969) *The Sound of our Time.* Quadrangle Books, Chicago, IL.
Laing, D. (1986) *One Chord Wonders: Power and Meaning in Punk Rock.* Open University Press, Milton Keynes.
Laing, D. (2008) World Music and the Global Music Industry: Flows, Corporations and Networks. *Popular Music History* 3, 213–31.
Lamont, M. (1995) National Identity and National Boundary Patterns in France and the United States. *French Historical Studies* 16, 349–65.
Lamont, M. and Aksartova, S. (2002) Ordinary Cosmopolitanisms: Strategies for Bridging Racial Boundaries among Working-Class Men. *Theory, Culture and Society* 19, 1–25.
Lamont, M. and Fournier, M. (eds.) (1992) *Cultivating Differences: Symbolic Boundaries and the Making of Inequality.* University of Chicago Press, Chicago, IL.

Lamont, M. and Molnár, V. (2002) The Study of Boundaries in the Social Sciences. *Annual Review of Sociology* 28, 167–95.

Landau, J. (1972) *It's too Late to Stop Now: A Rock and Roll Journal*. Straight Arrow Publishing, Los Angeles, CA.

Landry, R. and Bourhis, R.Y. (1997) Linguistic Landscape and Ethnolinguistic Vitality. *Journal of Language and Social Psychology* 16, 23–49.

Larkey, E. (1993) *Pungent Sounds: Constructing Identity with Popular Music in Austria*. Peter Lang, New York.

Larkin, P. (1995) *The Encyclopedia of Popular Music*. Enfield, Guinness Publishing.

Lash, S. (1990) *Sociology of Postmodernism*. Routledge, London.

Latour, B. (2005) *Re-Assembling the Social: An Introduction to Actor-Network Theory*. Oxford University Press, Oxford.

Lechado, J.M. (2005) *La Movida: Una Crónica de los 80*. Algaba Ediciones, Madrid.

Lena, J. (2004) Meaning and Membership: Samples in Rap Music, 1979–1995. *Poetics* 32, 297–310.

Lena, J. (2012) *Banding Together: How Communities Create Genres in Popular Music*. Princeton University Press, Princeton, NJ.

Lena, J. and Peterson, R.A. (2008) Classification as Culture: Types and Trajectories of Music Genres. *American Sociological Review* 73, 697–718.

Leyshon, A., Matless, D. and Revill, G. (eds.) (1998) *The Place of Music*. Guilford Press, New York.

Lilliestam, L. (1998) *Svensk rock. Musik, lyrik, historik*. Bo Ejeby Förlag, Gothenburg.

Lindberg, U. (2007) Writing the Nation: On Ulf Lundell's "Öppna Landskap." Paper presented at INTER: A European Cultural Studies Conference, Norrköping, Sweden.

Lindberg, U., Guðmundsson G., Michelsen, M. and Weisethaunet, H. (2005) *Rock Criticism from the Beginning*. Peter Lang, New York.

Lizardo, O. and Skiles, S. (2008) Cultural Consumption in the Fine and Popular Arts Realms. *Sociology Compass* 2, 485–502.

Lockard, C.A. (1998) *Dance of Life: Popular Music and Politics in Southeast Asia*. University of Hawai'i Press, Honolulu, HI.

Longhurst, B. (1995) *Popular Music and Society*. Polity, Cambridge.

Looseley, D. (2003a) *Popular Music in Contemporary France: Authenticity, Politics, Debate*. Berg, Oxford.

Looseley, D. (2003b) In from the Margins: Chanson, Pop and Cultural Legitimacy. In: Dauncey, H. and Cannon, S. (eds.) *Popular Music in France from Chanson to Techno*. Ashgate, Aldershot, pp. 27–40.

Looseley, D. (2005) Fabricating Johnny: French Popular Music and National Culture. *French Cultural Studies* 16, 191–203.

Macan, E. (1997) *Rocking the Classics: English Progressive Rock and the Counterculture*. Oxford University Press, Oxford.

Magaldi, C. (1999) Adopting Imports: New Images and Alliances in Brazilian Popular Music of the 1990s. *Popular Music* 18, 309–29.

Magaudda, P. (2003) Disco, House and Techno: Rethinking the Local and the Global in Italian Electronic Music. In: Gyde, A. and Stahl, G. (eds.) *Practicing Popular Music: Proceedings from the 12th Biennial IASPM Conference*. IASPM, Montreal, pp. 535–51.

Magaudda, P. (2009) Indie in Italy. Processes of Institutionalisation and "Symbolic Struggles" in the "Independent Music" Field in Italy. *Modern Italy* 14, 295–310.

Malm, K. and Wallis, R. (1992) *Media Policy and Music Activity.* Routledge, London.

Manuel, P. (1988) *Popular Musics of the Non-Western World.* Oxford University Press, Oxford.

Marchi, S. (2005) *El rock perdido.* Capital Intelectual, Buenos Aires.

Marcus, G. (1986) Critical Response. *Critical Studies in Mass Communication* 3, 79–82.

Marcus, G. (ed.) (1979) *Stranded: Rock and Roll for a Desert Island.* Knopf, New York.

Martin, B. (1998) *Listening to the Future: The Time of Progressive Rock, 1968–1978.* Open Court Publishing Company, Chicago, IL.

Martin, P.J. (2006) *Music and the Sociological Gaze: Art Worlds and Cultural Production.* Manchester University Press, Manchester.

Mayer, A.P. (2011) *"The Fist in the Face of God": Heavy Metal Music and Decentralized Global Cultural Diffusion.* Master of Arts Thesis, Department of Sociology, University of Cincinnati.

McClary, S. (1991) *Feminine Endings: Music, Gender, and Sexuality.* University of Minnesota Press, Minneapolis, MN.

McGuigan, J. (2005) The Cultural Public Sphere. *European Journal of Cultural Studies* 8, 427–43.

McLeod, K. (2001) Genres, Subgenres, Sub-Subgenres and More: Musical and Social Differentiation within Electronic/Dance Music Communities. *Journal of Popular Music Studies* 13, 59–75.

McMichael, P. (2005) "After all, you're a rock and roll star (at least, that's what they say)": Roksi and the Creation of the Soviet Rock Musician. *SEER* 83: 664–84.

Meintjes, L. (2005) Reaching "Overseas": South African Sound Engineers, Technology and Tradition. In: Greene, P.D. and Porcello, T. (eds.) *Wired for Sound: Engineering and Technologies in Sonic Cultures.* Wesleyan University Press, Middletown, CT, pp. 23–46.

Meyer, J.W. (2000) Globalization: Sources and Effects on National States and Societies. *International Sociology* 15, 233–48.

Meyer, J.W., Boli, J., Thomas, G.M. and Ramirez F.O. (1997) World Society and the Nation-State. *American Journal of Sociology* 103, 144–81.

Meyer, L.B. (1956) *Emotion and Meaning in Music.* University of Chicago Press, Chicago, IL.

Middleton, R. (1990) *Studying Popular Music.* Open University Press, Milton Keynes.

Middleton, R. and Manuel, P. (2010) Popular Music. *Grove Music Online,* Oxfordmusiconline.com/subscriber/article/grove/music/43179#S43179.

Minganti, F. (1993) Rock'n'Roll in Italy: Was It True Americanisation? In: Kroes, R., Rydell, R. and Bosscher D. (eds.) *Cultural Transmissions and Receptions: American Mass Culture in Europe.* VU University Press, Amsterdam.

Mitchell, T. (1996) *Popular Music and Local Identity.* Leicester University Press, London.

Mitchell, T. (ed.) (2001) *Global Noise.* Wesleyan University Press, Middletown, CT.

Mitchell, T. (2007) Tian Ci – Faye Wong and English Songs in the Cantopop and Mandapop Repertoire. Available at: www.localnoise.net.au/wp-content/uploads/2011/Tian%20Ci%20-%20Faye%20Wong.pdf (accessed 10 October, 2011).

Mitsui, T. (2005) Japan. In: Shepherd, J., Horn, D. and Laing, D. (eds.) *Continuum Encyclopedia of Popular Music of the World, vol. V: Asia and Oceania.* Continuum, London, pp. 132–56.

Molz, J.G. (2006) Cosmopolitan Bodies: Fit to Travel and Travelling to Fit. *Body and Society* 12, 1–21.

Moore, A. (2001) *Rock: The Primary Text: Developing a Musicology of Rock.* Ashgate, Aldershot.

Mōri, Y. (2009) J-Pop: From the Ideology of Creativity to DiY Music Culture. *Inter-Asia Cultural Studies* 10, 474–88.

Moser, I. and Law, J. (1999) Good Passages, Bad Passages. In: Law, J. and Hassard, J. (eds.) *Actor Network Theory and After.* Sociological Review and Blackwell, Oxford, pp. 196–219.

Muñoz, G. and Marín, M. (2006) Music is the Connection: Youth Cultures in Colombia. In: Nilan, P. and Feixa, C. (eds.) *Global Youth? Hybrid Identities, Plural Worlds.* Routledge, New York, pp. 130–49.

Negus, K. (1992) *Producing Pop.* Edward Arnold, London.

Negus, K. (1996) *Popular Music: In Theory.* Polity, Cambridge.

Negus, K. (1999) *Music Genres and Corporate Cultures.* Routledge, London.

Nettl, B. (1985) *The Western Impact on World Music: Change, Adaptation and Survival.* Schirmer, New York.

Niemi, M. (2003 [2000]) *Popular Music from Vittula* [a novel]. Seven Stories Press, New York.

Njogu, K. and Maupeu, H. (eds.) (2007) *Songs and Politics in Eastern Africa.* Mkuki na Nyota Publishers, Dar es Salaam.

Ntarangwi, M. (2010) African Hip Hop and Politics of Change in an Era of Rapid Globalization. *History Compass* 8, 1316–27.

Nugent, S.L. (1986) Critical Response. *Critical Studies in Mass Communication* 3, 83–5.

O'Connor, A. (2004) Punk and Globalization: Spain and Mexico. *International Journal of Cultural Studies* 7, 175–95.

Ollivier, M. (2004) Towards a Structural Theory of Status Inequality: Structures and Rents in Popular Music and Tastes. *Research in Social Stratification and Mobility* 21, 187–213.

Ollivier, M. (2008) Modes of Openness to Cultural Diversity: Humanist, Populist, Practical, and Indifferent. *Poetics* 36, 120–47.

Osumare, H. (2007) *The Africanist Aesthetic in Global Hip-Hop.* Palgrave Macmillan, New York.

Pacini Hernandez, D., L'Hoeste, H.F. and Zolov, E. (eds.) (2004) *Rockin' Las Américas: The Global Politics of Rock in Latin/o America.* University of Pittsburgh Press, Pittsburgh, PA.

Pardue, D. (2004) Putting *mano* to Music: The Mediation of Race in Brazilian Rap. *Ethnomusicological Forum* 13, 253–86.

Partan, O. (2007) Alla: The Jester Queen of Russian Pop Culture. *The Russian Review* 66, 483–500.

Pauker, I. (2006) Reconciliation and Popular Culture: A Promising Development in Former Yugoslavia? *Local-Global: Identity, Security, Community* 2: 72–81.

Peluse, M.S. (2005) Not Your Grandfather's Music: Tsugaru Shamisen Blurs the Lines between "Folk," "Traditional," and "Pop." *Asian Music* 36, 57–80.

Peterson, R.A. (1990) Why 1995? Explaining the Advent of Rock Music. *Popular Music* 9, 97–116.

Peterson, R.A. (1997) The Rise and Fall of Snobbery as a Status Marker. *Poetics* 25, 75–92.

Peterson, R.A. and Berger, D. (1975) Cycles in Symbol Production: The Case of Popular Music. *American Sociological Review* 40, 158–73.

Peterson, R.A. and Kern, R. (1996) Changing Highbrow Taste: From Snob to Omnivore. *American Sociological Review* 61, 900–7.

Peterson, R.A. and Simkus, A. (1992) How Musical Taste Groups Mark Occupational Status Groups. In: Lamont, M. and Fournier, M. (eds.) *Cultivating Differences: Symbolic Boundaries and the Making of Inequality.* University of Chicago Press, Chicago, IL, pp. 152–68.

Pickles, J. (2007) Punk, Pop and Protest: The Birth and Decline of Political Pop in Bandung. *RIMA: Review of Indonesian and Malaysian Affairs* 41, 223–46.

Pinch, T. and Bijsterveld, K. (2004) Sound Studies: New Technologies of Music. *Social Studies of Science* 34, 635–48.

Polychronakis, I. (2007) Anna Vissi: The Greek "Madonna?" Paper presented at INTER: A European Cultural Studies Conference, Norrköping, Sweden.

Pujol, S.A. (2002) *La década rebelde: los años 60 en la Argentina.* Emecé Editores, Buenos Aires.

Ramet, S.P. (1994a) Rock: The Music of the Revolution (and Political Conformity). In: Ramet, S.P. (ed.) *Rocking the State: Rock Music and Politics in Eastern Europe and Russia.* Westview Press, Boulder, CO, pp. 1–16.

Ramet, S.P. (ed.) (1994b) *Rocking the State: Rock Music and Politics in Eastern Europe and Russia.* Westview Press, Boulder, CO.

Ramet, S.P. (1999) *Balkan Babel: The Disintegration of Yugoslavia from the Death of Tito to Insurection in Kosovo.* Westview Press, Boulder, CO.

Rasmussen, L.V. (2002) *Newly Composed Folk Music of Yugoslavia.* Routledge, London.

Regev, M. (1986) The Musical Soundscape as a Contest Area: "Oriental Music" and Israeli Popular Music. *Media, Culture & Society* 8, 343–56.

Regev, M. (2000) To Have a Culture of our Own: On Israeliness and its Variants. *Ethnic and Racial Studies* 23, 223–48.

Regev, M. and Seroussi, E. (2004) *Popular Music and National Culture in Israel.* University of California Press, Berkeley, CA.

Richard, B. and Kruger, H.H. (1998) Raver's Paradise? German Youth Cultures in the 1990s. In: Skelton, T. and Valentine, G. (eds.) *Cool Places: Geographies of Youth Cultures.* Routledge, London, pp. 162–77.

Riley, T. (1987) For the Beatles: Notes on their Achievement. *Popular Music* 6, 257–72.

Ritzer, G. (1993) *The McDonaldization of Society.* Pine Forge Press, Thousand Oaks, CA.

Ritzer, G. and Liska, A. (1997) "McDisneyization" and "Post-Tourism." In: Rojek, C. and Urry, J. (eds.), *Touring Cultures: Transformations of Travel and Theory.* Routledge, London, pp. 96–109.

Ritzer, G. and Stillman, T. (2003) Assessing McDonaldization, Americanization and Globalization. In: Beck, U., Sznaider, N. and Winter, R. (eds.) *Global*

America? The Cultural Consequences of Globalization. University of Liverpool Press, Liverpool, pp. 30–48.

Robertson, R. (1995) Glocalization: Time-Space and Homogeneity-Heterogeneity. In: Featherstone, M., Lash, S. and Robertson, R. (eds.) *Global Modernities.* Sage, London, pp. 23–44.

Romanowski, P. and George-Warren, H. (eds.) (1995) *The New Rolling Stone Encyclopedia of Rock and Roll.* Firestone, New York.

Rose, T. (1994) *Black Noise: Rap Music and Black Culture in Contemporary America.* Wesleyan University Press, Hanover, NH.

Saada-Ophir, G. (2006) Borderland Pop: Arab Jewish Musicians and the Politics of Performance. *Cultural Anthropology* 21, 205–33.

Salas Zuniga, F. (2000) Gritos y Susurros: Vocalistas y casos del rock chileno. *Revista Musical Chilena* 54, 76–80.

Saldanha, A. (2002) Music, Space, Identity: Geographies of Youth Culture in Bangalore. *Cultural Studies* 16, 337–50.

Santoro, M. (2002) What is a "Cantautore?" Distinction and Authorship in Italian (Popular) Music. *Poetics* 30, 111–32.

Santoro, M. (2006) Introduction: Musical Identity and Social Change in Italy. *Journal of Modern Italian Studies* 11, 275–81.

Santoro, M. and Solaroli, M. (2007) Authors and Rappers: Italian Hip Hop and the Shifting Boundaries of *Canzone d'Autore. Popular Music* 26, 463–88.

Schmidt, J. (2012) Full Penetration: The Integration of Psychedelic Electronic Dance Music and Culture into the Israeli Mainstream. *Dancecult: Journal of Electronic Dance Music Culture* 4, 38–64.

Schmutz, V. (2005) Retrospective Cultural Consecration in Popular Music: *Rolling Stone*'s Greatest Albums of All Time. *American Behavioral Scientist* 48, 1510–23.

Schmutz, V., Van Venrooij, A., Janssen, S. and Verboord, M. (2010) Change and Continuity in Newspaper Coverage of Popular Music since 1955: Evidence from the United States, France, Germany and the Netherlands. *Popular Music and Society* 33, 501–15.

Schultz, D. (2001) Music Videos and the Effeminate Vices of Urban Culture in Mali. *Africa* 71, 345–72.

Seeger, C. (1960) On the Moods of a Musical Logic. *Journal of the American Musicological Society* 13, 224–61.

Semán, P. and Vila, P. (2002) Rock Chabón: The Contemporary National Rock of Argentina. In Clark, W.A. (ed.) *From Tejano to Tango: Latin American Popular Music.* Routledge, New York, pp. 70–94.

Semán, P., Vila, P. and Benedetti, C. (2004) Neoliberalism and Rock in the Popular Sectors of Contemporary Argentina. In Pacini Hernandez, D., L'Hoeste, H.F. and Zolov, E. (eds.) *Rockin' Las Américas: The Global Politics of Rock in Latin/o America.* University of Pittsburgh Press, Pittsburgh, PA, pp. 261–90.

Sewell Jr., W. (2005) *Logics of History: Social Theory and Social Transformation.* University of Chicago Press, Chicago, IL.

Shabtay, M. (2003) "RaGap": Music and Identity among Young Ethiopians in Israel. *Critical Arts* 17, 93–105.

Shepherd, J. and Wicke, P. (1997) *Music and Cultural Theory.* Polity, Cambridge.

Shilling, C. (2005) *The Body in Culture, Technology and Society.* Sage, London.

Shin, H. (2009a) Have you ever seen the Rain? And who'll stop the Rain?: The

Globalizing Project of Korean Pop (K-Pop). *Inter-Asia Cultural Studies* 10, 507–23.

Shin, H. (2009b) Reconsidering Transnational Cultural Flows of Popular Music in East Asia: Transbordering Musicians in Japan and Korea Searching for "Asia." *Korean Studies* 33, 101–23.

Shin, H. (2011) The Success of Hopelessness: The Evolution of Korean Indie Music. *Perfect Beat* 12, 147–65.

Shor, N. (2008) *Dancing with Tears in Our Eyes*. Resling, Tel Aviv (in Hebrew).

Shuker, R. (1998) *Key Concepts in Popular Music*. Routledge, London.

Shuker, R. (2001) *Understanding Popular Music*. Routledge, London.

Siriyuvasak, U. and Shin, H. (2007) Asianizing K-pop: Production, Consumption and Identification Patterns among Thai Youth. *Inter-Asia Cultural Studies* 8, 109–36.

Soffer, O. (2012) The Anomaly of Galei Tzahal: Israel's Army Radio as a Cultural Vanguard and Force for Pluralism. *Historical Journal of Film, Radio and Television* 32, 225–43.

Solomon, T. (2005) "Living Underground is Tough": Authenticity and Locality in the Hip-Hop Community in Istanbul, Turkey. *Popular Music* 24, 1–20.

Steinholt, Y. (2005) *Rock in the Reservation*. Mass Media Music Scholars Press, New York.

Sterne, J. (1997) Sounds Like the Mall of America: Programmed Music and the Architectonics of Commercial Space. *Ethnomusicology* 41, 22–50.

Stevens, C.S. (2008) *Japanese Popular Music: Culture, Authenticity and Power*. Routledge, London.

Stites, R. (1992) *Russian Popular Culture: Entertainment and Society since 1900*. Cambridge University Press, Cambridge.

Stokes, M. (ed.) (1994) *Ethnicity, Identity and Music: The Musical Construction of Place*. Berg, Oxford.

Stokes, M. (2004) Music and the Global Order. *Annual Review of Anthropology* 33, 47–72.

Stokes, M. (2007) On Musical Cosmopolitanism. *The Macalester International Roundtable 2007*. Paper 3. Available at: http://digitalcommons.macalester.edu/intlrdtable/3 (accessed February 15, 2012).

Straw, W. (1991) Systems of Articulation, Logics of Change: Communities and Scenes in Popular Music. *Cultural Studies* 5, 368–88.

Szemere, A. (2001) *Up from the Underground: The Culture of Rock Music in Postsocialist Hungary*. Pennsylvania State University Press, University Park, PA.

Szerszynski, B. and Urry, J. (2002) Cultures of Cosmopolitanism. *Sociological Review* 50, 461–81.

Szerszynski, B. and Urry, J. (2006) Visuality, Mobility and the Cosmopolitan: Inhabiting the World From Afar. *British Journal of Sociology* 57, 113–31.

Tagg, P. (1987) Musicology and the Semiotics of Popular Music. *Semiotica* 66, 279–98.

Tagg, P. (2012) *Music's Meanings: a Modern Musicology for Non-Musos*. Mass Media Music Scholars' Press, New York.

Taylor, T.D. (1997) *Global Pop: World Music, World Market*. Routledge, London.

Taylor, T.D. (2007) The Changing Shape of the Culture Industry; or, How Did

Electronica Music Get into Television Commercials? *Television & New Media* 8, 235–58.

Théberge, P. (1997) *Any Sound You Can Imagine: Making Music/Consuming Technology.* Wesleyan University Press, Hanover, NH.

Thornton, S. (1995) *Club Cultures: Music, Media and Subcultural Capital.* Polity, Cambridge.

Tomlinson, J. (1999) *Globalization and Culture.* University of Chicago Press, Chicago, IL.

Tomlinson, J. (2000) Proximity Politics. *Information, Communication and Society* 3, 402–14.

Toynbee, J. (2000) *Making Popular Music.* Arnold, London.

Toynbee, J. (2002) Mainstreaming, from Hegemonic Centre to Global Networks. In: Hesmondhalgh, D. and Negus, K. (eds.) *Popular Music Studies*, Arnold, London, pp. 149–63.

Toynbee, J. (2007) *Bob Marley: Herald of the Postcolonial World?* Polity, Cambridge.

Troitsky, A. (1987) *Back in the USSR: The True Story of Rock in Russia.* Omnibus Press, London.

Turino, T. (2000) *Nationalists, Cosmopolitans, and Popular Music in Zimbabwe.* University of Chicago Press, Chicago, IL.

Turner, V. (1969) *The Ritual Process: Structure and Anti Structure.* Aldine Publications, Chicago, IL.

Ulhôa, M.T. de (2004) Let Me Sing My *Brock*: Learning to Listen to Brazilian Rock. In: Pacini Hernandez, D., L'Hoeste, H.F. and Zolov, E. (eds.) *Rockin' Las Américas: The Global Politics of Rock in Latin/o America.* University of Pittsburgh Press, Pittsburgh, PA, pp. 200–19.

Urry, J. (1995) *Consuming Places.* Routledge, London.

Van Venrooij, A. (2009) The Aesthetic Discourse Space of Popular Music: 1985–86 and 2004–05. *Poetics* 37, 315–32.

Van Venrooij, A. and Schmutz, V. (2010) The Evaluation of Popular Music in the United States, Germany and the Netherlands: A Comparison of the Use of High Art and Popular Aesthetic Criteria. *Cultural Sociology* 4, 395–421.

Vila, P. (1987) Rock Nacional and Dictatorship in Argentina. *Popular Music* 6, 129–48.

Von Appen, R. and Doehring, A. (2006) Nevermind the Beatles, Here's Exile 61 and Nico: "The Top 100 Records of All Time" – a Canon of Pop and Rock Albums from a Sociological and an Aesthetic Perspective. *Popular Music* 25, 21–39.

Vroomen, L. (2004) Kate Bush: Teen Pop and Older Female Fans. In: Bennett, A. and Peterson, R.A. (eds.) *Music Scenes: Local, Translocal and Virtual.* Vanderbilt University Press, Nashville, TN, pp. 238–54.

Wagnleitner, R. (1994) *Coca Colonization and the Cold War: The Cultural Mission of the USA.* University of North Carolina Press, Chapel Hill, NC.

Waksman, S. (1999) *Instruments of Desire: The Electric Guitar and the Shaping of Musical Experience.* Harvard University Press, Cambridge, MA.

Wallach, J., Berger, H.M. and Greene, P.D. (eds.) (2011) *Metal Rules the Globe: Heavy Metal Music around the World.* Duke University Press, Durham, NC.

Wallis, R. and Malm, K. (1984) *Big Sounds from Small Peoples.* Pendragon Press, New York.

Walser, R. (1993) *Running with the Devil: Power, Gender, and Madness in Heavy Metal Music*. Wesleyan University Press, Hanover, NH.

Watson, J. (ed.) (1997) *Golden Arches East: McDonald's in East Asia*. Stanford University Press, Stanford, CA.

Weinstein D. (2000) *Heavy Metal: The Music and its Culture*, rev. edn. Da Capo Press, Cambridge, MA.

Weston, D. (2011) Basque Pagan Metal: View to a Primordial Past. *European Journal of Cultural Studies* 14, 103–22.

Whiteley, S., Bennett, A. and Hawkins, S. (eds.) (2005) *Music, Space and Place: Popular Music and Cultural Identity*. Ashgate, Aldershot.

Wicke, P. (1990) *Rock Music: Culture, Aesthetics and Sociology*. Cambridge University Press, Cambridge.

Williams, R. (1963) *Culture and Society*. Penguin, Harmondsworth.

Willis, P. (1978) *Profane Culture*. Routledge & Kegan Paul, London.

Wolff, J. (1987) The Ideology of Autonomous Art. In: Leppert, R. and McCalry, S. (eds.) *Music and Society: The Politics of Composition, Performance and Reception*. Cambridge University Press, Cambridge, pp. 1–12.

Yazıcıoğlu, E.T. (2010) Contesting the Global Consumption Ethos: Reterritorialization of Rock in Turkey. *Journal of Macromarketing* 30, 238–53.

Yúdice, G. (1999) La industria de la música en la integración América Latina-Estados Unidos. In García Canclini, N. and Moneta, C.J. (eds.) *Las industrias culturales en la integración latinoamericana*. Grijalbo, Mexico City, pp. 181–243.

Yurchak, A. (2003) Soviet Hegemony of Form: Everything Was Forever, Until It Was No More. *Comparative Studies in Society and History* 45, 480–510.

Zak III, A.J. (2001) *The Poetics of Rock: Cutting Tracks, Making Records*. University of California Press, Berkeley, CA.

INDEX

195